P9-CCZ-570

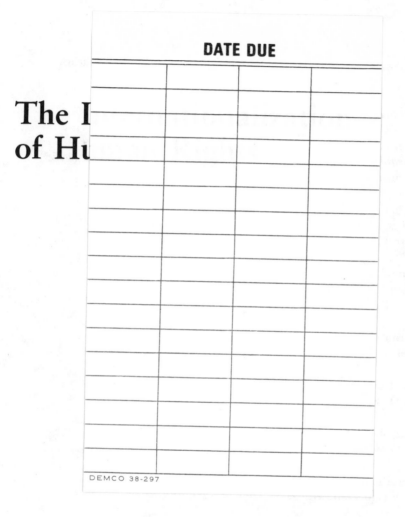

DATE DUE

The I
of Hu

DEMCO 38-297

Issues in World Politics Series

James N. Rosenau and William C. Potter, consulting editors

The Internationalization of Human Rights

David P. Forsythe
University of Nebraska

Lexington Books
D.C. Heath and Company/Lexington, Massachusetts/Toronto

WITHDRAWN

Tennessee Tech Library
Cookeville, TN

Library of Congress Cataloging-in-Publication Data

Forsythe, David P., 1941–
   The internationalization of human rights / David P. Forsythe.
      p.   cm. — (Issues in world politics series)
   Includes index.
   ISBN 0–669–21116–8 (case). — ISBN 0–669–21117–6 (pbk.)
   1. Human rights. I. Title. II. Series.
K3240.4.F683   1991
341.4'81—dc20   90–20052
                                                     CIP

Copyright © 1991 by Lexington Books

All rights reserved. No part of this publication may be reproduced
or transmitted in any form or by any means, electronic or mechanical,
including photocopy, recording, or any information storage or retrieval
system, without permission in writing from the publisher.

Published simultaneously in Canada
Printed in the United States of America
Casebound International Standard Book Number: 0–669–21116–8
Paperbound International Standard Book Number: 0–669–21117–6
Library of Congress Catalog Card Number: 90–20052

The paper used in this publication meets the minimum requirements of
American National Standard for Information Sciences—Permanence of
Paper for Printed Library Materials, ANSI Z39.48–1984. ∞™

Year and number of this printing:

91 92 93 94 10 9 8 7 6 5 4 3 2 1

Contents

Preface

Human rights is an issue no longer strictly within national purview but rather is the focus of widely accepted and growing international action. This book's central objective is to analyze and document that growing internationalization.

In the process of analyzing the internationalization of human rights, I pursue three other goals along the way. First, I give a substantive understanding of much of the meaning of this issue area in world politics at the end of the twentieth century, along with a survey of some of the more recent interpretive literature. Then I reinforce this first objective by showing, through several in-depth treatments, that one can cut into the subject of human rights from several different angles: the global, the regional, the national, the private transnational, and the individual. Finally, I speculate about the different prisms one can employ to try to understand better the dynamics behind international action for human rights.

The issue area of human rights is defined by porous boundaries, and thus the coverage is not without problems of definition and content. What is a human rights question as compared to a security question? Do human rights violations in El Salvador inherently touch upon U.S. security policy? What is a human rights question as compared to a question of economic development? Do gross violations of human rights in Somalia inherently touch upon its economic development and the availability of foreign developmental (and military) assistance? Given the messy world in which we live, the analytical treatment must inherently remain somewhat problematic.

Conceptions such as issue areas necessarily simplify a complex world, but this is what political scientists do. They simplify in order to gain insights without violating reality too much or in a significant way. They impose conceptions on a mass of specific happenings in the hope of bringing patterned understanding out of chaos. I have therefore been guided not by the quest for supposed completeness, much less celestial perfection, but have settled for some advance in understanding, however imperfect. Through the subject matter selected for analysis, I give a sense of the meaning of human rights in global context; in other words, I look at what rights are internationally recognized and to what extent implemented through international action on the eve of the twenty-first century. I also give some indication of the prospects for further development and understanding.

I begin by addressing basic questions. What is an internationally recognized human right? Is international action for human rights a form of cultural imperialism? Can there be international standards but particular variation in implementing those standards? I also stress what is new about the old subject of human rights, and I explain what political scientists call the level of analysis conception applied to human rights.

In the second chapter, I use primarily the global level of analysis to show that international relations, legally and politically, recognizes certain human rights and thereby generates pressure on states to implement them without formally negating state sovereignty; an analysis that shows, among other things, how to combine political and legal foci to maximize understanding. Law is both a reflection of political decision and an agent of political socialization on subsequent decisions.

I stay at the global level in chapter 3 to show increasing attention to human rights at the United Nations over time, and I suggest several causes for this remarkable transformation. This is not pure or chronological description but rather an analytic description that shows that one can gain insights into political behavior without rigorous theory or formal models. I discuss patterns of political behavior, the causes for change, and the significance of that change.

Then, in chapter 4, I show that regime theory and the theory of hegemonic leadership can help inform our understanding of human rights in the Western Hemisphere. Certain ideas, said to be theoretical because they make up a system of interconnected general statements, can help structure our analysis of the Organization of American States and its expansion of concern for human rights in member states. Thus I apply these two theories to basically a regional level of analysis.

I trace U.S. foreign policy and its treatment of human rights since 1945, and especially during the Carter and Reagan administrations, in chapter 5. I argue, ultimately, that internationally recognized human rights should be considered, ironically, a domestic (as well as foreign policy) subject for the United States—however startling an idea that may be to those who see the United States as a shining city on a hill for others to emulate. This is analysis primarily at the national level, although individuals, as well as global and regional international organizations, are covered.

In chapter 6 I analyze a subnational, private, transnational actor, the International Committee of the Red Cross. After providing description information, I analyze its activities by looking at its attempted influence on authorities, its mandate and style, and its organization. The ICRC is not entirely like any other human rights private actor, but its increased international activity is symptomatic of the larger role that private organizations play in making and implementing human rights policies.

I conclude by discussing the saliency of international human rights in American political science and legal circles, which says something about the information that citizens get—or fail to get—about that subject. International human rights will remain on the world's agenda; clearly both U.S. policymakers and citizens need a better understanding of this truly complex subject.

The sum total of this approach is to demonstrate many avenues to understanding internationally recognized human rights. I believe in an eclectic approach, one that is not wedded to any particular theory or school of thought but rather draws on different disciplines such as political science and law (or for that matter, philosophy and economics). Given the choice between a thinner survey of more material and a deeper treatment of less material, I have opted for the latter. Thus I cover part of the United Nations activity on human rights and the Organization of American States but do not analyze other intergovernmental international organizations such as the Council of Europe. And I study in depth the International Committee of the Red Cross but not Amnesty International or the International Commission of Jurists. I do, however, tell readers where information can be obtained on many subjects not treated extensively here.

This book represents a partial summation of much of my thinking and writing about human rights over a decade. There is necessarily therefore some overlap with my survey published for beginning students, *Human Rights and World Politics,* 2d rev. ed. (Lincoln: University of Nebraska Press, 1989). There is also some overlap with my published analyses of the United Nations, which appeared in different forms in several different sources and which in its first form appeared as "The United Nations and Human Rights, 1945–1985," *Political Science Quarterly* (Summer 1985). An analysis of the International Committee of the Red Cross, on which I have drawn here, was published as "Human Rights and The International Committee of the Red Cross" (*Human Rights Quarterly,* May 1990). I have also drawn on two published essays for the chapter on U.S. foreign policy. "The United States, the United Nations, and Human Rights," appeared as chapter 10 in Margaret P. Karns and Karen A. Mingst, eds., *The United States and Multilateral Institutions: Patterns of Changing Instrumentality and Influence* (Boston: Unwin Hyman, 1990), and "Human Rights and U.S. Foreign Policy: Retrospect and Prospect," appeared in the *Political Science Quarterly* (Fall 1990). This book, however, is mostly original as a publication, and where it relies closely on previously published material, that material has been altered and updated to take account of new events and further reflection.

I am grateful for comments obtained on drafts of various chapters from Richard Bilder, Richard Claude, Margaret Crahan, Jack Donnelly, Lawrence

Finkelstein, Leon Gordenker, David Hawk, Louis Henkin, Robert Hitchcock, Peter Juviler, Lawrence LeBlanc, Lowell Livezy, J. Paul Martin, James Nickel, Nick Onuf, Kathleen Pritchard, Howard Tolley, Jr., and Burns Weston. Three readers selected by Lexington Books read the entire manuscript and affected my revisions through their comments. Especially helpful and supportive were comments on the manuscript by James N. Rosenau, whose insights not only brought about important changes but also gave me added motivation during the difficult days of revision. Paul O'Connell of Lexington Books was a wise and understanding senior editor.

1
Human Rights in Global Perspective

Human Rights as an Old Subject

Human rights is an old subject in many ways. Most fundamental, it is one way to deal with a person's or persons' relation to public authority—and indeed to the rest of society. If one has a human right, one is entitled to make a fundamental claim that an authority, or some other part of society, do—or refrain from doing—something that affects significantly one's human dignity.[1] Human rights most fully understood involves not static property, something possessed, but rather a social and behavioral process. Human rights constitutes a fundamental means to the end of basic human dignity. To focus on this relationship between citizen and authority, or between citizen and society, is hardly novel. Touching as it does upon a central question of human existence, it has been much discussed. Human dignity, understandably enough, has never been precisely defined on the basis of consensus, but it accords roughly with justice or the good society. Libraries over the years have contained uncounted volumes about how the means of rights contributes to the end of justice. These tomes have been written by philosophers, theologians, historians, lawyers—and mere political scientists.

There is thus a long tradition, mainly Western in origin, of discourse—and even some action—about fundamental personal rights in relation to authority and society. This can be traced back to the Greeks and Romans, as has been shown in concise form.[2] While there was some implementation of fundamental rights in Greek and Roman public policy, much (if not most) of the discourse was relegated to the private sphere—to halls of learning and monasteries. This was especially true during the European Dark Ages, when religious and secular authority was mostly unrestrained by applied conceptions of fundamental personal rights. Thus whereas there was much intellectual consideration of personal rights in Western history, this was decidedly different from consistent applications of personal rights in public policy.

A fuller and closer nexus between intellectual debate and public policy emerged during the latter eighteenth century when European intellectuals affected the thinking of those who made the American and French revolutions. While there were antecedents, such as the Magna Carta in England, showing a linkage between rights of persons (at least of property-owning males) and public affairs, it was the United States and France after 1790 that were based explicitly on conceptions of human rights. Especially in the United States from about 1800, governments acting for the state were consistently limited by the human rights of U.S. citizens enumerated in the Bill of Rights. Indeed, the goal of implementing personal rights through state public policy became progressively characteristic of most of the states of Western culture during the last two centuries, although there were exceptions (including Portugal and Spain until the 1970s).

It seems evident, therefore, although some debate continues on the question, that limiting especially the state through the implementation of fundamental personal rights was—in point of historical evolution—basically a Western notion. Other areas of the world addressed public authority through cultural and religious maxims about correct rule, the just society, or the wise leader.[3] Intellectuals in all cultures have been concerned with right rule, but this is not the same as a concern with personal rights. It was only in the West that strong currents of intellectual debate focused on what was called in eighteenth-century sexist Europe the Rights of Man. And it was first in the West that this intellectual construct was put into significant, albeit severely limited, politico-legal practice.

Other cultures and other regions dealt with human dignity in the sense of human or social justice, but they did so for the most part through ideas and devices other than personal rights. In Islamic culture, both the Koran and the Sharia (a legal code derived from the religious precepts of the Koran) contain passages about tolerance between persons. But this tolerance is mandated as a rule of Allah and his Prophet; persons have the duty to implement the standard. This says nothing about personal rights to receiving correct treatment.[4] In Chinese-Confucian culture, there are precepts about the duties of the wise ruler to his subjects, but this is not the same as those subjects' having personal rights in order to restrain or commission the ruler.[5]

This introduction to fundamental personal rights raises the question of whether what is now called international human rights, which are supposed to be universal in scope, is a strictly Western construct. In other words, is the contemporary discourse on human rights a form of cultural imperialism?

In 1990 the leaders of Kenya, beneficiaries of a one-party state in which those demanding the creation of other political parties were arrested and sometimes mistreated, resisted growing international pressure consistent with internationally recognized human rights. On the one hand, the collapse of authoritarian governments in much of Eastern Europe in the late 1980s enboldened would-be political reformers in Kenya. On the other hand, President Daniel Arap Moi and his supporters argued that political pluralism, based on the civil and political rights enumerated in international documents, was a form of cultural imperialism that was inappropriate to Africa and likely to lead to the political fragmentation of Kenya because of the multiplicity of ethnic groups in that state.[6]

The charge that attention to international human rights was little more than cultural imperialism in various forms could also be found in the West. George Kennan is widely regarded as one of the United States's most distinguished diplomats and historians. He is usually credited not only with being the author of the containment doctrine, which stood as the cornerstone of U.S. foreign from about 1947 to the late 1980s, but also with a thoughtful view on foreign policy and international relations in general. In some of his publications, Kennan has shown a disregard for human rights, especially among the less industrialized countries. He has tended to see U.S. concern for human rights in these countries as a mixture of cultural imperialism, rampant moralism, and political selectivity. He has implied clearly that U.S. policy would be better off if it omitted the subject. Thus Kennan, like President Moi, would let each state, at least in the developing world, make its own unfettered decisions about personal rights, including the lack thereof.[7] This debate about human rights and cultural imperialism calls for further inquiry.

President Moi and Professor Kennan have had supporters in certain academic circles. There used to be a prominent school of anthropological thought arguing in favor of strong cultural relativism, meaning, for my purposes here, against universal human rights standards.[8] The argument was that all truth and goodness is relative to particular cultures. It followed that certain peoples, usually existing now within a state as indigenous-aboriginal peoples, have achieved both dignity and, equally important, a harmony with nature without the conception of rights. Relying mainly on social customs and not legal rights, these people, it was argued, have obtained a collective solidarity that prevents the abuses that legal rights, and their most fundamental version, human rights, were designed to prevent. It is now fair to say, however, that most anthropologists do not endorse pure or absolute cultural relativism. They accept certain universal standards (it is good to vaccinate to eradicate smallpox) though traditional customs may dictate otherwise.

Others, including some political scientists, also say that the contemporary movement in support of international or universal human rights constitutes cultural imperialism.[9] They argue that states like Saudi Arabia do not and will not accept the notion of human rights because it contradicts their cultural (including religious) heritage. States like Saudi Arabia object to many of the human rights now internationally recognized, such as freedom of religion, freedom from sexual discrimination, and freedom to participate politically. These observers conclude that universal human rights are inappropriate for a multicultural world. Whether these cultural relativists feel any unease when Saudi Arabia stones a woman to death for adultery is not a matter of record.

At the opposite end of the debate are those, mainly lawyers and political scientists, who reject the argument that the human rights movement equates with cultural imperialism. While acknowledging the Western origin of both the notion and the practice of human rights, these thinkers note that other ideas originated in the West but were voluntarily, even enthusiastically, accepted by non-Western parties. Both the idea of the nation-state and its accompanying idea of national sovereignty were Western in intellectual origin and politico-legal practice, and both became universally accepted (with minor and usually temporary exceptions). Those who endorse Marxism as universal truth would make the same argument, and they would note the examples of China, North Korea, and Vietnam as non-Western states that vigorously endorsed a version of Marxism even though Marx was German, lived in the United Kingdom, and was propelled to write as he did because of the Western industrial revolution. Clearly an idea can prove universally valid as a perceived response to social need, through global and voluntary acceptance, although emanating from a particular place and time.

Virtually all non-Western states have not only become a party to the United Nations Charter (a treaty), with its human rights provisions, but have given voting or verbal endorsement to the Universal Declaration of Human Rights (a U.N. General Assembly resolution translating the generalities of the charter into relatively more precise principles pertaining to human rights). No state has ever accepted the U.N. Charter, in effect a global constitution, but reserved against its human rights provisions. Only eight states out of fifty-five abstained on the 1948 vote in favor of the Universal Declaration, and some of those abstainers like the Soviet Union and its former European allies changed their position in the 1980s and endorsed the declaration.

Many non-Western states have written human rights provisions into their national constitutions, and some of these same states have even compiled a respectable record of implementing these rights in practice.[10] (There is no evidence that these non-Western national constitutions endorsing internationally recognized human rights were the products of Western pressure. Cultural influence, even if via colonialism, is not the same as cultural imperialism. Ideas about individual freedom, for example, may have been spread by colonialism, but such ideas were voluntarily accepted by many of the new leaders of former colonies.) Thus this politico-legal record (legal positivism to the lawyers, empirical proof to the political scientists) mandates against the charge of cultural imperialism.

It has been said, however, that individual rights are a Western invention inappropriate to nonindividualistic cultures, an argument heard frequently with regard to the extended family orientation of African culture.[11] But what is important is the modern power of the state, or perhaps the majority in society, which needs restraining and commissioning by means of personal legal rights. One can agree that traditional African culture has been less individualistic than in the West while also noting that the extended family structure in Africa has proved powerless to prevent systematic and extensive abuse by national rulers. The extended family structure has not prevented attempts at genocide between ethnic groups in Rwanda and Burundi. An African willingness to provide temporary relief to distant cousins in distress is a poor substitute for personal, legal mandates on governing authority or on powerful ethnic groups. One has only to look at the poor quality of human dignity across Africa, despite the continuation of family and ethnic-tribal allegiances—indeed because of the continuation of these allegiances in conjunction with powerful national rulers—to see the need for internationally recognized human rights there. Similar arguments could be made about the nonindividualistic Asian societies. Personal rights can be seen as a valid response to a contemporary need, despite previous traditions deemphasizing rights.

In addition to the cultural relativists who argue for disparate local standards of correct behavior and those supporting universal human rights standards, there are also those who adopt a mediating or synthetic position, sometimes called an argument in support of weak cultural relativism. This position argues in favor of universal human rights but acknowledges that some concessions should be made to particular cultural differences or that cultural differences will affect the interpretation and implementation of the universal principles.

Although the United States and the Netherlands are both Western democracies sympathetic to human rights in principle, they differ widely in their specific public policies implementing human rights principles. In Holland there is ". . . Legal prostitution. Coffee houses that sell marijuana to teenagers. Free abortions on request. Free needles for heroin addicts. Special rooms for prisoners to conduct liaisons with outside partners, even of the same sex. Euthanasia in hospitals."[12] How many white, middle-class Americans over the age of thirty or forty would agree with Holland's specific interpretations of human rights principles governing interpersonal relations? If the United States and the Netherlands agree that ". . . No one shall be held in slavery or servitude" (Universal Declaration, Art. 4), is prostitution a form of servitude? If the United States and the Netherlands agree that "everyone has the right to a standard of living adequate for . . . health and well-being" (Universal Declaration, Art. 25), does that include the right to free needles for drug addicts?

A more complex version of cultural relativism, not widely known, pertains to the United States. Many native Americans within the boundaries of the United States have been exempted from much federal and state law.[13] Native Americans from federally recognized tribes have achieved a type of measured separatism, which can lead to a "federally sanctioned serfdom" for some. That is, native Americans are exempted from much federal civil rights legislation, to the detriment of some of them. Some native American women do not have the same civil rights, say, regarding property and divorce that American women have under the federal and state law.

Here we have an example of the fact that human rights provisions can conflict with each other, and the resolution of this conflict can depend on either cultural preferences or a willingness to defer to cultural differences. (Some native Americans in Connecticut may have no rights at all since they have apparently been exempted from federal and state law, but have no legal standards and court systems of their own.)[14]

International law now recognizes the right to self-determination as a collective human right of peoples (Art. 1 of both the U.N. Covenant on Civil and Political Rights and the U.N. Covenant on Economic, Social, and Cultural Rights). In implementing native Americans' right to self-determination, U.S. authorities have accepted a violation of certain individual civil rights as defined by U.S. and international law. Since native American conceptions of human dignity differ from those found in U.S. law, cultural relativism prevails on some specific issues.

At the same time, should one native American tribe engage in genocide, no doubt U.S. federal authorities would act despite any claims to native American legal jurisdiction. Genocide would be considered today (somewhat ironically in the light of past U.S. policies toward native Americans) as a major violation of fundamental human rights, whereas native American gender discrimination within their jurisdiction is tolerated as a disagreeable but unavoidable violation of fundamental human rights—if the principle of collective self-determination is to be honored. One could try to persuade native Americans to move away from gender discrimination over time, but for the moment it exists and is legally sanctioned. Such are some of the policy trade-offs in the human rights domain, and cultural relativity is involved. Universal standards coexist with cultural relativism in implementation.

Are there any human rights that can be said to constitute a primary core and that because of their importance to human dignity permit only the weakest type of variation in implementation? One can arrive at such a primary core by looking at what states indicate should be primary. Nevertheless, state practice indicates many things, and debate will continue on what should be of primary importance in the area of human rights.

One theorist argues that the thirty rights principles found in the Universal Declaration of Human Rights of 1948, the contemporary Magna Carta of rights, are all equally fundamental in a moral sense and that they should be considered a universally valid and indivisible whole. (That some theorist would permit a weak form of cultural relativity in the implementation process. He also acknowledges that actors may have to prioritize rights in the name of practical use of scarce resources.)[15] Another theorist suggests that three clusters of rights are most fundamental or basic: rights to subsistence, security, and liberty. To him, these are the truly universal rights, necessary for the practice of other rights.[16] Others have arrived at different lists of what is truly universal because of being most important. By implication, other rights would be either not universal or, if universal, derogable on various grounds.[17] Clearly disagreement rules.

A focus on the theory of rights magnifies disagreement, making it easy to lose sight of how many times political actors have reached agreement on rights definition and action.[18] If we look at state practice in contemporary times, we can construct an argument that runs as follows: there are truly universal and nonderogable human rights (permitting only variation in implementation); there are also human rights that, although apparently universal, may be suspended or delayed. There are also human rights in a gray area, falling short of being basic in the past but perhaps changing their character—as determined by state practice. For example, Pope John Paul II was quoted as saying that "the right to a safe environment" should be part of a revised Universal Declaration of Human Rights.[19] That view has been frequently articulated, but it has never been adopted in treaty form and several powerful states, including the United States, thus far have been unwilling to view environmental protection as a human right.

Rather than rely on abstract moral theory as found in nongovernmental argument, one should look at what states indicate, by their consent to treaties and resolutions adopted by international organizations, as the primary values of international relations. International treaty law and quasi-law in the form of major intergovernmental resolutions reflect state practice rather than academic or other private argument. International law, both conventional (treaty) and customary, arises from state practice, not from the lectures of some law professor. It is a great misconception to think of international law and the resolutions of intergovernmental organizations as theory, somehow apart from state practice.

I am using the reality of international relations to show something about universal, nonderogable values. I am using empiricism to arrive at norms. I am using state practice, mostly treaty laws and the quasi-law of intergovernmental declarations, to show what is widely considered to be universally good public policy.

This process might start with what international lawyers call jus cogens applied to human rights, or those rights that are nonderogable and which—as trumps, so to speak—override all other legal concerns. From a strictly legal view, however, although most international lawyers agree on the concept of jus cogens, they do not always agree, nor do states, on the exact content of it.[20]

One could also look at the wording of extant human rights treaties, which, in several instances, specify derogable and nonderogable rights based on situations that threaten the life of the nation.[21] This approach not only fails to deal directly with cultural relativism but also is limited to civil and political rights only. The U.N. Covenant on Civil and Political Rights, the European Convention on Human Rights (which deals only with civil and political rights), and the American Convention on Human Rights contain articles on derogation. Since this second look at our subject cannot address social, economic, cultural, and any other human rights (the treatment of such rights in the American Convention is cursory), it proves deficient in helping us answer the question about which universal rights might be basic across cultures. Our first look at jus cogens found a substantive void; our second look at conventional nonderogable rights found severely limited scope.

In seeking guidance from state practice, this leaves us with the option of looking for those human rights so widely endorsed, and whose violation is so widely condemned where extant, that on empirical evidence they seem to constitute the clearly universal and nonderogable core, at least for a given point in time. Because there is no precise list of trump rights in international law, and because the treaties specifying which human rights can never be violated cover only civil and political rights, to be comprehensive in our inquiry we have to look to state practice broadly considered.

It is highly relevant to note those actions that under international law give rise to universal jurisdiction (and by noting that most of them involve abuses of persons that are so morally reprehensible that any state that legally obtains jurisdiction over the perpetrator is authorized to prosecute for the stated crime or extradite, without regard for other rules of jurisdiction). That list of crimes giving rise to universal jurisdiction includes piracy; slavery, the slave trade, and slavelike practices; genocide; torture; aerial hijacking; and major war crimes (grave breaches of the laws of war).[22] This is not academic theory but rather a legal codification of what states regard in contemporary times as especially reprehensible, as defined by diplomatic-legal practice. All of these crimes, which by implication clearly involve violations of human rights, with perhaps the exception of aerial hijacking, are condemned by the contents of major human rights treaties and by extraconventional behavior. Not only does a 1984 treaty establish universal jurisdiction in regard to torture, but no state endorses and openly admits to torture (although Amnesty International has made clear that as many as one-third of the states of the world tolerate torture as a systematic practice).[23]

Not only do several treaties establish universal jurisdiction in regard to slavery, but no state endorses it and its related evils. Even those Arab, African, and Asian states that still allow the practice of slavery do not endorse it but lay the blame on private parties beyond the control of the state.[24] As the columnist George Will wrote in the *Washington Post* when focusing on the Anti-Slavery Society, "Social traditions no longer sanctioned by laws—traditions of caste and class—can still be as strong as iron fetters." He was particularly concerned about slavery affecting children—whether in sex shops, at carpet looms, or sold into bondage as collateral for loans.[25]

Genocide—the intent to destroy or harm a national, ethnic, racial, or religious group in whole or in part—leads to universal jurisdiction under a 1948 treaty and is condemned in principle by all states (although there is persuasive evidence that genocide continues to be practiced).[26] On the basis of clear universal jurisdiction plus state practice, the specific content of piracy, such as violent attacks on persons on the high seas for monetary or sexual gratification, should be added to the core (though piracy still exists, especially in the South China Sea). The Geneva Conventions of 1949 designed to protect victims of war, plus the 1977 Additional Protocols, not only define major war crimes stemming from armed conflict, such as harming combatants who are out of the fight or attacking civilians and civilian objects, but also establish universal jurisdiction for purposes of implementation.[27]

With regard to all of these actions, the connection to universal jurisdiction plus state public pronouncements and the bulk of applied policy clearly and universally indicate opposition to certain practices on grounds of a fundamental denial of human rights, even if legal status and official pronouncements outstrip implementation efforts. No exceptions are acknowledged because of culture or any other reason, such as stage of economic development or public disorder. While some private action and de facto governmental policy is otherwise, the overwhelming evidence from formal state pronouncements is that the listed norms deserve primary and global support.

One might want to remove aerial hijacking per se from the core on the grounds that it reflects basically a state of concern with orderly air transport (although a prohibition on the taking of hostages seems an older and more pervasive part of international law).

A strong case could be made for adding to the universal core widespread opposition to summary execution and racism, and widespread support for provision of basic sustenance, even though treaty law does not establish universal jurisdiction in connection with them. No state officially endorses and openly carries out summary execution (although it occurs at least with the connivance of states).[28] No state endorses and openly admits to starvation of its own people (although it occurs if not with the connivance of states, at least with the omission of policies that could stop it).[29] With regard to basic sustenance, the 1977 Geneva Protocols for victims of war prohibit starvation of civilians even in wartime, and the 1990 U.N. Security Council resolution mandating a trade embargo on Iraq for its aggression against Kuwait exempted foodstuffs that would correct starvation. Freedom from racism has not only been repeatedly endorsed, but also racism has been practically fought where it continues to exist—which is probably everywhere.[30]

Finally, several treaties clearly state that even in times of national emergency threatening the life of the nation, no derogation is permitted from prohibitions of summary execution, torture, and mistreatment.[31] These bans are reinforced by that part of the law of human rights in armed conflict covering internal armed conflict, which stipulates that even in what journalists call civil wars, these same prohibitions remain.[32]

The attempt to establish a core of human rights from which no derogation is possible even on grounds of cultural relativism, or on other grounds such as state security or economic development, is not free of all problems. In this process one is charting a list of what is, in the view of states, rather than what should be, in the view of moral theorists. This can lead to an incomplete list, at least in terms of what should be. Moreover, even if one employs a list of most basic human rights derived from politico-legal empiricism, a practical problem inheres in this apparent consensus. It is not always easy to translate general consensus into specific consensus and thus to specify whether certain actions fall within the conception of proscribed action.

The agreement that freedom from slavery is such a basic human right that no derogation is possible even on grounds of cultural tradition (or economic necessity) leads to the question of whether prostitution is really a slavelike practice. It is, after all, legally sanctioned and regulated by democratic states in places other than the Netherlands. Is the practice of female child marriage a slavelike practice? It can, after all, lead to great psychological trauma and physical damage to young women.[33] Does alteration or removal of the clitoris in the young women of North Africa and parts of sub-Sahara Africa according to local cultural tradition constitute torture or mistreatment?[34] What about infibulation (sewing closed the vulva of young women, which is still practiced in parts of Africa in order to guarantee virginity at marriage, with high probability of resulting medical problems)?

There is a more troubling critique of the empirical-positivist approach to establishing a nonderogable core of universal human rights: are not some practices such an infringement on human dignity as to necessitate rights in the nonderogable core in and of themselves? Do we not need to recognize rights against clitorectomies, infibulation, and child marriages on a universal scale regardless of state-approved law and state practice at any given time?

This line of thinking closes the circle by raising the old issue of whether that which seems a universal abomination to some, needing elimination through the recognition of trump rights, may not be seen in a different light to others. Presumably certain feminists would disagree with U.S. federal authorities that gender discrimination within native American jurisdiction is a permissible price to pay for implementing the collective human right of self-determination.[35] Moreover, why should something so important as internationally recognized human rights be left only to state practice, since states are notorious for violating rights and for being slow in developing international human rights legal standards? Do we not need a moral theory to inform us about what should be rather than an empirical survey of state practice to tell us what is?

There are internationally recognized human rights comprising a primary core as evidenced by international public policy. Although not an ultimate source of rights, extant public policy indicates what states and derivative public authorities (such as intergovernmental organizations) consider to be rights at a given time. More "ultimate" sources of rights beyond the "intermediate" source of public policy may exist, but we do not know with certainty what those sources are or what rights they encompass. Each theorist knows, at least to his or her satisfaction, what human rights are, but what seems so obvious to one seems a bone of contention to others.

Theorists are prone to emphasize the source of rights inherent in personhood;[36] or rights found in natural law;[37] or rights necessary for the collective good;[38] or rights that can be justified according to moral reasoning.[39] But they do not agree among themselves, and no one approach has proved widely persuasive to public authorities. In the meantime, those concerned with implementation of rights are compelled to focus on empiricism. After all, absent international public policy, state X has no legal obligation to implement right Y just because it was articulated by theorist Z. Law based on consent restrains cultural imperialism.

Empiricism defines universal human rights mostly according to international instruments (mainly treaties, evidence of customary international law, and major U.N. resolutions usually called declarations). Such sources—legal or quasi-legal ones rather than ultimate moral ones—produce the International Bill of Rights as the central focal point of fundamental human rights. But it is important to emphasize that human rights are not comprised of a list set down forever in year X but rather constitute a changing set of standards over time as deprivations of human dignity change (or as public policy evolves on moral or expediential grounds—that is, deprivations can remain the same but perceptions and responses can evolve).[40]

In a behavioral or empirical sense, rights exist only if they are recognized as such by public authorities. One can argue for a moral theory of rights. However one might argue for a moral theory encompassing economic human rights, U.S. nationals cannot make effective claims in this regard against the U.S. government because the U.S. Constitution and Bill of Rights do not acknowledge them; the United States has not become a full party to the U.N. Covenant on Economic, Social, and Cultural Rights; and U.S. courts will not give controlling weight to arguments based on economic rights.[41] For practical purposes, economic rights do not exist within the U.S. jurisdiction, whatever theorists might argue. A moral right with no support from public law and policy is not an effective or practical right. The right to freedom from racism in South Africa is becoming a practical or effective right because other states, acting at the United Nations and outside it, have acknowledged the right. The purely moral right to freedom from racism has no practical meaning without its translation into political-legal form.

Within the broad range of human rights internationally recognized, there is a universally valid core of nonderogable human rights comprising freedom from: violent attacks on persons for money or sex (derived from piracy), slavery and related practices, torture, summary execution, mistreatment, starvation, hostage taking (derived from aerial hijacking and the laws of war), racism, and major war crimes.

This is not to say that other internationally recognized human rights, such as freedom of religion or freedom of information, are not important means for achieving human dignity. It is only to say that the empirical evidence of their acceptance and practice is somewhat weaker than the core. One can say that if the full spectrum of the thirty-odd rights mentioned in the Universal Declaration of Human Rights is partially denied, there cannot be a life with true human dignity.[42] This may or may not be true in terms of pure moral theory. I interpret state practice in contemporary times to say the violation of the listed core rights is fundamentally debilitating to a life with dignity; denial beyond the core is debilitating and short of full potential but not fundamentally so. At the moment, state practice seems to say that one cannot lead a dignified life while under torture or starving; one can lead such a life even without the right to emigrate or periodic holidays with pay.

If internationally recognized human rights are not fixed permanently, neither is the definition of the core, which can change through politico-legal evidence. Given the demise of European communism at least in its Stalinist form, a stronger case is evolving for adding to the list of core, nonderogable rights as based on state practice.

Somewhat paradoxically, implementation of human rights through public policy in any given historical era is affected by culture. For example, had U.S. culture in particular or Western culture more generally been more sensitive and sympathetic to economic, social, and cultural rights, given the power of United States and the rest of the West, such rights would have been internationally recognized sooner and more widely.

This is not to say that all parts of the West have been so opposed as the United States to treating such objects as adequate food, clothing, shelter, and health care as essential for human dignity and thus meriting designation as human rights. Parts of the West have long dealt with essential socioeconomic subjects in terms of rights. Some Western states manifest provisions pertaining to such subjects in their constitutions, and a number of them not only now accept the validity of such rights but also provide in their public policy such things as comprehensive public health care and linguistic rights.[43] Still, the Western priority to civil and political rights, combined with the power of the West in world affairs, shows the effect of cultural influences on acknowledgment and practice of rights, both core and beyond. Thus culture is important in a discussion of human rights, but at the same time there can be a core of universal human rights mostly immune to cultural relativism.

Some cultural relativism seems to be necessary given what is perceived at a particular time as a politically wise management of contradictions (as I have explained in reference to U.S. federal authorities and native Americans).[44] Contemporary dynamics seem to be expanding the arena of universalism and shrinking domain of the culturally particular (with the exception of pockets of indigenous peoples). One example of expanding universalism is the acceptance by important European Marxists of civil and political rights. One example of the countervailing exception is the increased attention within the United Nations to the exceptional collective rights of indigenous peoples to choose a way of life not entirely consistent with the international bill of rights.[45]

The last point about the paradox of universalism cum exceptions completes the circle with the first point about universal human rights and merits commentary. Clearly in the industrialized European states formerly called Marxist, communist, or socialist, there is a clear and widespread movement to accept those civil and political rights long associated wtih "bourgeois democracies." The vision of the Gorbachev faction of the Communist party of the Soviet Union, no less than of the Bulgarian communist party, is to emulate Sweden. Marxist socialism, at least in the Soviet Union and many of its former allies, appears to seek the same goals of democratic socialism as found in the Scandinavian and European continental social democratic parties. This entails an acceptance of the human rights defined by international law.

Against the background of history from 1917 to the late 1980s, it is remarkable that Hungary in 1988–1989 consented to the right of its nationals to petition a U.N. agency if they believed their civil or political rights, as defined in the 1966 U.N. treaty on the subject, had been violated. It is equally remarkable that the same right of individual petition is being publicly debated in the Soviet Union, with some prospect that the Soviet Union will follow the Hungarian lead in accepting the relevant treaty provision. While Hungary (and Poland and Czechoslovakia) might have been expected to embrace the international version of human rights—when given the freedom to do so— because of their Western cultural heritage, the same cannot be said for the Soviet Union with its history of ambivalence about openings to the West. Thus Soviet developments are even more remarkable than some others.

And even in other Marxist polities such as the People's Republic of China, one can easily see the appeal of the idea of human rights even by citizens not educated in the West and even if claims to such rights are still systematically denied by the authorities. The demand for such human rights, as affected by transnational communications and other aspects of international relations, is greater than ever before. Those demanding greater attention to human rights in Mongolia are not doing so because of Western compulsion.

Although in much of the noncommunist less developed world the evidence is more ambiguous than in what used to be called the Soviet bloc, the clear aspiration of many (if not most) intellectuals and other citizens is to be associated with universally recognized rights, even if prevailing conditions make that achievement difficult. For example, in non-Westernized Burma (Myanmar) and Nepal, not to mention places like South Korea, Taiwan, and the Philippines, the appeal of human rights has been so great as to affect politico-legal reality. This is not to say that culture is irrelevant to human rights acceptance, and it is not by accident that a resurgence of fundamentalist Islam has proved inhospitable to effective implementation of human rights in places like Iran.

But if we take a historical perspective, empirical evidence supports the argument of a growing acceptance across the globe of the basic idea of human rights. That idea is more important in public policy than ever before. There is a growing global agreement on what is meant by human rights, at least in a formal sense and in the sense of defining its outer parameters. That is, there is growing agreement that a list of treaties and declarations define human rights in contemporary times. At the same time, there is no denying that such agreements are subject to continuing attempts at revision or amendment, continuing debate over precise meaning, and continuing debate over choices in manner and priority of implementation.

Despite such continuing controversy over rights policies, public authorities endorse internationally recognized human rights (even if they continue to violate them or defer to the violation of them by others). Individuals and their nongovernmental organizations pressure states as never before to close the gap between state promise and performance. Many problems of definition, application, and policy choice remain, but the evolution of international relations itself does not sustain the notion that the subject of human rights is a culture-bound construct being foisted upon an unwilling world through Western power. President Carter was essentially correct when he said in 1977, "The basic thrust of human affairs points toward a more universal demand for fundamental human rights."[46]

Human rights is an old subject precisely because it addresses a persistent question of human existence—the relationship of person(s) to state and society—that reoccurs not only across time but across cultures. That the idea of human rights has proved attractive across cultures, as a means for dealing with public authority and the larger society, mainly attests to its substantive content. In this most fundamental sense, its Western origin is largely irrelevant.

Human Rights as a New Idea

What is new about the old subject of human rights is its emergence as part of international relations. No doubt most intellectuals grappling with the subject of personal rights, and certainly those associated with the European enlightenment, thought they were articulating rights possessed by all humans everywhere. Even when allowing for the biases of the times pertaining to gender, race, and class, the central argument about human rights was, at a minimum, that all men of a certain race and class possessed inalienable rights, although most philosophers did not put the argument in such crass terms. These intellectual points notwithstanding, the political practice was that human rights was a matter for the nation-state. From roughly 1648 and the Peace of Westphalia endorsing supreme territorial authority, to 1945 and the U.N. era, human rights were regarded as mostly within the competence of the nation-state. This changed fundamentally in both legal theory and diplomatic practice starting in 1945 with the U.N. Charter and its provisions mandating all member states to promote observance of fundamental human rights without "distinction as to race, sex, language, or religion" (Art. 55).

This international attention to human rights did not spring totally new from the San Francisco Conference creating the United Nations. There were historical antecedents of two types. The first was based on moral opprobrium. Examples were the progressive outlawing of slavery, the slave trade, and slavery-like practices, which occurred throughout the nineteenth and twentieth centuries; the progressive protection of humane values in warfare, which started with the first Geneva Convention for the protection of sick and wounded in land warfare in 1864 and continued into present times (the most recent addition being two 1977 protocols added to the 1949 Geneva Conventions for the protection of human rights in armed conflict); and sporadic diplomatic intervention by some great powers to protect those being abused in foreign states (Britain and France occasionally took moral interest in the cause of various peoples in the Turkish empire). The overwhelming motivation for such international action was moral, even if some supporting rationales could be based on expediency (to offer humane treatment of combatants upon capture is to induce surrender from opponents rather than a fight to the finish).

The second type of human rights measure was based, at least to considerable degree, on state self-interest. The minority treaties of the interwar period, for example, attempted (rather unsuccessfully) to implement the collective human rights of certain minorities in certain European states because of the contribution of minority problems to the outbreak of World War I. State interest in avoiding the practical problem of war was the primary factor producing those treaties. The provisions of the League of Nations mandates system pertaining to the welfare of dependent peoples can be best understood as a political means to soften the continuation of a form of colonialism. Similarly, attempts to protect the rights of aliens were primarily based on attempts to preempt the international conflict that frequently accompanied alien mistreatment.

This is not to say that some or even all international action could not be based on a combination of moral and expediential concern. The attempts at international protection of labor rights from 1919 via the International Labour Organization (ILO) perhaps reflect this synthetic type of concern. Moreover, other expediential factors besides an effort to prevent international war could also come into play. Domestic political pressure in behalf of foreign minorities played some role in the state policies that produced the minority treaties.

But all of these pre-1945 attempts at international action in behalf of human rights, whether morally or politically motivated, represented small exceptions to the basic principle that human rights was normally a domestic affair of nation-states. Most of the international action for human rights prior to 1945 did not intrude on the state's authority within its territorial jurisdiction in any significant way. The international law on alien rights pertained to a relatively small fraction of persons and provided no means of implementation beyond state bargaining over rules.[47] The international law of armed conflict pertained to a situation already internationalized by the fact of international war (that law did not cover internal armed conflict until 1949) and did not provide even partial means of supervision until 1949.

The minority treaties were not generalized but pertained only to those states either defeated in World War I or emergent from defeated empires (other minorities were completely unprotected even in legal theory). The minority treaties did at least contain some monitoring mechanisms and did provide experience with the idea of private complaints.[48] The treaties banning slavery, the slave trade, and slavelike practices did not provide for centers of authority that could contest state policy. Indeed, the international instruments against slavery provided no special means of implementation, save for the concept of universal jurisdiction for states. Had Great Britain and its powerful navy not provided at least the threat of implementation measures, it is doubtful that the movement against slavery would have fared so well. (But this is, more positively, an example of the difference one great power can make when it is committed to seeing the protection of an internationally recognized human right implemented.) This leaves international action against labor abuses as the sole example of creation of international authority of broad scope to contest state policy within its territorial jurisdiction.

The significant point about the benchmark year of 1945 is not just that the U.N. Charter, as legal theory, broke with the dominant tradition of national sovereignty over human rights issues. Rather, it is that the charter represented a broad foundational stepping-stone leading to a continuing series of decisions that cumulatively internationalized human rights. After ratification of the charter came the passage of the Universal Declaration of Human Rights, accompanied by the creation of the U.N. Human Rights Commission, the passage by the Organization of American States (OAS) of the American Declaration on Human Rights, and the adoption by the Council of Europe of the European Convention on Human Rights. It was during this 1945–1950 period that a beginning was made on drafting many specific human rights treaties in an effort to translate the legal and quasi-legal principles already adopted into more specific, as well as presumably more binding, form.

Whereas legal theory and legal principles began to change in 1945, most global developments pertaining to human rights in a specific sense occurred only from 1967. Between 1967 and 1970, the two sweeping covenants on civil-political and economic-social-cultural rights came into legal force for adhering states; the U.N. Economic and Social Council (ECOSOC) authorized the U.N. Human Rights Commission to inquire into the human rights situation of specific states; and ECOSOC authorized a systematic procedure for the processing of private complaints pertaining to a systematic and gross violation of human rights (leading over time to the publication of a list of states engaged in such violations). By 1970, therefore, it was clear not only in legal theory but also in politico-legal practices that human rights had been internationalized on a global basis.

Regional developments supplemented these global trends. By 1970 in Western Europe, the international system of protection related to the European Convention had produced both international court cases of considerable number and quasi-cases handled in an extrajudicial process.[49] After 1970 in the Western Hemisphere, the American Declaration was supplemented not only by the Inter-American Convention and Court on Human Rights but also by the relatively dynamic Inter-American Commission on Human Rights. If other regional organizations lagged behind the Council of Europe and the OAS in human rights matters and if state behavior did not always match the human rights principles that states adopted in regional international organizations, nevertheless the direction of diplomacy was unmistakable.

International relations underwent a fundamental change from 1945 to 1970 in the sense that human rights ceased to be generally considered a matter fully protected by state sovereignty. As the Permanent Court of International Justice had said in a dictum in 1923: "The question whether a certain matter is or is not solely within the jurisdiction of a State is an essentially relative question; it depends on the development of international relations."[50] By 1970, states had consented to all sorts of treaties, had voted for all sorts of resolutions and declarations, and had engaged in all sorts of diplomatic practices that cumulatively had the effect of internationalizing the subject of human rights. The *New York Times* was essentially correct when it editorialized at the end of 1989: ". . . no dictatorship . . . could plausibly argue that human rights were purely an internal matter."[51]

There were two driving forces behind all of these developments: moral and expediential. The U.N. Charter represents a political rationale for the internationalization of human rights, but this may reflect an effort to give moral impulse a political facade. It is difficult, if not impossible, to say which was the primary or real motivating force in the contemporary internationalization of human rights, but it may prove insightful to reflect on the two wellsprings.

The U.N. Charter, Article 55, reads as follows:

> With a view to the creation of conditions of stability and well-being which are necessary for peaceful and friendly relations among nations based on respect for the principle of equal rights and self-determination of peoples, the United Nations shall promote: . . .
>
> c. universal respect for, and observance of, human rights and fundamental freedoms for all.

Hence, in charter theory, violation of human rights is seen as a source of international conflict; protection of human rights would eliminate a source of international instability. Simply put, protection of human rights is necessary for international peace—a point of view that has been articulated by a number of persons over the years. Woodrow Wilson gave salience to the argument that authoritarian states (which violate civil and political rights) cause wars, whereas democratic states (which protect civil and political rights) are peace loving.[52] Probably every U.S. president since Wilson has said something similar. According to President Reagan in 1985, "We've learned from history that the cause of peace and human freedom is indivisible. Respect for human rights is essential to true peace on earth. Governments that must answer to their peoples do not launch wars of aggression."[53]

There seems to be some truth embodied in this maxim about democratic states, but one can simplify too much. Some evidence strongly supports the thesis that democratic states do not make international war on each other, and it seems well established that no major democratic state has gone to war against another democratic polity in the twentieth century.[54] However, that evidence also shows that democratic states do make war on nondemocracies. A classic case is the tripartite democratic invasion of Egypt in 1956. Another is the Spanish-American War, forced on Spain by an imperial United States whose democratic procedures did not restrain its violent version of manifest destiny. And in fact, contrary to Reagan's statement, the Spanish-American War seems to show that public opinion in a democracy can push a government into a war that it does not initially want.

Moreover, not all authoritarian states are inherently aggressive. Franco's fascist Spain stayed neutral during World War II and attacked no one thereafter. Numerous communist states such as Hungary, Rumania, and Yugoslavia after 1945 proved more or less as less peace loving as democratic Norway or Italy. In these matters of international peace or war, it is obvious that much more is involved than the authoritarian structure of the state—which entails violation of civil and political rights. There are factors affecting the decision to go to war involving the distribution of power, personal leadership, alliance partnership, and others.[55] A complicating fact is that democracies also violate some human rights. The United States, for example, was a blatantly racist society until at least the 1960s, especially in the South. By the late 1980s, Guatemala combined free and fair elections with the forced disappearance of persons. In 1990 South Korea combined democratic elections with political prisoners.

Of course, an idea does not have to be true to be believed, and it is possible that the political theory about the linkage between human rights and peace was genuinely believed—even if partially true and partially false—by the U.N.'s creators. The legislative history or documentary record on these points is not clear.

That means it is also not clear whether those at the San Francisco Conference were driven by moral repugnance after the fascist atrocities of the 1930s and 1940s. Some argue, without conclusive proof, that revulsion toward the Nazi holocaust and other German and Japanese atrocities led to the internationalization of human rights in the U.N. era. Beyond the U.N. Charter, such legal instruments as the treaty against genocide or the one against torture seem primarily a moral expression rather than one based on political calculation about steps to peace. If torture led to war, more than fifty states would be so engaged in any given year, questions of power aside. If genocidal acts led to war, Burundi and Rwanda would be among the most war prone. Since such calculations seem far fetched, it is unlikely that many diplomats so calculated when they voted to approve human rights instruments or saw to it that their states became parties to them. This means that a moral impulse lay at the root of the human rights movement and that the internationalization of human rights rested more on moral than political foundations.

It is not well established how typical Jimmy Carter was as a national leader, but it is possible that a moral approach to human rights lay at the foundation of his human rights policy. In his memoirs, for example, he discussed his controversial human rights policy first in political or expediential terms. He wrote about restoring the American spirit and heading off leftist movements in foreign countries. But then he added a moral maxim about these policies: "And it was the right thing to do."[56]

It is possible that in the minds of statesmen in and around 1945, the two pillars were thought to support the same structure. Human rights could have been internationalized because of both a believed linkage between rights and peace and a moral revulsion to fascist atrocities. Policymakers do not always have the clearest of motives, nor do they usually have the time to reflect on and prioritize the ultimate reasons for policy choice. Perhaps it is in the synthesis of two different dynamics that the origins of international human rights reside, although it remains of interest to scholars to determine the extent to which the animating beliefs are true.

The point that should be stressed is a redundant one: international relations is not what it was. Since 1945 state authority, jurisdiction, and policy have been challenged in the name of human rights at an accelerating pace. The subject matter of human rights has been internationalized, and the states that seek to ignore the meaning and import of internationally recognized human rights, under the guise of claims to national sovereignty and domestic jurisdiction, do so at their peril—as a long list of discredited and disempowered dictators and repressive political parties will attest. This last point leads naturally into a third characterization of human rights.

Human Rights as a Political Idea

The study of human rights lends itself to many different perspectives. Philosophers and lawyers have understandably dominated the study of human rights in North America. Philosophers have frequently concerned themselves with what should be the good society, and what should be the personal rights related to that society, and lawyers, or at least law professors, have pioneered in dissecting the personal rights contained in international legal instruments.

One can also utilize the perspective of the economist in the study of rights. One of the perennial questions is whether the level or stage of economic development centrally affects rights performance.[57] Another is whether the manipulation of economic leverages can advance the cause of human rights.[58] A third is whether one can come at the subject of human rights from the religious, sociological, historical, or literary angle.[59]

Lying at the heart of the notion of human rights, however, is political process. The process of establishing and then implementing human rights is a political one in which claims are made against public authority. By definition this is a political process, since one meaning of *political* is the struggle through the exercise of power—influence—to make and implement public policy. Human rights are fundamental entitlements that allow persons to make claims vis-à-vis public authority pertaining to human dignity.

There is no reason to deny that philosophy can inform this political process, particularly in the form of discourse over what human rights should be recognized. There is also no reason to deny that one form of public policy is law. Law is formalized policy, resulting from a political process and leading to a further part of the political process in which the legislated standards are implemented.[60] But the central feature of the human rights movement is the struggle to get accepted in public policy the notion of human rights. The establishment and implementation of rights are not achieved in detachment from power and public policy. Much of the history of the human rights movement, both national and international, should be understood as claims by the have-nots, by the masses, against the haves, the elites, those with wealth and authority.[61] What David Heaps has written about democracy could be applied to a broad range of human rights: "It evolves indigenously [but in an interdependent world] over time through a political symbiosis of enlightened leadership and responsible citizenry."[62] This is precisely what politics is all about: the authoritative allocation of values as a result of struggle involving power in the form of influence.[63]

Thus the quintessence of human rights is politics, and that is the perspective I take in this book. There will be considerable attention to law but in relation to politics. The emphasis is on the political struggle to produce and then implement the law. Implementation is conceived as a broad political process, with enforcement referring to adjudication as a small subset of implementation. There will also be considerable emphasis on law as an agent of political socialization. That is, the international law of human rights will be viewed as reflective of policy values written into law through political process, and that same law will be viewed as communicating political values to actors in international relations.

There will be considerable attention to international organizations created through use of international law. Once again the emphasis will be on policy choice and the policy values that states and other actors impart to international organizations. Then the question will be, What is the extent to which these international organizations, once created and mandated, affect the policy choice of states?

Given this emphasis on political process, there will not be very much direct attention to the question of what rights should be recognized or whether the rights already recognized in the policy process can be justified philosophically. This is what philosophers do primarily, and there is no reason to try to critique that vast literature here.[64] Nor will there be much attention to what internationally recognized rights were intended to cover according to the legislative history of international legal instruments. That, too, has been attempted elsewhere.[65]

My central purpose is to give a sense of the international political process through which claims about human dignity are made. Which human rights have been recognized (an introduction to this has already been given), what does this indicate about policy values, how are the recognized rights implemented (to the extent that they are), and what are the prospects of further international action on human rights?

Levels of Political Analysis

One of the few widely accepted maxims for the study of international politics is that one can profitably utilize the idea of levels of analysis. Popularized by Kenneth Waltz, "levels of analysis" means that one can look at international affairs through different prisms.[66] In Waltz's terms, one can develop different images of international politics: the image or level of the individual, of the state, and of the international political system. Others have employed four or five levels. Thus one could use the individual, the subnational, the state, the regional, and the global.[67] By taking different looks at, or different angles on, a question, one can understand it most fully. And the level or image chosen may determine the results of inquiry.

In this book, I use four levels of analysis and mention a fifth. Using the global level first does not rule out attention to other levels or images. It is difficult, if not impossible, to speak of the global political system without reference to states and their foreign policies, which is analysis at the national level. Political scientists have never been very clear about the difference between a political system and actors within the system because a system is made up in part of actors. The language of levels of analysis refers mainly to differing emphases, not to airtight compartments of thought. It is difficult, if not impossible, to speak of a national level of analysis without mentioning individuals, for the governments that speak for states that represent nations are all made up of individuals. Again, one can speak of differing foci, emphases, or images to highlight certain points, but there cannot be total separation of the differing levels since they are but images of an integrated whole and since the only fundamental actor is the individual.

At the first or global international level, we look at international politics as a whole, with attention to actors that manifest a global scope to their action. We look at the functioning of international law, primarily as an agent of political socialization, in relation to human rights. Then we examine the United Nations, at least its principal human rights organs, over time. The cumulative impact should be to confirm that international relations has changed significantly with regard to the status of human rights.

There are certainly other possibilities for examination at the global level. One could examine human rights in the light of the evolution of global markets. By so doing, one could search for explanation in terms of global economic forces under the control of the core political economies, noting the resulting effect on dependent political economies.[68] Or, acknowledging one of the larger gaps in our knowledge, one could examine the global communications revolution and inquire into its impact on human rights. (While we have a number of studies about the legal right to information flows and/or a free press, we have almost no studies about how the media cover human rights issues and the effect of this coverage on policymakers.[69]) Or one could examine other global actors and their impact on human rights conditions. We have some studies of actors such as the U.N. Human Rights Commission[70] but need updated studies of actors such as the ILO[71] and further studies of important actors such as the World Bank and International Monetary Fund.[72]

At the level of regional international politics, chapter 4 will deal with human rights and the OAS. This is a little-studied phenomenon, at least by political scientists, perhaps because of the complexity of trying to explain the evolution of this human rights regime. Nevertheless, an attempt is made to utilize the concept of regime in a fairly rigorous way to delve into the dynamics of promoting and protecting human rights on a hemispheric basis.

Again, there are other possibilities for analysis at the regional level. Perhaps the most studied developments in this regard have been in Western Europe, where the Council of Europe's action in the field of civil and political human rights has led to a vast literature. This voluminous coverage stems not only from the openness of the process but also from the extensive case law from the European Court of Human Rights and (in a quasi-legal sense) the European Commission on Human Rights.[73] The European Social Charter, covering socioeconomic rights, has also been studied.[74]

More difficult is an analysis of the impact of the Helsinki process over time. This European regional process (with Canada and the United States accepted as honorary Europeans, as it were), centering on the Helsinki Accord of 1975 and its Basket Three on human rights and humanitarian principles, has been widely regarded as having an important impact on evolving human rights standards in Eastern Europe, but this is difficult to prove. Basket Three refers to the part of the Accord dealing with human rights and humanitarian principles; the other two "Baskets" deal with security and economics. Here one is not examining court or commission cases and their impact on public policy but rather searching for threads of influence from conference documents and state foreign policies out of a welter of conflicting events. We have much formal documentation, and even some perceptive studies, of the Helsinki process, but we need more.[75]

And we now have the African Charter of Human and People's Rights, under the aegis of the Organization of African Unity. The constituent documents have been analyzed, with speculation about actual functioning.[76] In the future, we will gain some understanding of how the norms and agencies will actually function in political context. Also, one can make some limited analyses of the human rights activity undertaken in conjunction with the Arab League and follow the beginnings of some regional action for human rights in Asia or parts of Asia.

One of the more fruitful levels of analysis, given the authority and power of the nation-state, is the state level. Chapter 5 provides an overview of U.S. foreign policy on human rights, showing how various administrations and the Congress have wrestled with the perplexing choices that are inherent in this subject matter. Since the 1970s the study of U.S. approaches to international human rights has become a growth sector, and the volume of literature is just short of overwhelming, but there is always room for more understanding. U.S. policy changes not only with administrations but with moods of Congress.[77] How a state organizes itself to fashion a human rights policy abroad may change.[78] The human rights conditions in particular countries change, as do the perspectives about what should be learned from previous country experiences.[79] No doubt there is more to learn about the effects of manipulating foreign assistance in the name of human rights.[80]

Beyond the United States, there are numerous states with a human rights component to foreign policy. Most of the OECD states (industrialized, democratic-capitalist states that are members of the Organization for Economic Cooperation and Development) have created special offices in their foreign ministries for the administration of human rights policy. All of these countries, from Canada to Spain, from Australia to Austria, have developed specific foreign policies about human rights. Most of these state policies on human rights have not been studied in any rigorous way and certainly not in comparative perspective, although we know some bits and pieces.[81]

One of the most interesting developments concerning the formerly Stalinist states of Eastern Europe is the evolution of their policies toward human rights. In the late 1980s, Hungary engaged in protracted conflict with Rumania over the latter's treatment of ethnic Hungarians and even introduced a resolution of condemnation in the United Nation over this issue (cosponsored by Sweden, it passed the U.N. Human Rights Commission in 1989). Hungary's shift concerning East German emigration, rationalized in terms of international human rights commitments, drew world attention in 1989. The Soviet Union has created a human rights office in its Forein Ministry and has altered a number of its approaches to international human rights. It has, for example, accepted the compulsory jurisdiction of the International Court of Justice concerning five human rights treaties (torture, genocide, political rights of women, traffic in prostitution, and racism).[82] All of this activity by rapidly changing states merits careful tracking and analysis.

Many of the less developed countries have taken action on international human rights. Senegal, for example, has often played a key role in brokering deals at the United Nations that have improved that organization's monitoring of human rights situations. The same could be said for some of the smaller states members of the OAS. India has been an important actor on matters pertaining to human rights in Sri Lanka (apparently both positively and negatively if the press reports are to be believed).[83] One cannot accurately understand the fate of the Vietnamese boat people without reference to refugee policy by Malaysia, Singapore, and Hong Kong. In general we need to know much more about Third World foreign policy on human rights.

One can also utilize what can be called the private transnational level or prism. It is a level designed to get at the impact of nongovernmental organizations (NGOs). The idea of transnational relations has been defined in several ways.[84] I use it here not in reference to parts of state bureaucracies, which may act relatively independently as actors across international boundaries, but rather only in the sense of private groups that—while headquartered in one country and perhaps even with a membership of one nationality—have an international focus to their work. A case study deals with the International Committee of the Red Cross (ICRC) and its work with victims of armed conflict and victims of politics (viz., political prisoners).

A number of other human rights NGOs have been studied, such as Amnesty International.[85] New private groups are appearing all the time, frequently stimulated by the repression and deprivation that their members experience.[86] The boundaries of this type of inquiry are amorphous, for any private group—such as a church or labor union—can become a human rights group depending on its activities.[87] One can analyze the tasks or specific roles these groups perform, such as fact finding and publicity, trial observation, formal lobbying of public authorities, provision of material and medical assistance, and mediation of policy disputes.[88] An unfortunately necessary new specialization is the provision of centers for coping with the aftermath of torture.[89] Moreover, some private groups are worth studying for their impact on human rights even if their primary raison d'être is profit seeking. One of the major actors here is the multinational or transnational corporation, which because of its resources or monopoly position can have an enormous impact on the implementation—or lack thereof—of human rights. A provocative example entailed Coca-Cola in Guatemala.[90] A more positive example pertained to the British corporation, Booker McConnel, in Kenya.[91]

Finally, there is the individual level or focal point. While one can debate whether it is impersonal forces or individuals that make history, it is obvious that whether one empowers a Jimmy Carter or a Ronald Reagan, a Leonid Brezhnev or a Mikhail Gorbachev, a Sihanouk or a Pol Pot does make a difference for human rights.[92] From a slightly different perspective, the presence or absence of a Nelson Mandela, Lech Walesa, Mother Teresa, or Adolfo Perez Esquivel can make some impact on human rights. There is at least some truth to the old saying that political analysis without biography (and/or autobiography) is just a form of taxonomy.

Here the problems of analysis are formidable. First is the problem of access of the researcher to the personage in question or to the documentary evidence of his or her private thoughts; and it is for reasons of lack of any special access that there is not an illustrative chapter in this book. Beyond that barrier, there is the question of how best to analyze the individual studied, whether living or deceased. There are various theories of personal leadership or influence in general, some Freudian and some not.[93] Then one has to apply the chosen approach to the issue area of human rights.

Did Carter really stumble into an emphasis on human rights during his 1976 campaign as an effective way to appeal to American voters,[94] and thus should one look for domestic political calculation behind his human rights pronouncements? Is this why he seemed to find it so easy to discard his human rights emphasis when visiting the shah of Iran or the royal family of Saudi Arabia? Or was there a personal moral impulse to his public policy stances, which caused him to speak out on human rights before understanding the complexity of the subject, especially in international perspective? Is this why he wrote in his memoirs, "I did not fully grasp all of the ramifications of our new [human rights] policy"?[95] The answers to such questions at the individual level would do much to explain some of the dynamics of human rights action in a given era.

It is likely that the fullest analysis of human rights inquiries will be based on a combination of different levels of analysis or different foci.[96] Yet it is usually helpful to disaggregate different inquiries for reasons of simplicity and organization. If one wants to comprehend the political process that controls the recognition and implementation of human rights on an international basis, systematically distinguishing levels of analysis is helpful.

Yet our methodological concerns should not obscure or make unnecessarily complex our substantive concerns. Internationally recognized human rights are making a different world. Their acknowledgment and implementation, however incomplete the process on both accounts, represents a fundamental change in international relations. The late Andrei Sakharov, father of the Soviet H-bomb and leading crusader for human rights, stated his provocative view of the ultimate potential of human rights:

> The global character of human rights is particularly important. [Its] ideology is probably the only one that can be combined with such diverse ideologies as communism, social democracy, religion, technocracy, and those that are national and indigenous. It can serve as a foothold for those who do not wish to be aligned with the theoretical intricacies of dogmas, and who have tired of the abundance of ideologies, none of which has brought mankind simple human happiness. The defense of human rights is a clear path toward the unification of peoples in our turbulent world, and a path toward the relief of suffering.[97]

Anything with such alleged potential deserves careful study.

Notes

1. Ronald Dworkin, *Taking Rights Seriously* (Cambridge: Harvard University Press, 1977).

2. Burns Weston, "Human Rights," in *Encyclopaedia Britannica,* 15th ed. (London: Encyclopaedia Britannica, 1985), 714–22.

3. Jack Donnelly, "Human Rights and Human Dignity," *American Political Science Review* 76, 2 (June 1982): 433–49.

4. See further Abdullahi A. An-Na'im, "Religious Minorities under Islamic Law and the Limits of Cultural Relativism," *Human Rights Quarterly* 9, 1 (February 1987):

1–18. Khalifa Abdul Hakin, *Fundamental Human Rights* (Lahore: Institute of Islamic Culture, 1955). Khalid M. Ishaque, "Human Rights in Islamic Law," *Review of International Commission of Jurists* 12 (June): 30–39. Donna Arzt, "The Application of Human Rights Law in Islamic States," *Human Rights Quarterly* 12, 2 (May 1990): 202–31.

5. See further James C. Hsiung, ed., *Human Rights in East Asia* (New York: Paragon House Publishers, 1986). David J. Wessels, "Advancing Human Rights: Japan, East Asia, and the World," Research Paper A-49, Institute of International Relations, Sophia University (Japan) (1986). Claude E. Welch, Jr., and Virginia A. Leary, eds., *Asian Perspectives on Human Rights* (Boulder, Colo.: Westview, 1990).

6. See further *New York Times,* July 17, 1990, A15.

7. See, for example, George Kennan's *Cloud of Danger* (London: Hutchinson, 1978).

8. For a discussion of the anthropologists like Franz Boas and Melville Herskovits who argued for a strong cultural relativism, and of the decline of this school of thought in that discipline, see, among others, Wilcomb E. Washburn, "Cultural Relativism, Human Rights, and the AAAS," *American Anthropologist* 89, 3 (September 1987): 939–42, and Henry H. Bagish, "Confessions of a Former Cultural Relativist," in *Annual Editions: Anthropology* (Guilford, Conn.: Dushkin Publishing Group, 1990), 30–37.

9. See further some of the essays in Adamantia Pollis and Peter Schwab, eds., *Human Rights: Cultural and Ideological Perspectives* (New York: Praeger Publishers, 1980).

10. David P. Forsythe, ed., *Human Rights and Development: International Views* (London: Macmillan, 1989), chaps. 18–20.

11. Compare Josiah Cobbah, "African Values and the Human Rights Debate: An African Perspective," *Human Rights Quarterly* 9, 3 (August 1987): 309–31. See further Josiah Cobbah and Munyonzwe Hamalengwa, eds., "The Human Rights Literature on Africa: A Bibliography," *Human Rights Quarterly* 8, 1 (February 1986): 115–26. And see Abdullahi An-Na'im and Francis Seng, eds., *Human Rights in Africa* (Washington, D.C.: Brookings, 1990).

12. David Morris, "Holland: A Social Conservative's Nightmare," *Charlotte (N.C.) Observer,* October 15, 1989, C1.

13. Charles F. Wilkinson, *American Indians, Time, and the Law* (New Haven: Yale University Press, 1987).

14. *New York Times,* July 10, 1990, 10.

15. Jack Donnelly, *Universal Human Rights in Theory and Practice* (Ithaca, N.Y.: Cornell University Press, 1989), chap. 2.

16. Henry Shue, *Basic Rights: Subsistence, Affluence, and U.S. Foreign Policy* (Princeton, N.J.: Princeton University Press, 1980).

17. Various views are reviewed in Donnelly, *Universal Human Rights,* chap. 2.

18. David P. Forsythe, *Human Rights and World Politics,* rev. 2d ed. (Lincoln: University of Nebraska Press, 1989).

19. *New York Times,* December 6, 1989, 7.

20. Gerhard von Glahn, *Law Among Nations: An Introduction to Public International Law,* 5th ed. (New York: Macmillan, 1986), 510: "Others reply that state practice as well as certain treaty provisions demonstrate convincingly that *jus cogens* does not exist (the present writer shares that view)."

21. U.N. Covenant on Civil and Political Rights: Article 4; European Convention on Human Rights: Article 15; American Convention on Human Rights: Article 27.

22. von Glahn, *Law among Nations,* 282. von Glahn also lists terrorism, but he is in error since terrorism is not found in conventional law, is not clearly found in customary law, and presents no agreed-upon definition. If an act cannot be defined, it cannot be a crime giving rise to universal or any other jurisdiction. von Glahn also lists crimes against humanity. While this is not a clear error, it is dubious; most of the Germans and Japanese tried after World War II were not tried for a crime against humanity, and, since that time, to my knowledge, only Israel and France have incorporated a crime against humanity into national law. This concept remains controversial, constituting more sporadic victor's justice than established positive international law.

23. Herman Burgers and Hans Danelius, eds., *The United Nations Convention against Torture* (Dordrecht: Kluwer Academic, 1988). Amnesty International, *Report on Torture* (New York: Farrar, Straus, and Giroux, 1975), plus various AI reports since.

24. Slavery and slavelike practices are common in much of Africa and Asia. See especially the publications of the Anti-Slavery Society, based in London. See further the United Nations report covered by the *New York Times* and reprinted as "Report: 100,000 Enslaved," *Lincoln Journal,* August 26, 1981, 10, focusing on Mauritania.

25. George F. Will, "Slavery Exists—and It Still Pays," *Washington Post,* June 21, 1990, A19.

26. Ted Robert Gurr and James R. Scarritt, "Minorities Rights at Risk: A Global Survey," *Human Rights Quarterly* 11, 3 (August 1989): 375–405.

27. E.g., Third Geneva Convention of 1949: Article 129.

28. Summary executions are prohibited by treaties on human rights in both peace and armed conflict. Then there is the growing problem of unofficial summary execution. See further U.N. Center for Human Rights, *Enforced or Involuntary Disappearances* (Geneva: United Nations, 1989). While a "disappeared person" is not always a victim of summary execution, in all too many cases, there is congruence between the two terms.

29. Protocol I of 1977, additional to the Geneva Conventions of August 12, 1949, for victims of war, prohibits starvation of civilians as an act of international armed conflict. See Article 54. This is the first time conventional law has contained such an explicit prohibition in time of armed conflict. In situations of famine in peacetime, there is usually an international program of humanitarian relief, with concomitant pressure on the government involved to permit that relief to enter national territory. See Gil Loescher and Bruce Nichols, *The Moral Nation: Humanitarianism and U.S. Foreign Policy Today* (Notre Dame, Ind.: University of Notre Dame Press, 1989), esp. the chapter by Frederick C. Cuny.

30. See esp. Paul Gordon Lauren, *Power and Prejudice: The Politics and Diplomacy of Racial Discrimination* (Boulder, Colo.: Westview Press, 1988).

31. See note 21.

32. Common Article 3 of the Geneva Conventions of August 12, 1949, supplemented by Protocol II of 1977.

33. "A Nigerian Shame: The Agony of the Child Bride," *New York Times,* July 17, 1987, 7. This should be read in the context of Yougindra Khushalani, *Dignity and*

Honour of Women as Basic and Fundamental Human Rights (Dordrecht: Kluwer Academic, 1983). And Natalie Kaufman Hevener, *International Law and the Status of Women* (Boulder, Colo.: Westview, 1983).

34. Alison T. Slack, "Female Circumcision: A Critical Appraisal," *Human Rights Quarterly* 10, 4 (November 1988): 437–86. See also *New York Times*, January 15, 1990, 4, on female circumcision in Africa, and, more generally, Arvonne S. Fraswer, *The U.N. Decade for Women: Documents and Dialog* (Boulder, Colo.: Westview Press, 1987).

35. See further Riane Eisler, "Human Rights: Toward an Integrated Theory for Action," *Human Rights Quarterly*, 9, 3 (August 1987): 287–308, arguing for priority to women's rights.

36. Donnelly, *Universal Human Rights*.

37. Hersch Lauterpact, *International Law and Human Rights* (Hamden, Conn.: Archon Books, 1968). Compare H.L.A. Hart, "Are There Any Natural Rights," *Philosophical Review* 64, 2 (April 1955): 175.

38. Jeremy Bentham and the utilitarians are usually cited here. For a discussion of this school of thought, see Forsythe, *Human Rights and World Politics*, chap. 7.

39. John Rawls, *A Theory of Justice* (Cambridge: Harvard University Press, 1971).

40. Donnelly, *Universal Human Rights,* esp. pp. 21–23.

41. U.S. courts have said that if the Congress or state legislatures wish to provide, through voluntary discretion, welfare programs, these programs must meet due process (civil) rights. But Congress and the various legislatures are not obligated to provide such programs. Thus welfare programs are not obligatory duties on the part of public authorities in response to human rights. They are socioeconomic benefits that may be provided; if provided, they must meet civil standards of equality and fairness. See further Martha H. Good, "Freedom from Want: The Failure of United States Courts to Protect Subsistence Rights," *Human Rights Quarterly* 6, 3 (August 1984): 335–65. See further "Shelter Is Not a Right, Court in Jersey Holds," *New York Times,* December 10 [human rights day], 1986, 15.

42. Donnelly, *Universal Human Rights.*

43. Forsythe, *Human Rights and World Politics.*

44. On foreign policy as entailing the management of contradictions, see Stanley Hoffmann, "The Hell of Good Intentions," *Foreign Policy*, no. 29 (Winter 1977–1978): esp. 5.

45. Douglas Sanders, "The U.N. Working Group on Indigenous Populations," *Human Rights Quarterly* 11, 3 (August 1989): 406–33. Wolfgang Heinz, *Indigenous Populations, Ethnic Minorities, and Human Rights* (Berlin: Quorum Verlag, 1988). United Nations, *The Rights of Indigenous Peoples,* Human Rights Fact Sheet 9 (Geneva and New York: United Nations, 1990).

46. Department of State, *News Release,* March 17, 1977, 3.

47. See further Richard Lillich, *The Human Rights of Aliens in Contemporary International Law* (Manchester: Manchester University Press, 1984).

48. Inis L. Claude, Jr., *National Minorities: An International Problem* (Cambridge: Harvard University Press, 1955). See further Vernon van Dyke, *Human Rights, Ethnicity and Discrimination* (Westport, Conn.: Greenwood Press, 1985).

49. Council of Europe, *Yearbook of the European Convention on Human Rights*

(Strasbourg: Council of Europe, annual). Jacob Sundberg, ed., *Laws, Rights and the European Convention on Human Rights* (Littleton, Colo.: F.B. Rothman, 1986). Vincent Berger, *A Casebook on the European Court of Human Rights* (Savage, Md: Rowman and Littlefield, 1989). Ralph Beddard, *Human Rights and Europe: A Study of the Machinery of Human Rights Protection of the Council of Europe,* 2d ed. (London: Sweet and Maxwell, 1980.

50. *Nationality Decrees in Tunis and Marocco,* Permanent Court of International Justice, Series B, No. 4: World Court Report 143.

51. "Human Rights: Now the Hard Part," *New York Times,* December 30, 1989, 14. This editorial was correct in its conclusion but should have cited legal sources in addition to recent political events. Recent political events do not legitimize the internationalization of human rights as much as longstanding legal and diplomatic practice.

52. See further Kenneth Waltz, *Man, the State and War* (New York: Columbia University Press, 1959).

53. "Safeguarding Human Rights," *Current Policy,* December 10, 1985, 1.

54. Michael W. Doyle, "Liberalism and World Politics," *American Political Science Review* 80, 4 (December 1986): 1151–70.

55. Among many sources, see Geoffrey Blainey, *The Causes of War* (London: Macmillan, 1988). Compare Seyom Brown, *The Causes and Prevention of War* (New York: St. Martin's Press, 1987).

56. Jimmy Carter, *Keeping Faith: Memoirs of a President* (New York: Bantam Books, 1982), 143.

57. See further Forsythe, *Human Rights and Development.*

58. Ibid.

59. The contents of *Human Rights Quarterly* supports this statement.

60. Werner Levi, *Law and Politics in the International Society* (Beverly Hills, Calif.: Sage Publications, 1976).

61. Rhoda Howard, *Human Rights in Commonwealth Africa* (London: Rowman & Littlefield, 1986).

62. David Heaps, "Paving the Way to Democracy by Upholding Human Rights," *Christian Science Monitor,* July 25, 1988, 21.

63. This formulation is the Forsythe variation of David Easton's core concept in *The Political System,* 2nd ed. (New York: Knopf, 1971).

64. A useful view is A.J.M. Milne, *Human Rights and Human Diversity: An Essay in the Philosophy of Human Rights* (Albany, N.Y.: SUNY Press, 1986). Compare James W. Nickel, *Making Sense of Human Rights: Philosophical Reflections on the Universal Declaration of Human Rights* (Berkeley: University of California Press, 1987).

65. Louis Henkin, ed., *The International Bill of Rights* (New York: Columbia University Press, 1981). Marc Bossuyt, *Guide to The "Travaux Preparatoires"* of the International Covenant on Civil and Political Rights (Dordrecht: Kluwer Academic, 1987).

66. Waltz, *Man, the State and War.*

67. See further Paul R. Viotti and Mark V. Kauppi, eds., *International Relations Theory: Realism, Pluralism, Globalism* (New York: Macmillan, 1987), esp. chap. 3.

68. E.g., Immanueal Wallerstein, *The Modern World System* (New York: Academic Press, 1974).

69. One of the very few studies is Asbjorn Eide and Sigrun Skogly, eds., *Human Rights and the Media* (Oslo: Norwegian Institute of Human Rights, 1988). See also Kathleen Pritchard, "Human Rights: A Decent Respect for Public Opinion" (paper presented for the International Studies Association's annual meeting, Washington, D.C., April 1990).

70. Howard Tolley, Jr., *The U.N. Commission on Human Rights* (Boulder, Colo: Westview, 1987).

71. For an older, in-depth and analytical treatment of the ILO and human rights, see Ernst B. Haas, *Human Rights and International Action: The Case of Freedom of Association* (Stanford: Stanford University Press, 1970).

72. E.g., Margaret Conklin and Daphne Davidson, "The I.M.F. and Economic and Social Human Rights: A Case Study of Argentina, 1958–1985," *Human Rights Quarterly* 8, 2 (May 1986): 227–69. Robert L. Ayres, *Banking on the Poor: The World Bank and World Poverty* (Cambridge: MIT Press, 1983).

73. See note 49.

74. D. Harris, *The European Social Charter* (Charlottesville: University Press of Virginia, 1984).

75. See William Korey, "Helsinki, Human Rights, and the Gorbachev Style," *Ethics and International Affairs* 1, 1 (1987): 113–34. Compare A. Bloed and P. van Dijk, ed., *Essays on Human Rights in the Helsinki Process* (Dordrecht: Kluwer Academic 1985), and Votech Mastny, *Helsinki, Human Rights, and European Security* (Durham, N.C.: Duke University Press, 1986).

76. Olusola Ojo and Amadu Sessay, "The O.A.U. and Human Rights: Prospects for the 1980s and Beyond," *Human Rights Quarterly* 8, 1 (February 1986): 89–103.

77. David P. Forsythe, *Human Rights and U.S. Foreign Policy: Congress Reconsidered* (Gainesville: University Presses of Florida, 1988).

78. Edwin S. Maynard, "The Bureaucracy and Implementation of U.S. Human Rights Policy," *Human Rights Quarterly* 11, 2 (May 1989): 175–248.

79. E.g., David D. Newsom, ed., *The Diplomacy of Human Rights* (Lanham, Md.: University Press of America, 1986).

80. Different studies of this genre have led to conflicting results. See the literature review in Thomas E. Pasquarello, "Human Rights and U.S. Bilateral Aid Allocations to Africa," in David L. Cingranelli, ed., *Human Rights: Theory and Measurement* (New York: St. Martin's Press, 1988), 236–54.

81. There are many studies of some aspect of U.S. foreign policy and human rights. There are very few studies of other states. But see Robert O. Matthews and Cranford Pratt, eds., *Human Rights in Canadian Foreign Policy* (Montreal: McGill/Queens University Press, 1988). There are fewer still comparative studies. But see Forsythe, *Human Rights and Development,* pt. 2, with attention to the foreign policies of the Federal Republic of Germany, the Netherlands, the United States, Canada, and others. See in general R.J. Vincent, *Foreign Policy and Human Rights: Issues and Responses* (Cambridge: Cambridge University Press, 1986).

82. *New York Times,* March 19, 1988, 1, 4.

83. Ibid., May 17, 1989, 6.

84. E.g., Viotti and Kauppi, *International Relations Theory,* chap. 3.

85. E.g., Egon Larsen, *A Flame in Barbed Wire: The Story of Amnesty International* (London: Frederick Muller, 1978). Jonathan Power, *Against Oblivion: Amnesty International's Fight for Human Rights* (London: Fontana, 1981).

86. Lowell W. Livezey, Nongovernmental Organizations and the Idea of Human Rights (Princeton, N.J.: Princeton University Press, 1988). Forsythe, Human Rights and Development, pt. 7.

87. Forsythe, Human Rights and World Politics, chap. 6.

88. Ibid.

89. "Grim Specialty Emerges As Therapists Treat Victims of Torture," New York Times, April 25, 1989, 19–20.

90. Henry J. Frundt, Refreshing Pauses: Coca-Cola and Human Rights in Guatemala (New York: Praeger, 1987). More generally see parts of Antonia Cassesse, ed., U.N. Law/Fundamental Rights (Alphen van den Rijn: Sijthoff and Noordhoff, 1979).

91. Susan George, How the Other Half Dies: The Real Reasons for World Hunger (Montclair, N.J.: Allanheld, Osmun & Co., 1977), 155–58. This source should be read in the context of Philip Alston and Katarina Tomasevski, eds., The Right to Food (Dordrecht: Kluwer Academic, 1984).

92. John G. Stoessinger, Why Nations Go to War, 2d ed. (New York: St. Martin's Press, 1978).

93. The bibliography on personal leadership and influence is too vast for repetition here. For some leading examples, see James David Barber, Politics by Humans: Research on American Leadership (Durham, N.C.: Duke University Press, 1988). Compare the provocative and Freudian interpretations of political action and leadership in E. Victor Wolfenstein, The Revolutionary Personality (Princeton, N.J.: Princeton University Press, 1967).

94. Elizabeth Drew, "Reporter at Large: Human Rights," New Yorker, July 18, 1977, starting at p. 36.

95. Carter, Keeping Faith, 144.

96. Even if one focuses on the Carter period, for example, and on the president's personal inputs on human rights issues, his views must still be translated into a policy that can be diffused throughout the bureaucracy. On this point, see Lincoln P. Bloomfield, "From Ideology to Program to Policy: Tracking the Carter Human Rights Policy," Journal of Policy Analysis and Management 2, 1 (Fall 1982): 1–12. To the personal focus, and the bureaucratic, must be added the congressional, the public, and the international.

97. Quoted in Heaps, "Paving the Way to Democracy."

2
Human Rights and International Law: Basic Values

A quarter of a century ago, William Coplin pointed out that international law, in addition to being a direct control on state behavior, was also an agent of political socialization.[1] In this socializing function, international law acted to communicate assumptions about the state system. Three assumptions were traditionally fundamental: (1) the international system was statecentric, and the highest value was state security; (2) law recognized the exercise of state power and made ample allowance for war; (3) there was a need to maintain minimum order, a value in tension with the first two.

In this generally perceptive essay, Coplin noted that whereas there had been broad concensus in support of the three basic assumptions, with a legal consensus reflecting a political consensus, there had arisen a state of "arrested ambiguity."[2] International law no longer communicated clear conceptions about the nature of international politics because legal doctrines were unclear. Underlying this legal confusion were "social and institutional revolutions," which had changed the nature of international politics.[3]

One of these social revolutions was a growing emphasis in world politics on individual human rights, as contrasted with state interests and state security policy. Part of the institutional revolution was a growing number of international organizations, both public and private, that focused on human rights.

This chapter revisits Coplin's general thesis with particular regard to the place of human rights in contemporary international relations. Twenty-five years ago he argued: "Although the role of the individual in international law is small and the chances for its rapid development in the near future slight, it represents a more vital challenge to traditional international law and to the assumptions of the state system than either international or regional organizations."[4]

There is some ambiguity about the meaning of the role of the individual in Coplin's original treatment. On the basis of his wording, as well as on the logic of his general argument, it is reasonable to equate "role of the individual" with internationally recognized human rights, both that law which grants actor status to individuals and that which regulates states for the rights of more passive individuals.

I believe that Coplin's views about the place of the individual in international relations have proved partially erroneous for three reasons, entailing both mistaken forecasts and mistaken conceptualization. First, the place of individual human rights in international law has developed rapidly, and international law is increasingly clear about many human rights obligations. On this point much law is no longer in a state of arrested ambiguity. Second, the status of individual human rights has developed largely in tandem with international governmental organizations, not as an alternative challenge to the state, and indeed in a most fundamental sense the state has challenged itself. Finally, the development of individual human rights in international law can be compatible with an international system in which states retain considerable legal and political importance.

The Role of the Individual

Whatever the earlier status of individuals and other nonstate entities in the law of nations, by the nineteenth century *international law* referred to a public international law brought into being by state consent and regulating only states directly.[5] As for both substance and procedure, states were the only subjects of international law; other entities were mere objects, affected by the law through state behavior. The dignity of individuals was largely a matter of domestic jurisdiction. As Coplin correctly observed, states were much more interested in using international law to promote their authority and independence than to promote human dignity.

Coplin was less than precise in observing an increasing role of the individual in international law. At times he spoke of the individual as an actor recognized by international law. At other times he spoke of the individual as an absolute value, but this could be a value or goal implemented by states as actors, with the individual legally a passive beneficiary. So too when Coplin spoke of the individual as point of policy reference, he could be referring to object status as well as subject status. Clearly he was referring overall to the substantive and procedural rights of humans, as compared to states and intergovernmental organizations. But human rights can entail state action, as well as encompassing legally recognized individual action. It is also clear that Coplin was not referring to other roles of individuals, such as executive heads within an intergovernmental organization. On balance, it is reasonable to interpret Coplin as saying that internationally recognized human rights constitutes one of the new challenges to traditional international law.

Coplin observed the beginnings of the emphasis on the rights of individuals in international law, with law a reflection of politics and a socializing agent thereof. That emphasis on individual human rights has been advancing in a revolutionary, accelerating, and continuing process during the last half of the twentieth century. The development of international human rights law can be viewed in three different but related ways: (1) human rights is increasingly a well-established issue area of international politics; (2) states are increasingly obligated to respect human rights norms; and (3) individuals have increasingly obtained legal personality, in the form of partial subjectivity, with regard to human rights matters.

Politically human rights is a clearly accepted issue area of international relations manifesting a core regime plus additional regional and functional regimes.[6] If we use the idea of an issue cycle—genesis, crisis, ritualization, dormancy, decision making, and authoritative allocation—we get a sense of political overview.[7] The genesis of change for the issue of international human rights occurred in the middle of the nineteenth century when movements to protect victims of war and of slavery succeeded in obtaining state endorsement of their concerns. Somewhat later movements were successful (in the formal legal sense) in protecting laborers, refugees, minorities, and others.[8]

Crisis occurred during World War II when the Holocaust (and to a lesser extent Japanese atrocities) appalled moral sensitivities. Moral outrage led to the ritualization, or institutionalization, of a general concern for individual dignity in world affairs through the adoption of the International Bill of Rights (Article 55 of the U.N. Charter, the 1948 Universal Declaration of Human Rights, and the two U.N. Covenants on Civil and Political Rights and Economic, Social, and Cultural Rights).[9] This was the normative foundation of the core regime on international human rights, supplemented by functional regimes on genocide, refugees, racial discrimination, labor, torture, and other issues and also by regional regimes under the Council of Europe, OAS, and Organization of African Unity.

There was a global period of dormancy between 1956 (when the two covenants were completed de facto) and the late 1960s when more serious decision making at the United Nations began to address the question of implementing human rights standards in specific countries and that of responding more seriously to private petitions about human rights violations.[10] There also evolved more serious concern for integrating human rights values into national foreign policies at about this same time. In the United States, for example, Congress dealt with the subject in considerable detail from about 1973, and the administrations did so from 1977.[11] This transition from dormancy to more serious status was also formalized by Basket Three of the 1975 Helsinki Accord pertaining to human rights and humanitarian principles in East-West negotiations.

Authoritative allocation of human rights values has, for the most part and certainly in a formal sense, been absent at the global level. There are only two cases in which the U.N. Security Council has reached a binding decision pertaining to human rights (mandatory economic sanctions on the white minority regime of Rhodesia from 1966 to 1979; and a mandatory arms embargo on the Republic of South Africa from 1977 to the present). The International Court of Justice has handed down few judgments on human rights. The international authoritative allocation of human rights values is far more developed in Western Europe and slightly more developed in the Western Hemisphere.[12]

A traditional legal view would trace developments in different terms, but the outcome would be the same. While a political concern for issue cycles facilitates an overview of regime formation and development, a traditional legal view enriches with detail. It has long been acknowledged that international law recognized individuals in the sense of imposing duties. It proscribed such individual acts as piracy, slavery, war crimes, crimes against humanity, and planning or waging aggressive war.[13] It has not been so well known that international law, even before the U.N. period, also recognized individual rights. These were mostly legal rights unrelated to human rights. Individuals were empowered to act in legally recognized ways under the terms of the Central American Court of Justice, the Mixed Arbitral Commissions stemming from the Versailles Peace Conference, the Polish-German Convention on Upper Silesia, the Polish-Danzig Treaty, the minority treaties in the interwar years, and, indirectly, the Mandates Commission of the League of Nations.[14] But it should be stressed that the recognition of international human rights has taken two essential forms, and only one of them entails individual procedural rights.

Rights have been conferred on individuals as a means to human dignity, and states have been obligated to respect them, even when individuals have not been empowered to act for themselves. This can be demonstrated by reference to the Geneva Conventions and Protocols for the protection of victims of war (increasingly referred to as the core of human rights law in armed conflict). The fact that individuals are not legally empowered to any great extent to act for themselves does not mean that prisoners of war, civilians in a war zone and occupied territory, or sick or wounded combatants have no rights. Specified persons in specified situations have specified rights, whether or not protected persons qua individuals are afforded procedural rights. States that have consented to these standards are fully obligated to respect them. The question of procedural rights, and more generally supervision of rights, pertains to issues of effective implementation rather than to the existence of rights ab initio.[15]

Thus, if international law restricts state behavior by legislation of human rights in order to increase the dignity of persons, human rights exist in the formal-legal sense. This can have, at times, nothing at all to do with whether a natural individual is a subject or an object of international law. In this first form, human rights can exist, in the sense of being formally recognized by states, without subjectivity (meaning legal personality) for natural (or juridical) persons. Any view that deals with the place of individual human rights in international relations must accommodate this first characterization in order to appreciate reality, even though individual procedural rights may not be involved. Increasingly states are restricted by the role of the individual as an entity recognized by international law and possessing rights, with a corresponding duty by states to respect them. This is an increasingly important role.

But even this clarification has become frequently moot, for modern international law clearly recognizes at least partial subjectivity for individuals. Increasingly the law provides for individuals to act in their own capacity in order to try to implement their human rights afforded by international law. This second form of human rights law is most developed in Western Europe.

Individuals in states that are members of the Council of Europe and parties to the European Convention on Human Rights, when such states have consented to the specific rules in question and have in general exhausted local remedies, can submit an individual petition to the European Human Rights Commission in pursuit of redress of grievance. If the matter remains unresolved and if the state in question has consented to the specific rule, the commission, on behalf of the individual, can petition the European Court of Human Rights, with the individual's legal counsel participating in deliberations. According to case law, the individual can be represented in an international tribunal by both international agency and personal attorney. The individual has direct locus standi in the commission and indirect standing in the court. The commission may also refer the matter to the Committee of Ministers, in which case the individual is represented indirectly in a second international body.[16]

A related but often ignored point is that when human rights standards become involved in economic proceedings under the Treaty of Rome creating the European Communities, individuals in states party to that treaty can petition the European Court of Justice for redress of grievance against community institutions (but not directly against states). Moreover, community standards (including human rights standards derived from the Council of Europe) have been incorporated directly into the various European municipal legal orders, and individuals have recourse to protection under those standards through national courts.[17]

These remarks pertain only to the procedural capacity of natural individuals to secure implementation and enforcement of their internationally recognized human rights in Western Europe; they do not encompass action permissible by either states or juridical persons (commercial enterprises).

Most of the human rights case law emanating from the regional bodies in Western Europe originates from individual action.[18]

Individual legal subjectivity can also be seen in the Western Hemisphere where individuals in OAS member states have automatic access (without the necessity of state acceptance of a specific legal rule) to the Inter-American Commission on Human Rights and the added advantage that the commission will accept the individual's version of events if the state in question does not respond to petition within a specified time. A slightly different set of rules governs individual petitions under the American Convention on Human Rights. As in Western Europe, if the commission, as a collective ombudsman, cannot resolve the matter and if the state in question has so consented, the commission may take the case to the Inter-American Court of Human Rights, which began to function in 1979.[19] In its most important case thus far, and one started by individual petition, the court handed down a binding judgment with regard to death squads and disappeared persons in Honduras.[20]

Even when one moves to global international law and even when acknowledging lack of individual procedural capacity in the International Court of Justice, important events have transpired with regard to the recognition of partial subjectivity for individuals. Although large numbers of individuals complained of human rights violations to the United Nations, from 1945 until the late 1960s such action resulted in nothing more than the construction of an elaborate trash basket procedure.[21] In 1967 the ECOSOC, in resolution 1503, authorized a somewhat more responsible processing of private petitions (which could be individual or collective, the latter category referring to nongovernmental organizations). Such petitions were to be processed and evaluated by the U.N. Human Rights Commission and its subcommission, and practice eventually led to the publication of a list of states where there appeared to be a pattern of gross violation of internationally recognized human rights.[22]

In 1977 the U.N. Human Rights Committee began to function, since the U.N. Covenant on Civil and Political Rights had entered into legal force the preceding year. That committee was authorized, when adhering states had consented to an optional protocol, to receive individual petitions about violations of civil and political rights. Almost forty states had provided that consent by 1989, and the committee had acted rather vigorously, albeit diplomatically, in response.[23]

There were other parts of the U.N. system in which private petitions, including individual or collective communications, were utilized, such as by the ILO and also the committees that oversaw the Conventions on Racial Discrimination and on Torture. It still remains true that individuals cannot sue states directly in international tribunals, but short of that situation, the matter of individual (and other private) petitions has become part of routinized international relations. A U.S. district court said in 1987 that it would "dispose" of the "contention that international law pertained only to the relationship among nations rather than individuals"; U.S. courts "expressly disavowed" this view, "at least in so far as it concerns individual injuries under the international law of human rights." Under this law, the court accepted that individuals have a legal right of action in U.S. courts.[24]

Clearly, whether one takes a political view centering on human rights as an issue area cum regimes, or a legal view tracing state acknowledgment of human rights (with or without individual procedural capacity), human rights is a fully recognized part of international relations. The United Nations alone has adopted more than two dozen human rights treaties and has made as many major declarations on human rights.[25] Africa has joined Western Europe and the Western Hemisphere in producing regional standards on human rights.[26] And there are other instruments that do not fit into these categories, such as the Geneva Conventions and Protocols and the Helsinki Accord.[27]

Most of these human rights developments have transpired since 1945, and most of the more serious considerations of global international human rights have occurred since 1967. (Council of Europe and OAS developments became important in the early and late 1950s, respectively.) The development of human rights as a serious issue in international relations has been rapid since about 1970, though there are historical antecedents of considerable duration. And one should not collapse the larger question of international human rights into the important but smaller question of individual procedural capacity. The role of the individual encompasses both. International law now clearly communicates many general principles about individual human rights, the basic norms of which are supported by overwhelming formal consensus— and not a little substantive consensus.[28]

Clarity of Individual Human Rights

One of the persistent criticisms of international human rights is that the principles are vague. There is some truth to this charge, but the point can be overstated, and many standards are being made precise. If a true international regime is characterized not only by general principles but also by more specific rules and decision-making procedures so as to comprise a regulatory mechanism for an issue area, then there do exist core, functional, and regional regimes.[29] International human rights are not always so vague or otherwise deficient as to prove meaningless in international relations. There has been a real change in international relations, not just a rhetorical change based on states' hypocritical lip-service to human rights values (although certainly this latter behavior can be observed at times throughout the international system).

Most constitutional, fundamental, or basic laws manifest an element of vagueness by virtue of being principles. This is as true of internationally recognized human rights as of the U.S. Constitution. Standing alone as a first principle, the internationally recognized right to life, or to adequate nutrition, is no more clear (or no more vague) than U.S. principles concerning equal protection of the law, due process, cruel or unusual punishment, or freedom of speech. Indeed, some vagueness is commendable, permitting the legal principles to be adjusted to new and unforeseen circumstances. The question rather is whether mechanisms exist to translate the principles into rules applicable to specific situations. For the international law of human rights, this is now occurring in the slow, decentralized, and uneven process so common to all of international law.

Political and civil rights are the clearest internationally recognized human rights, despite allegations that the United Nations has neglected them in favor of other rights.[30] It is not just that most of the rights mentioned in the Universal Declaration of Human Rights from 1948 are civil and political, that the detailed Covenant on Civil and Political Rights first entered into legal force in 1976 for adhering states, or that other detailed treaties exist on such rights as freedom from torture, racial discrimination, and gender discrimination.

There is considerable monitoring of the endorsed rights in order to give them specific application. The U.N. Human Rights Committee has been functioning for more than a decade to clarify obligations under the Civil-Political Covenant.[31] Although the process of rule specification and application is slow, the trend is clear. The U.N. Human Rights Commission, in utilizing the 1503 procedure to list states manifesting a persistent pattern of gross violations of internationally recognized human rights, appears to have focused mainly on civil and political rights,[32] using rapporteurs and working groups to focus on specific countries and specific problems.[33] The same general focus is evident in the U.N. Sub-Commission on Human Rights.[34] An international view of considerable specificity does exist concerning many violations of individual civil and political rights.

It is possible that what is communicated by these positions is nothing more than a sense of political bias—a charge that has been levied particularly at the U.N.'s handling of human rights issues. And some research does show that large amounts of time in the General Assembly, its standing Third Committee, and ECOSOC are devoted to a limited range of human rights issues, such as apartheid in South Africa, Israeli policies in the occupied territories, and economic development.[35] One's judgment as scholarly observer may depend on what part of the large beast known as the U.N. system one is dealing with. But even careful critics acknowledge that there has been a decline of bias in some parts of the United Nations, and overall there is increased seriousness of purpose in its handling of civil and political rights issues.[36]

Moreover, there is extensive case law in the Council of Europe on the civil and political rights guaranteed by the European Convention on Human Rights.[37] Under the OAS, the quasi-legal positions adopted by the Inter-American Commission on Human Rights are numerous, even if not immediately legally binding.[38] The few advisory and binding judgments thus far by the Inter-American Court on Human Rights deal with civil and political rights.[39]

Perhaps equally important, some internationally recognized human rights of a civil and political nature have become so clear that national courts have started utilizing them, directly or indirectly, as part of customary international law. This is true in the United States for several cases concerning torture[40] and arbitary detention.[41] U.S. courts have long referred to international civil standards concerning refugees.[42] One U.S. court in 1988 accepted the concept of forced disappearance, among other concepts, as pertaining to a clear right giving rise to a cause of individual legal action.[43]

While controversies may abound about any given civil or political right (such as the right to life), or about the exact boundary of this category of rights (the familiar problem of categorizing rights to education or collective bargaining as civil, social, or economic), the position cannot be maintained in general that internationally recognized civil and political rights lack specificity or are treated with such bias that they lose their status as legal standards. International agencies may not pronounce authoritatively on violations of these rights in the sense of providing binding court judgments (although these exist frequently in Western Europe and at least more frequently than formerly in the Western Hemisphere), but they do pronounce diplomatically. The human rights values communicated are frequently clear and without taint of strategic bias. That this is so can be seen by the fact that national courts have begun to utilize these standards, at least in the United States, although the number of such cases is still small (and it is not clear what judgments other national courts might be issuing).

There are, however, two categories of international human rights that remain so vague as to have exercised minimum influence on actual behavior in international relations: the second generation of socioeconomic rights, which are clear enough as general principles but not yet clear as specific rules, and the third-generation rights of solidarity (rights to development, peace, common heritage, safe environment, humanitarian assistance), which remain so controversial as to be debated still at the level of general principle. (Especially the third-generation rights are said to be collective rather than individual, but insofar as they pertain to individual rights they are briefly included here for completeness.)

The U.N. Covenant on Social, Economic, and Cultural Rights, while negotiated in 1956, approved in 1966, and brought into force for the first time in 1976, remained essentially moribund for its first legal decade. Formal acceptance was accompanied by neglect, since many of the state reports required under its terms were tardy or nonexistent, and there was little effective monitoring. It was only in the late 1980s that a new committee of experts was created to breathe some life—and some specificity—into the process. One is still at the stage of establishing minimum standards for the least fortunate in the various national societies with regard to nutrition, health, shelter, and other categories.[44]

In Western Europe, the situation with regard to international socioeconomic standards is somewhat better, since the European Social Charter has been taken more seriously by state members of the Council of Europe (although perhaps not as seriously as the European Convention on civil and political rights). Still, there remains a certain vagueness to the standards, and it is not so clear how those standards have affected national public policy.[45] Under the OAS, the Inter-American Commission on Human Rights has paid relatively little attention to socioeconomic rights[46] and the Inter-American Court none since the American Convention deals with civil and political rights.

On balance, international law—global and regional—is communicating very little to states about their legal obligations concerning socioeconomic rights. The situation may be changing given new dynamics in the monitoring of the U.N. Covenant concerned and some effort within the OAS to produce a new protocol on socioeconomic rights. The situation would be altered if international agencies active in the socioeconomic realm presented their programs as responses to human rights rather than nonobligatory activities designed to improve health, education, and economic growth. For a considerable time, agencies like the World Health Organization and the U.N. Development Program have not officially integrated their activities with human rights standards.[47]

Finally, the third generation of solidarity rights remains mostly demanded rather than endorsed. Aside from the right to self-determination, which preceded the international emphasis on human rights language and has already been written into the two U.N. covenants, and in any event is a collective rather than individual right, none of the claimed rights exists in global treaty form. The other third-generation right closest to formal acceptance is the right to national economic development, which has been endorsed by a large majority in the General Assembly. Even with that diplomatic acceptance as a U.N. declaration, it is still not clear what specific rights and duties are entailed in the collective right and what this means for individuals, as the assembly has itself implicitly acknowledged by asking for a study on meaning.[48] Other claimed rights in this category are questioned by most of the West (such as the right to peace) or rejected by the Third World (for example, the right to humanitarian assistance since it implies a diminution of national sovereignty), or mostly devoid of specific and individual content (as with rights to common heritage or healthy environment).

Third-generation rights may (or may not) evolve into accepted legal principles and specific legal rules, but they are neither yet, nor are there monitoring agencies. Consequently they do not communicate very much to states about obligatory policies and certainly nothing very much about individuals.

Individual Human Rights and Challenges to the State

William Coplin suggested that the state was being challenged from above by international organizations with their attempts to regulate security issues and from below by individuals and their human rights. What has been transpiring in fact is that the rapid and reasonably clear, if uneven, development of the international law of individual human rights entails a hemming in of the state from above and below simultaneously. (Coplin proved correct, however, in his argument that developments concerning human rights would prove more important than international measures concerning security as traditionally understood and as related to the contempt of the just war.)

States themselves have consented to the restrictions on their freedom of decision making entailed in human rights law. Especially in the form of treaties, international human rights law reflects not so much a pure external challenge, whether from international organizations or individuals, as an auto-challenge; states in effect challenge themselves to meet human rights standards. Only in the form of customary law, despite the concept of implicit consent, do states find that they are obligated without having given intended consent. Thus in the United States, the official policymaking branches have found themselves bound by court decisions holding the United States obligated under international customary law on human rights, even though those branches had not expressly consented to the relevant human rights treaties.[49]

It may be true that states give their initial consent to be bound by international human rights standards on the assumption that they will never be called to account in any serious way under the regimes they have created. Even in Western Europe, where the basic political culture indicates serious interest in human rights, states have shown a reluctance to activate the regional regime, since by far most petitions to the commission—and ultimately to the court— originate with individuals. The same reluctance by states can be seen in other regimes permitting state-to-state complaints. And it has been often remarked that most states seek human rights regimes that will be largely promotional rather than protective, largely devoid of decisive international authority, in order to retain their real freedom of decision despite formal adherence to the standards. History proves Coplin correct in focusing on pressures from individuals and international organizations in the transformation of international law, especially if one gives due weight to NGOs as private associations of individuals. States are pressured in various ways to implement human rights standards, but in a formal sense they have initially challenged themselves to meet those standards.

Nevertheless, individuals alone usually cannot challenge state policy on human rights at the international level, or, in more traditional legal terms, by using international instruments concerning human rights. First, international organizations must approve the standards at issue. Second, it is to international organizations that individuals frequently appeal for redress of delicts committed by states or in the jurisdiction of states. Thus it is the combination of action by international organizations and individuals that has led to the place of human rights in international law and politics, along with state consent.

Once the standards have been endorsed by international organizations, it is possible that individuals might be able to use national courts rather than international organizations in pursuit of redress of grievances. This is a large and complicated subject, involving varying national laws and juridical traditions concerning such subjects as the doctrine of incorporation, non-self-executing treaties, deference to the executive branch, act of state doctrine, and so on. The point remains that only if national courts will provide protection based on the international law of human rights can individuals act apart from international organizations. Even if national courts will so act, international organizations are almost always involved in the prior steps of negotiating and approving treaties or contributing to customary law through their activities.[50]

The fundamental point remains that Coplin was in error conceptually in presenting the development of individual human rights law as a challenge originating external to the state and a challenge from below rather than from above. States have, at least initially, essentially challenged themselves, with pressures from both above and below acting in tandem.

Individual, State Security, and System Modification

In grappling with the sum total of his subject, Coplin could only conclude, beyond his argument about the arrested ambiguity of international law as an agent of political socialization, that "a subtle transformation of some kind is taking place."[51] His imprecision may have been appropriate given the time of his analysis. The overall thrust of his argument, however, was to suggest that the rise of individual human rights in international law stood in opposition to the historical concern for state security and in opposition to the centrality of the state in international affairs. This suggestion has proved both true and false.

His view is true in the sense that incorporation of human rights values into international law, when combined with effective machinery for implementation and enforcement, means that the state has to share the international stage with individuals and international organizations. We see this both in Western Europe and the Western Hemisphere, where human rights courts exercise supranational authority, primarily in indirect response to individual complaints, at least for those states consenting to the relevant rules. A more modest transformation has occurred in other parts of international relations concerning human rights, where the regimes depend more on implementation than enforcement—that is, on political pressures rather than juridical commands. The general transformation effected through creation of the human rights regimes has been from a pure to a modified nation-state system.

His view is false in the sense that states have not disappeared as significant actors in international relations and in fact are actually made more secure by adherence to and implementation of international human rights standards—a perspective generally neglected in the literature on human rights.[52] States in compliance with internationally recognized human rights manifest an added degree of legitimacy in addition to the legitimacy provided by national traditions, state efficiency in problemsolving, and adherence to formal ideology. The nation-states of Western Europe are among the most secure in the world, in part because they face little threat of widespread internal revolt. (Probabilities of internal revolt in the states of Western Europe are limited and historically unique, as in Northern Ireland and Basque Spain.) Internationally supervised standards on human rights contribute to this security. Paradoxically, state identification and longevity is undergirded by commitment to human rights values beyond the state.

States no doubt see ample reason to be concerned with external threats to their security, but they (or more precisely the governments that represent them) frequently become insecure—in fact are overthrown—because of internal revolt as in Iran under Shah Mohammed Reza Pahlevi, Nicaragua under Anastasio Somoza, Haiti under Jean-Claude Duvalier, Argentina under the junta, Sudan under Jaafar Numeiri, and the Philippines under Ferdinand Marcos. In all of these cases, gross violations of internationally recognized human rights contributed to internal rebellion. One of the most fundamental points communicated by contemporary international law is that the state that protects human rights is a more secure state than otherwise—at least from internal threats. International commitment increases internal security.

At the same time, the government that tries to implement international human rights standards may provoke internal opposition if it faces powerful forces antagonistic to rights. This seems true especially in some countries in which a weak civilian government must face a powerful military that has recently yielded power. Presidents Raúl Alfonsin in Argentina and Vinicio Cerezo in Guatemala typified this dilemma, as did new civilian governments in Uruguay and Chile. If they moved to enforce international human rights standards against former rulers, they increased the probability of a coup. Thus in some situations, governmental security may be adversely affected in the short term by a commitment to rights. In the long run, however, should the civilian government persist and should it be able to establish a national tradition of commitment to international human rights, the security of a rights-oriented government is strengthened.

Some evidence also suggests that implementation of some human rights can strengthen external security as well. Although this is a large and much debated subject, it does seem to be the case that democracies do not war on each other.[53] Thus it is not completely or always true that human rights and external (or internal) security have to be in tension.

The central point remains: the international law of human rights is not ultimately antagonistic to states as legal-political entities, and its values do not run counter to all state security. Individual human rights standards may—and indeed should—limit the freedom of states, but that very process of limitation may make the state more viable and enduring. Neither the United Kingdom nor Honduras has reduced the bond between people and state by adhering to the regional human rights treaty, acknowledging the right of individual petition, or accepting the general obligatory jurisdiction of the regional human rights court. Even losing "cases" in the regional commission and court has not undermined the state but rather has compelled the government to address policies that it left unattended might themselves have undermined popular commitment to the state, or at least to its government.

The international law of human rights requires that states recognize the universal human rights of their nationals. From the international legal perspective, not just any state is legitimate by virtue of possessing a defined people and territory and functioning government, but only those states implementing at least the core human rights regime. And the only way to certify such commitment is through a modified nation-state system in which states (usually acting through international organizations) establish the standards, which are then monitored by international organizations (public or private) and by individuals themselves. Coplin noted a quarter of a century ago that the absolute value of the state was under attack.[54] By 1990, it had been essentially rejected, at least according to a coherent reading of international law. The essence of this transformation was captured in a quotation attributed to Mikhail Gorbachev: "No system has the right to exist unless it properly serves a human being."[55]

Conclusions

In an incremental revolution, internationally recognized individual human rights have become a routinized part of international relations. Human rights constitute one of the primary three or four functional issue areas comprising international relations (the others are external security, economics, and perhaps environmental protection).[56] In political terms, human rights is on foreign policy agendas, and international rights regimes do exist. In traditional legal terms, public authorities are increasingly obligated to respect human rights, and individual procedural capacity is widespread even if individuals lack the full subjectivity or legal personality accorded to other actors. Rights as a means to individual human dignity is no longer exclusively a matter of domestic jurisdiction.

If one utilizes the three basic ideas from the notion of international regimes—principles, rules, and decisions—one can observe over time not only the establishment of reasonably clear principles but also the progressive clarification of more specific rules applicable to specific governments and situations. This is most pronounced with regard to civil and political rights, less so concerning economic and social rights (with some variation), and least of all with solidarity rights. Intergovernmental international organizations, interacting not only with states but also with nongovernmental organizations and with individuals, have played an essential role in this process of clarification and specification. What matters most in terms of systemic dynamics is the ongoing process that produces clearer socialization in rights values with each passing decade. What was written in 1982 will be even truer in 1992: human rights has become "a permanent part of the way we think about relations between nations."[57]

International law is no longer completely in a state of arrested ambiguity about the place of individual human rights in world politics. Tensions remain among the values found in international public law, such as occasionally between external security and human rights, or state independence of action and international order, or individual and other procedural capacity. But in dealing with these tensions, modern international law increasingly communicates something reasonably clear. For example, certain civil rights remain inviolable even in times of national emergency threatening the life of a nation, and the claim to national emergency is subject to an international review process of varying degrees of authority.[58]

Despite increasingly clear socialization about rights from a modern international law that—on the basis of state consent—has modified world politics over time, states and their governments are hardly withering away. States remain the primary legal and political actor in international relations. Although state consent to international human rights has led to challenges by both intergovernmental organizations and individuals (acting separately or in private associations), states that implement internationally recognized rights generally strengthen their internal security and perhaps also their external security. Thus while from one perspective internationally recognized rights may lead to challenges to state behavior, from another perspective rights operate to secure the permanence of states, although on a world stage shared by other actors.

None of the above suggests that nirvana is at hand. Legal socialization is often accompanied by legal violations. At best there is a time lag between adoption and then clarification of the law on the one hand, and compliance on the other—as the slow gains attest concerning slavery and slavelike practices. Violations of international human rights are widespread, suggesting the passing of considerable time before major improvements transpire in the action of national authorities. Yet the trends of the past half-century are unmistakable. Many individual human rights have been internationally routinized in a relatively short time, at least some of them have become more clearly specified with each passing year, and the nation-state system has been modified in important ways even as it remains for the most part statecentric.

Incremental revolutions lead to situations not easy to summarize in their totality, given uneven and incomplete developments. But it can no longer be maintained that international law fails to communicate many clear principles—and not a few specifics rules as well—about state obligation in the field of individual human rights. The central issue for the next fifty years will be implementation and enforcement, along with the continuing socialization that inheres in such direct protection efforts.

Notes

1. William D. Coplin, "International Law and Assumptions about the State System," *World Politics* 17, 4 (July 1965): 615–35.

2. Ibid., 625.

3. Ibid., 633.

4. Ibid., 629.

5. For a good review of this subject, see Mark W. Janis, *An Introduction to International Law* (Boston: Little, Brown, 1988), 163–70. For a modern case dealing with whether individual rights were included within the "law of nations," see *Tel-Oren v. Libyan Arab Republic*, 716 F.2d 774 (D.C. Cir., 1984). See also Rosalyn Higgins, "Conceptual Thinking about the Individual in International Law," in Richard A. Falk et al., *International Law: A Contemporary Perspective* (Boulder, Colo.: Westview Press, 1985), 476–94.

6. The best scholarly treatment on international human rights from a regime perspective is Jack Donnelly, "International Human Rights: A Regime Analysis," *International Organization* 40, 3 (Summer 1986): 599–642. See the regime literature Donnelly cites.

7. John A. Vasquez and Richard W. Mansback, "The Issue Cycle and Global Change," *International Organization* 37, 3 (Summer 1983): 257–79.

8. See further David P. Forsythe, *Human Rights and World Politics,* 2d ed. (Lincoln: University of Nebraska Press, 1989), chap. 1.

9. See the discussion in chapter 1 about the moral and expediential bases of international action for human rights.

10. For an analysis that emphasizes the importance of decisions taken at the United Nations during the late 1960s for the evolution of international human rights, see David P. Forsythe, "The United Nations and Human Rights, 1945–1985," *Political Science Quarterly* 100, 1 (Summer 1985): 249–69.

11. For an analysis of U.S. human rights policy as the result of congressional-presidential interaction, see David P. Forsythe, *Human Rights and U.S. Foreign Policy: Congress Reconsidered* (Gainesville: University of Florida Press, 1988).

12. The council resolution on South Africa mentioned both racism and international aggression as threats to or breaches of the peace meriting binding decision, UNSC/RES/418, November 4, 1977. The council's first binding decision on Southern Rhodesia stressed rebellion from the United Kingdom, UNSC/RES/232, December 16, 1966. When the council moved from selective to comprehensive mandatory sanctions, it mentioned both rebellion and human rights, UNSC/RES/253, May 29, 1968.

In the 115 cases of the International Court of Justice listed by Thomas M. Franck in *Judging the World Court* (New York: Priority Press, 1986), very few legal questions pertain centrally to human rights: guardianship of infants, treatment of American airline crews in Hungary, whether apartheid violates international law, whether the Nicaraguan contras violated human rights in armed conflict, and whether India violated the rights of Pakistani prisoners of war.

Regional authoritative allocation of human rights values is treated below.

For an argument that international organizations do authoritatively allocate values but in a political process lacking supranational formal authority, see Lawrence J. Finkelstein, ed., *Politics in the United Nations System* (Durham, N.C.: Duke University Press, 1988), esp. chap. 1.

13. For one overview of this topic, see Hans Kelsen, *Principles of International Law,* 2d ed. (New York: Holt, Rinehart, Winston, 1967), 203–20.

14. See especially H. Lauterpacht, *International Law and Human Rights* (Hamden, Conn.: Archon Books, 1968). See also W. Paul Gormley, *The Procedural Status of the Individual Before International and Supranational Tribunals* (The Hague: Martinus Nijhoff, 1966).

15. Detainees in an international armed conflict have the procedural right to confidential interviews with the ICRC. Otherwise their rights must be implemented by other actors. See David Weissbrodt, "The Role of International Organizations in the Implementation of Human Rights and Humanitarian Law in Situations of Armed Conflict," *Vanderbilt Journal of Transnational Law* 21, 2 (Spring 1988): 313–65, and David P. Forsythe, *Humanitarian Politics: The International Committee of the Red Cross* (Baltimore: Johns Hopkins University Press, 1977).

16. European Convention on Human Rights, Articles 25–56; see also the *Lawless* case from 1960;* Of twenty-one eligible states, seventeen have permitted individual petitions, and nineteen have accepted binding court authority. For a general overview, see P.T. Muchlinski, "The Status of the Individual under the European Conven-

---

Yearbook of the European Convention on Human Rights (Dordrecht, the Netherlands: Martinus Nijhoff, 1960) v. 3, p. 492; v. 4, p. 438; v. 5, p. 442.

tion on Human Rights and Contemporary International Law," *International and Comparative Law Quarterly* 34, 2 (April 1985): 376–82.

17. See further H.H. Weiler, "Eurocracy and Distrust: Some Questions Concerning the Role of the European Court of Justice in the Protection of Fundamental Human Rights within the Legal Order of the European Communities," *Washington Law Review* 61, 3 (July 1986): 1103–1144, and Jurgen Schwarze, "The Administrative Law of the Community and the Protection of Human Rights," *Common Market Law Review,* no. 23 (1986): 401–17.

18. European Commission on Human Rights, *Stocktaking on the European Convention on Human Rights, the First Thirty Years; 1954 until 1984* (Strasbourg: European Commission, 1984). There are periodic updates, as in Directorate of Human Rights, "Human Rights: Information Sheet No. 20" (Strasbourg: Council of Europe, 1987).

19. A basic overview is provided in Thomas Buergenthal, "The Inter-American System for the Protection of Human Rights," in T. Meron, ed., *Human Rights in International Law* (Oxford: Clarendon Press, 1984) 2: 439–91.

20. *Velasques Rodriguez Case,* Series C, No. 4, 28 ILM 291 (1989). For an analysis see *New York Times,* July 30, 1988, 2. Of thirty-three eligible states, eleven have accepted binding court authority.

21. John P. Humphrey, *Human Rights and the United Nations: A Great Adventure* (New York: Transnational Publishers, 1984).

22. See Howard Tolley, Jr., *The U.N. Commission on Human Rights* (Boulder, Colo.: Westview Press, 1986), chap. 6, esp. 128, for a list of thirty governments reviewed over 1978–1986 as possible gross violators of human rights.

23. U.N. Human Rights Committee, *Selected Decisions under the Optional Protocol: Second to Sixteenth Sessions,* U.N. Publication No. E, 84.XIV.2 (1984). One scholar concludes that the committee "has been able to develop a valuable body of caselaw interpreting and applying the Covenant and Protocol." Thomas Buergenthal, *International Human Rights in a Nutshell* (St. Paul, Minn.: West Publishing Co., 1988), 42. See further P.R. Ghandi, "The Human Rights Committee and the Right of Individual Communication," *British Yearbook of International Law,* 57, 201–51.

24. *Forti v. Suarez-Mason,* 672 F. Supp. 1531 (N.D. Cal. 1987).

25. United Nations, *United Nations Action in the Field of Human Rights,* U.N. Publication No. E.83.XIV.2 (1982), and United Nations, *The United Nations and Human Rights,* U.N. Publication No. E.84.I.6 (1984). See also United Nations, *Human Rights: A Compilation of International Instruments,* U.N. Publication No. E.83.XIV.1 (1982).

26. This chapter does not treat the African Charter on Human and Peoples Rights since it has only recently come into force. See Olusola Ojo and Amadu Sesay, "The O.A.U. and Human Rights: Prospects for the 1980s and Beyond," *Human Rights Quarterly* 8, 1 (February 1986): 89–103. The African Charter acknowledges collective as well as individual rights. It provides no provocative procedural rights for individuals or promising measures for implementation.

27. See Forsythe, *Human Rights and World Politics.*

28. As of the time of writing, 90 states, or 56 percent of those eligible, had formally consented to the U.N. Economic Covenant; 86 states, or 54 percent, to the U.N. Political Covenant (and 38 or 23 percent to the optional protocol on individual peti-

tion). Some other figures: 124 states (78 percent) on racial discrimination; 86 states (54 percent) on apartheid; 93 states (58 percent) on gender discrimination; 97 states (61 percent) on genocide; 99 states (64 percent) on refugees; 98 states (61 percent) on ILO freedom of association; 165 states (96 percent) on Geneva Conventions of 1949. These figures pertain to formal adherence, not actual implementation or enforcement. It is common knowledge that many adhering states fail to submit required reports concerning implementation on time or at all, and a number have a poor record regarding actual protection of the rights formally accepted.

29. From the voluminous literature on regimes, see especially Steven Krasner, ed., *International Regimes* (Ithaca, N.Y.: Cornell University Press, 1983).

30. This charge, articulated by numerous public figures, has been subjected to scholarly analysis by Jack Donnelly in "Recent Trends in U.N. Human Rights Activity: Description and Polemic," *International Organization* 35, 4 (Autumn 1981): 633–55. An effective rebuttal is found in Philip Alston, "The Alleged Demise of Political Human Rights at the U.N.: A Reply to Donnelly," *International Organization* 37, 3 (Summer 1983): 537–46.

31. Supra, note 23.

32. Tolley, *U.N. Commission on Human Rights.*

33. Ibid.

34. Ibid.

35. Jack Donnelly, "Human Rights at the United Nations 1955–85: The Question of Bias," *International Studies Quarterly* 32, 3 (September 1988): 275–303.

36. Donnelly, ibid., acknowledges that there is improved impartiality in the U.N. Human Rights Commission (p. 296), that the overall U.N. record contains both positive and negative elements, and that he has chosen to emphasize the latter (p. 300, no. 35). Even officials of the Reagan administration said that by 1988, the U.N.'s treatment of civil and political rights was much improved. See the statement by Richard S. Williamson, assistant secretary of state for international organization affairs, in "Status of U.S. Participation in the United Nations System, 1988," *Hearings*, Subcommittees on Human Rights and International Organizations, and International Operations, Committee on Foreign Affairs, House, 100th Cong., 2d sess., September 23, 1988, esp. 16. See further Thomas J. Farer, "The United Nations and Human Rights: More Than a Whimper, Less Than a Roar," *Human Rights Quarterly* 9, 4 (November 1987): 550–86.

37. European Commission on Human Rights, *Stocktaking.*

38. *Inter-American Commission on Human Rights, 1959–1984: 25 Years of Struggle for Human Rights in the Americas* (Washington, D.C.: OAS, 1984). There has not been a major and analytical study of the commission since Anna P. Schreiber, *The Inter-American Commission on Human Rights* (Leiden: Sijthoff, 1970). But see Burns H. Weston et al, "Regional Human Rights Regimes: A Comparison and Appraisal," *Vanderbilt Journal of Transnational Law* 20, 4 (October 1987): 585–637. And see C.M. Quiroga, *The Battle of Human Rights: Gross, Systematic Violations and the Inter-American System* (Dordrecht: Martinus Nijhoff, 1988).

39. Thomas Buergenthal, "The Advisory Practice of the Inter-American Human Rights Court," *American Journal of International Law* 79, 1 (January 1985): 1–27.

40. The key case is *Filartiga v. Pena-Irala*, 630 F.2d 876 (2d Cir., 1980). Compare the inconsistent *Tel-Oren v. Libyan Arab Republic*, 726 F.2d 774 (D.C. Cir.,

1984). Note the bypassing of *Tel-Oren* in *Forti v. Suarez-Mason,* 672 F. Supp. 1531 (N.D. Cal., 1987) and its companion cases.

41. *Fernandez v. Wilkinson,* 505 F. Supp. 787 (D. Kan., 1980), affirmed but on different reasoning, 654 F.2d 1382 (10th Cir., 1981).

42. For an overview, see Gilburt D. Loescher and John A. Scanlan, "The Global Refugee Problem: U.S. and World Response," *Annals* 467 (May 1983), especially essays by Astri Suhrke and Naomi Flink Zucker. See also G.P. Loescher and John Scanlan, *Calculated Kindness: Refugees and the Half Opened Door* (New York: Free Press, 1987). For examples of the use of international refugee standards to inform judgments striking down administration policy, see *Haitian Refugee Center v. Civiletti,* 503 F. Supp. 442, 509 (S.D. Fla, 1980), and *INS v. Cardoza-Fonseca,* 55 LW 4313 (March 9, 1987).

43. *Forti.* This is an important case because it reaffirms and expands the ruling found in *Filartiga.*

44. U.N. ECOSOC, Official Records, Suppl. no. 17, U.N. Doc. E/1987/28, *Report of the First Session of the Committee on Economic, Social, and Cultural Rights* (March 1987); and U.N. ECOSOC, Official Records, Suppl. no. 4, U.N. Doc. E/1988/14, *Report of the Second Session of the Committee on Economic, Social, and Cultural Rights* (February 1988). See further *Human Rights Quarterly* 9, 2 (May 1987), special issue on implementing the International Covenant on Economic, Social and Cultural Rights, and particularly the Limburg Principles on the specific meaning of the covenant.

45. There are fourteen state parties to the European Social Charter. In 1988 a new protocol was added extending some rights; 27 *International Legal Materials* 575 (March 1988). For an overview, see A. Glenn Mower, Jr., *International Cooperation for Social Justice: Global and Regional Protection of Economic/Social Rights* (Westport, Conn.: Greenwood Press, 1985), chaps. 8–10.

46. Lawrence J. LeBlanc, "The Inter-American Commission on Human Rights and Socioeconomic Rights" (paper prepared for at the International Studies Association's annual convention, London, March 28–April 1, 1989).

47. For a contemporary overview of this longstanding problem, see Theo van Boven, "Human Rights and Development: The U.N. Experience," in David P. Forsythe, ed., *Human Rights and Development: International Views* (London: Macmillan, 1989). Van Boven is a member of the U.N. Sub-Commission on Minorities and was Director of the U.N. Human Rights Centre.

48. U.N. ECOSOC/CN. 4/1987/10, *Report of Working Group of Governmental Experts on the Right to Development,* January 29, 1987. Thus even an overwhelming vote in favor of a U.N. resolution does not lead to clear political socialization if there is subsequent indication that the specific meaning of the vote is in doubt.

49. In the *Filartiga* case, the Carter administration intervened to urge the court to rule as it did, thus suggesting informal consent by the executive branch. By contrast in the *Suarez-Mason* cases, there was no such executive consent expressed by the Reagan administration.

50. In *Thompson v. Oklahoma* 487 U.S.—, 101 LEd 2d 702, 108 S.Ct.—, the U.S. Supreme Court said in 1988 that the U.S. Constitution's prohibition of cruel and unusual punishment proscribed execution of those under the age of sixteen; in reaching this judgment, the Court took into account "civilized standards of decency" as found

in the international law of human rights, especially as indicated by the United Nations, the OAS, and the Geneva Diplomatic Conferences on Humanitarian Law. See also notes 40–43.

51. Coplin, "International Law," 631.

52. But see R.J. Vincent, *Human Rights and International Relations* (Cambridge University Press, 1988), esp. 151–52.

53. Michael W. Doyle, "Liberalism and World Politics," *American Political Science Review* 80, 4 (December 1986): 1151–70.

54. Coplin, "International Law," 629.

55. Quoted by Fyodor M. Burlatsky, "New Thinking about Socialism," in *Breakthrough: Emerging New Thinking,* ed. Anatoly Gromyko and Martin Hellman (New York: Walker and Company, 1988), 263.

56. Elites have clearly recognized security and economics, and now human rights. Environmental concern seems to be emerging. For an official view that these four constitute the major issue areas, see the publications of the World Order Models Project, as represented by Samuel S. Kim, *The Quest for a Just World Order* (Boulder, Colo.: Westview Press, 1984).

57. Anthony D'Amato, "The Concept of Human Rights in International Law," *Columbia Law Review* 82, 6 (October 1982): 1110.

58. These principles exist in the U.N. core regime and the Western European and Western Hemispheric regimes as well.

3
Human Rights and the United Nations: Change and Its Significance

The U.N. system has seen three political eras. The first occurred from the founding of the organization until the early 1960s, when the Western political grouping, led by the United States, dominated proceedings. The second ran from roughly 1965 to 1985 when an influx of newly independent states from the Third World, frequently backed by the Warsaw Pact countries, comprised a large majority on most issues. While the West in general and the United States in particular still exercised considerable influence through financial contributions or votes in the Security Council, this second era saw a decisive shift in voting power within most of the United Nations. The third political era started soon after the rise to power of Mikhail Gorbachev in the Soviet Union in 1985. Soviet policy began to shift on a number of policy questions including the importance of the United Nations. After the European political revolusions of 1989, leading to the effective dissolution of the Warsaw Pact and Soviet control over most of Eastern Europe, not to mention continuing momentous events in the Soviet Union itself, there was no longer a Stalinist bloc of votes. On many issues at the United Nations, the former members of this bloc were more likely to side with the Western political grouping than with the Third World.

Implicit in this analysis is the fact that what happens in the name of the United Nations, or at the United Nations, or in the United Nations, is highly dependent on state policy. "The United Nations" is rarely an independent actor in its own right. It is more a framework for other actors than an independent actor.[1] Nevertheless, at the same time one can look for some independent influence, to some extent, for those acting in the name of the United Nations but not representing states. Individual members of the Secretariat as well as expert individuals on U.N. bodies who are not officially instructed by states may also generate some impact on policy. Other factors at play include the activity of NGOs, which function as interest groups, and climates of opinion (or what passes for world public opinion).

Developments at the United Nations may reflect, in changing ways on changing issues, a complex of causal factors. The analyst may be on safe ground in assuming that state foreign policy, when linked to intranational politics, is the most important factor. But one might also be well advised to be alert to influence from other sources as well. What happens at the United Nations may at times equal more than the simple sum of state members' foreign policy. This is the case in the issue area of human rights.

The evolution of U.N. developments concerning internationally recognized human rights has not exactly paralleled overall political developments, although the latter have certainly affected the former. From 1945 until 1967, the United Nations (meaning those who took action there) emphasized what is usually called standard setting; that is, there was an effort to develop declarations and treaties specifying the meaning of statements found in the U.N. Charter. It is only a slight oversimplification to say that this was the exclusive human rights activity of the United Nations, narrowly understood. It is also true, however, that the United Nations in a broader sense (including the specialized agencies such as the ILO, and special agencies such as the United Nations Educational, Scientific, and Cultural Organization) undertook other human rights activity beyond standard setting.

It was not until 1967 that the United Nations proper moved in any systematic way from standard setting to other human rights activity: making investigations about specific states, conducting studies of specific problems like torture or disappeared persons, responding even half-seriously to private complaints about human rights violations, and providing technical assistance to states that might want to improve their human rights records. This transition to more specific, more systematic, and somewhat more authoritative action on human rights was affected by the shift in membership and concomitant voting power that started about 1955. But there was a time lag between the introduction of new Third World members and changed human rights activity, and some of the more important changes reflected not just a different majority of states within the organization but a different interplay of a complex of factors.

It is probable that the third political era (from 1985) will result in significant changes in U.N. human rights developments, although it is premature to argue that the demise of the Stalinist bloc will definitely lead to broad changes in the U.N.'s human rights performance. Some changes are already evident (for instance, Hungary's cosponsorship of a resolution condemning Rumania's human rights record in early 1989), and more changes can be forecast (if the Soviet leadership continues to emphasize glasnost or civil and political freedom at home, it could oppose or abstain in similar issues abroad only with the greatest of difficulty). But it is preferable to focus on the verifiable fact that the United Nations has increasingly moved from the setting of international standards, with application left to states members, to the more delicate task of trying to get states, by varying organized international action, to apply to their nationals the rights internationally recognized. So far there have been essentially two U.N. eras for its human rights activity: from about 1948 and from about 1968. A third probably will run from about 1988, the nature of which should be left to a future essay. This chapter remains focused on the important changes that have already transpired.

Those who write about human rights have not developed clear meanings of widely used terms that would help in precise analysis of important processes and transformations. One can read frequently of the promotion and protection of human rights, of implementation and enforcement, or direct and indirect protection, of strong and weak regimes, of declaratory regimes engaged in standard setting. It is unlikely that a few words here will settle ongoing debates, but it is necessary to clarify the use of key terms.

In my view, the United Nations has increasingly moved from promoting rights to trying to help protect them (along with continued promotion). By *promotion*, I mean standard setting and education and dissemination. In adopting treaties and thereby opening them for signature, the General Assembly sets standards and socializes into those standards. That is promotion, as is the holding of conferences and seminars to spread the word about human rights values found in the international documents. Generally worded resolutions, calling on all states to take unspecified human rights action at their discretion, are also promotional devices.

By *protection*, I refer to implementation and enforcement action. I conceive of enforcement as the issuing of a command linked to the threat or application of sanctions. Among U.N. agencies, only the Security Council and the International Court of Justice can engage in enforcement action; only they make a law or issue a binding judgment. The council can threaten or vote sanctions in relation to its own previous actions or that of the court. Enforcement is thus the authoritative application of human rights. All other action beyond promotion but short of enforcement I consider implementation efforts.

Implementation thus includes passing nonbinding resolutions about specific problems or states, publishing lists of violative states or actions, engaging in diplomacy to try to solve specific problems, and providing goods or services helpful for the practice of human rights. When a U.N. agency approves a resolution calling on a specific state to take specific human rights action, I consider this an effort to generate political pressure on the target and thus an effort at protection, not just promotion. All of these examples I consider to be protection in the realm of implementation.

Agencies that see themselves engaged in the protection of human rights do not spend great amounts of time and effort trying to define it. This is as true of U.N. agencies as those outside the United Nations. Neither the U.N. High Commissioner for Refugees (UNHCR) nor the ICRC has ever published a doctrinal statement defining precisely its protection activities.[2] Both consider themselves, however, to be engaged in the business of helping to protect human rights. Thus, one may have to be content with a general distinction between promotion and protection, recognizing the relativity of semantical choice that stems from the difficulty of putting various human endeavors into neat categories. Even promotion, with some reason, can be considered indirect protection, since it is the background against which protection occurs.

It is important to distinguish direct from indirect protection. The United Nations engages mostly in indirect protection, with direct protection being mostly the preserve of states. By indirect protection (and excluding for the moment promotion which I continue to view as more general educational activity), I mean that an actor calls upon or commands another to take specific and short-term action so that nationals can exercise human rights.

By direct action, I mean that an actor itself assumes primary responsibility so that an individual can exercise his or her human rights. I can think of only two types of direction protection by a U.N. agency. If the Security Council legally requires a state to engage a human rights policy (for instance, terminate minority governance since it constitutes a threat or breach of the peace) and then legally requires sanctions in support of its majoritarian policy, that constitutes a direct protection attempt even though it is states (and private parties within states) that must apply the policy. Second, if a U.N. agency is allowed to operate in country to provide socioeconomic goods and services, that is a direct protection attempt in support of economic and social rights. Both positive and negative action can be taken to protect rights. The fact that states or private agencies are involved in some way does not change the fact that it is a U.N. agency that itself and in a primary, specific, and immediate way seeks to guarantee the exercise of human rights.

It may be argued that there is no pure example of direct protection of human rights at the international level or by international agencies, since all such action depends either on borrowed state power or on the granting of state consent. In this sense, not even the European Court of Human Rights, which has compulsory jurisdiction from twenty state parties and ultimate authority to interpret the European Convention on Human Rights, exercises direct protection because its judgments go to the European Committee of Ministers and because its functioning depends on state cooperation. But then by that logic there could be almost no pure examples of direct protection by states either, for states (of the governments that speak for them) call upon or rely on others to apply national protection. To protect against torture, for example, states call upon police and jailers to take, or not take, certain actions. In this sense, every protective action is indirect except personal action taken in direct contact with the specified person. This is too rigorous a definition of direct protection, denying the commonsense observation that historically it has been territorial states that have been directly responsible for guaranteeing the exercise of human rights.

Even when the United Nations is engaged in protective actions, it is mostly—even overwhelmingly—calling upon its states members to take action. The United Nations rarely takes direct protective action itself, that is, primary responsibility for guaranteeing the exercise of rights. Beyond promotion, the United Nations engages mainly in indirect protection through implementation efforts designed to push or encourage states into allowing the exercise of human rights.

Others can provide insights into this subject matter by use of different terminology and (usually implicit) definitions.[3] But their semantics are not problem free, and my approach is not only explicit but as clear as possible given the complexity of the subject.

That the treatment of human rights at the United Nations has changed over the years can be proved without any doubt. More controversial are efforts to formulate precisely the accurate significance of the change that has clearly occurred. It seems clear enough that institutional and procedural changes at the United Nations in the field of human rights have been striking. It also seems clear that there is some legal significance to the changes that have occurred. At least it can be said that states have accepted a number of new legal obligations and that the record includes numerous cases in the broadest possible sense that can be used as precedents should actors choose to do so in pursuit of human rights values.

Controversy begins to set in when one tackles the subject of the practical significance of these changes for the condition of human rights beyond U.N. meeting rooms. On this subject, there is considerable disagreement, including a debate on what constitutes progress in human rights and how to discern it. Opinion about practical significance is affected by the time span employed and by how the problem to be overcome is defined. In the short term and with regard to one individual or one situation, many U.N. actions clearly fail to generate decisive influence. In the long term and with regard to the collective mind-set of an actor, however, it may be that U.N. action contributes importantly to the exercise of human rights. If progress in human rights is most fundamentally characterized by acceptance of the idea of human rights and a willingness by public authorities to respond favorably to personal claims based on human rights, then over time perhaps U.N. agencies may make significant contributions, along with other causal factors.[4]

Between 1946, when India first raised the question of apartheid in the General Assembly, and 1990, when the South African government released Nelson Mandela from detention and legalized the African National Congress, one might have said that U.N. action on apartheid was insignificant. Persons of color continued to be killed, tortured, mistreated, discriminated against in countless ways, denied meaningful political participation, and so forth. On the other hand, historians looking back from the twenty-first century may judge U.N. action on the question of apartheid in South Africa as significant, in combination with other factors. If the key factor in ending apartheid was convincing the white elite that change had to occur, the United Nations may have played a role. Time span and definition of problem affect how significance is treated.

The Process: Six Organs

There are a variety of views on the historical evolution of the United Nations and human rights.[5] Clearly from 1945 to 1954 human rights diplomacy at the United Nations focused primarily on promotion or on the drafting of norms—the elaboration of the charter provisions on the subject. Some observers see a new period beginning about 1954 when U.N. human rights activity supposedly turned to different promotional efforts through the holding of seminars and the publication of various studies on human rights problems in general, without the naming of countries or specific patterns of behavior. Other observers see no real change between 1954 and 1967, despite a supposed U.N. action plan on promoting human rights. This second view is basically persuasive, although numerous persons at the United Nations were active on several human rights matters. The Eisenhower administration, however, traded away much activity on human rights at the United Nations in return for the demise of the movement in Congress for the Bricker amendment to the U.S. Constitution, which would have limited executive authority in foreign affairs.[6] Since the United States dominated U.N. proceedings during this period and since it was unwilling to push for vigorous U.N. action on human rights, one can say with assurance that there was no important change in U.N. developments on human rights between 1954 and 1967.

A distinctive period clearly started around 1967 when the United Nations began selective specific protection attempts or the targeting of specific countries like South Africa and Israel for human rights consideration. These targets had long been diplomatically attacked by other states in the General Assembly. After 1967 other parts of the U.N. system began to deal with human rights specifics in these and other states. At some point, these efforts at protection became almost global, especially after the two major covenants—or treaties—on human rights came into legal force. Countries were not guaranteed freedom from some type of U.N. supervision of their rights record. Because this change represented an effort by U.N. agencies to monitor state performance in the field of human rights and to generate diplomatic pressure or encouragement on the basis of state performance, this is an exercise of protection activity, not just more promotion.

Given that the definition of most historical eras is partly arbitrary, I will speak of before and after 1967. This simple bifurcation allows one to note clearly the change that has taken place at the United Nations on human rights. Before 1967, there was a timidity on the part of member states toward the human rights issue, and almost all expectations were low about utilizing the United Nations to act on human rights questions.[7]

The superpowers and great powers were not interested in precise legal obligations and international action on human rights at the San Francisco Conference. As noted, only vague principles were endorsed in the charter. This timid climate of opinion continued during the early years of the United Nations, although specific debates and finger pointing occurred. The U.N. Commission on Human Rights (a body whose members are instructed by their governments) reporting to ECOSOC, issued a self-denying ordinance in 1947 holding that it had no authority to hear specific complaints about human rights violations addressed to the United Nations. The commission functioned basically as a research and drafting organ. As part of the action—or inaction—plan of the 1950s, states were asked to report voluntarily on their rights policies. Reports were generally self-serving and not subjected to careful review. When the commission's expert—viz., uninstructed—Sub-Commission on Prevention of Discrimination and Protection of Minorities appointed a rapporteur who became assertive and tried to push an analytic summary drawn from state reports, the subcommission buried the project. Western states sought the termination of the commission's subgroups, ironically succeeding concerning the one on freedom of information. The one on discrimination and minorities was barely saved by other coalitions.[8] The one on women continued as a separate commission. Sporadic resolutions on particular subjects like forced labor did not change the dominant pattern of this early period, a pattern marked more by lip-service to human rights than by specific protection efforts.

During this early period, the Universal Declaration of Human Rights was adopted in 1948, and the two major covenants were negotiated (one on Civil and Political, the other on Economic, Social, and Cultural Rights). These instruments came to have considerable salience legally and politically. However necessary this drafting was, in this first period it was accompanied by considerable foot dragging. Even Eleanor Roosevelt, a champion of international standards on human rights, repeatedly defended the idea of a nonbinding declaration. As instructed by the State Department, she fought the efforts of some who wanted a legally binding instrument.[9] The covenants, while substantially completed by 1954, were not approved by the General Assembly and opened for signature until 1966 and did not reach the number of adherences required for entry into legal force until 1976. Most states, including the United States, were not anxious to accept specific and binding obligations concerning international human rights, and they did not want the U.N. Commission on Human Rights or other organs of the U.N. system to be assertive in the cause of human rights. Vague principles were acceptable; specific and binding obligations, with intrusive monitoring mechanisms, were not.

Prior to 1967 a number of other human rights instruments were developed beyond the International Bill of Rights. Concern with labor rights and slavery carried over from the time of the League of Nations. New legal instruments were created concerning refugees, genocide, and women's political rights. Toward the end of this first period, treaties were drafted on the prevention of educational and racial discrimination. It was as if states could not avoid drafting documents proclaiming high-minded standards, even if their specific policies fell short of the values they were approving, which may explain their reluctance to accept authoritative international monitoring of the standards they endorsed. After 1955, many Third World states championed the cause of nondiscrimination, especially related to race. Many of these same states eventually failed to submit required reports to the Committee on the Elimination of Racial Discrimination (CERD) after adhering to the nondiscrimination treaty.[10] Endorsement of principles outstripped efforts at application.

In the second twenty years of the United Nations, the situation changed markedly. Efforts increasingly moved from the general and the abstract to the specific and the concrete, although some standard-setting efforts continued—for example, on a special instrument concerning torture and also on the rights of the child. That is, continuing promotion was accompanied by increasing protection attempts. Most of these protective efforts took the weaker form of implementation rather than enforcement; nevertheless, an incremental and diplomatic revolution occurred. The United Nations accepted the principle of the permissibility of private petitions claiming rights violations and created several mechanisms to deal with them. Increasingly U.N. bodies used publicity as a means of pressure against specific states. Targets were not limited to South Africa and Israel—or even Chile. Increasingly across the U.N. system, there was a fragile but persistent movement toward improved supervision of states' policies on human rights. More and more human rights treaties came into legal force, and various agencies tried to see that they were implemented. Mainstream U.N. rights agencies created new monitoring mechanisms to supervise states' policies, and some new agencies were set up. A brief synopsis of some U.N. organs on human rights will highlight the process.

Human Rights Committee

The U.N. Covenant on Civil and Political Rights came into legal force for adhering states in 1976. Since then, the number of parties had grown to about ninety states as of the late 1980s. These elect an eighteen-member expert committee (of uninstructed persons) to review state reports and to hear private petitions from persons whose states have accepted an optional protocol permitting such action (about forty states at the time of writing). The committee officially does not take instructions from states or U.N. bodies, but it reports to the General Assembly through ECOSOC and interacts with the Secretariat. By most accounts, since 1978 the committee has been energetic and assertive, seeking to make the review process as rigorous as possible but staying within the bounds of a generally cooperative attitude toward states.[11] Particularly its treatment of private petitions has drawn high praise.[12]

Developments in 1980 show how incremental but important change can occur. There arose in the committee a discussion about its authority in the light of Article 40, paragraph 4 in the civil-political covenant: "The Committee shall study the reports submitted by the States Parties to the present Covenant. It shall transmit its reports, and such general comments as it may consider appropriate, to the States Parties. The Committee may also transmit to the Economic and Social Council these comments along with the copies of the reports it has received from States Parties to the present Covenant."

A majority of the thirteen committee members participating in the debate wanted to give considerable scope to the word *study* and not be deterred from vigorous action by the word *general*. This majority was made up of Third World as well as Western members. Clear support for an active Human Rights Committee came from the members from Ecuador, Jordan, Tunisia, and Senegal, as well as West Germany and Norway. The members from Eastern Europe—especially from the Soviet Union, East Germany, and Rumania—were a distinct minority. Eventually a compromise statement was reached: "general comments" would be addressed to state parties; the committee could comment on the implementation of the covenant; protection of human rights—not just promotion—was a proper subject for the committee; the committee could take up the subject of "the implementation of the obligation to guarantee the rights set forth in the Covenant"; the committee might later consider further what duties it would undertake; the Secretariat would be asked to make an "analysis" of states' reports and the pattern of questions by members. Subsequently other comments by members indicated that many would continue to push for a serious review process and that an attempt would be made to be systematic in order to establish pattern over time.[13] If this compromise seemed in the short run a concession to the East Europeans, it contained ample language to legitimize expansive and assertive action by the Western and Third World members. Since 1980 "general comments" have been used to interpret the covenant in a specific way.

To take one year at random, in 1981 the committee publicly criticized Uruguay for its treatment of certain individuals. The committee in effect rejected a report from Chile and criticized the inadequacies of several other reports. It also requested the Secretariat to put pressure on Zaire for its failure to file a report on time. Many states have been questioned closely about their reports and policies; frequently additional information is requested and provided. Aside from the Soviet Union and its close allies, the nature of questioning did not usually follow ideological alignments. In 1983, the member from Yugoslavia seemed tough on the subject on Nicaragua's treatment of Miskito Indians. Also in 1983, the member from West Germany was exceedingly tough in addressing the presenter of the report from France. The member from Tunisia led the effort to put pressure on Zaire.[14]

The Human Rights Committee has not functioned for very long, and its authority, procedures, and impact are still in flux. It seems clear thus far that the majority on the committee, irrespective of turnover, intends to have as much impact as it can generate. Future committee members from Eastern Europe and/or the Soviet Union should boost its assertiveness. National laws in Sweden and Senegal and perhaps elsewhere have been changed, apparently as a result of committee questioning.

Human Rights Sub-Commission

Over time the Sub-Commission on Prevention of Discrimination and Protection of Minorities has become an expert body on human rights in general, functioning under the charter and under whatever mandates might be received from its parent commission, the ECOSOC, or the General Assembly and under whatever initiatives it might seize for itself.[15] Its membership has not been that different from its instructed parent, which elects its twenty-six members. In 1982, to choose one year arbitrarily, according to the index of Freedom House, ten members came from "Free," seven from "Partly Free," and nine from "Not Free" nations.[16] Many individuals have served as instructed representatives of states in other bodies and also as supposedly uninstructed members of the subcommission. This is a prevalent personnel pattern not limited to Stalinist delegations, one that reappears in the Human Rights Committee as well.

The members of the subcommission have been so assertive at times that its superior bodies have tried to suppress its activity, ignore its projects, change its mandates, or change its membership. It has been more willing than its superiors to use public pressure on states. It has sought to do as much as it can on a number of problems, including detained or disappeared persons. It has tried a variety of procedures to improve its functioning, such as working groups and special rapporteurs that act beyond its regular session to address particular geographical or topical problems. The working group on slavery and the one on indigenous peoples have generated considerable attention and perhaps some influence over time.[17] The subcommission is the U.N. body of first recourse for private communications under important resolutions, and it has performed that review with seriousness of purpose since 1972. At times it has broken new ground in protective efforts—for example, in taking extraordinary steps to try to protect the rights of a Rumanian member of the sub-commission in 1988.[18]

At one time there was some fear that the expansion of the subcommission's membership—and thus an increase in Third World members—would destroy its credibility. This has not happened. In the early 1980s, members from Eastern Europe, joined by the one from Pakistan, tried to establish the principle that the subcommission would act only by consensus. This would have given a blocking role to a minority that might wish to curtail the persistently assertive subcommission. This move was rejected, with a number of Third World members lining up with Western members.[19] Given the changes in the Soviet Union and Eastern Europe in the late 1980s, one can assume that this attempt to emphasize minority blocking rights has been completely laid to rest. The subjects taken up by the Human Rights Sub-Commission, the states criticized, and the resolutions passed do not show a simple East-West or North-South bias. By the late 1980s an increase in cooperation and consensus within the subcommission could be observed.[20] The subcommission seems as serious and assertive now as in the past—and as seriously circumscribed.

Commission on Human Rights

The U.N. Commission on Human Rights is an instructed body, elected by ECOSOC and now comprising forty-three states, that has become the focal point of much of the U.N.'s human rights activity. Increasingly it is the diplomatic hub of the wheel making up U.N. human rights action. According to the rating system of Freedom House, in 1982 the commission was made up of seventeen states classified as "Not Free," ten as "Partly Free," and sixteen as "Free."[21] If 63 percept of states making up a human rights body show major deficiencies in their own records concerning civil and political rights, one might reasonably expect that body to be less than enthusiastic in its activity—at least on those rights. This assumption is not completely substantiated by the facts.[22]

In the decade of the commission after the drafting of the covenants and later after two expansions of its membership, doctrinal disputes over the relationship of socioeconomic and civil-political right—and over which had priority—gave way to an increasing focus on the protection of specific civil and political rights.[23] There is still a bias in the agenda of the commission, since it tends to focus on civil rights of primary interest to the Third World, such as racial nondiscrimination. It also devotes a disproportionate amount of time to such subjects as national self-determination, apartheid in South Africa, Israeli practices in the occupied territories, and other subjects of interest to the Third World. But during the earlier era (1947–1967), it also displayed a slant to its work, only then it was a bias stemming from the Western states that controlled the agenda.[24]

It is not just the Third World, or in the past the Stalinist bloc, that played politics with human rights in the Human Rights Commission. In the late 1980s the United States sought to have the commission focus on Cuba out of all proportion to human rights violations in Cuba, relative to situations constituting a systematic pattern of gross violations of human rights. Cuba did manifest serious violations, but they paled in significance compared to those in the Sudan, South Africa, Israeli-controlled territory, El Salvador, and elsewhere. In Cuba, thousands of political opponents were not summarily executed as in the Sudan or Somalia. Death squads did not operate in Cuba, as they did in El Salvador. Large numbers of prisoners did not die in police custody, as in South Africa. Large numbers of youth were not detained in harsh conditions, with a stated policy of mistreatment, as in Israeli-controlled territory. Governmental indifference to famine and illiteracy did not exist in Cuba as it did in Ethiopia. Yet the United States, during both the Reagan and Bush administrations, continued to make U.N. monitoring of Cuba its top priority in the commission, to the point of engaging in considerable friction with the U.N. secretary-general.[25]

Despite the various biases or slants that different governments brought to the commission, one could nevertheless chart some improvement in systematic attention to a broad range of rights problems. The commission, like its subcommission, appointed independent rapporteurs for nonpartisan reports. It voted working groups to focus on special problems beyond regular meetings. In addition to promotion through standard setting, it tried to help implement rights through condemnatory resolutions, using the standard procedure of embarrassment by publicity. During the 1980s, according to one source:

> The West has become increasingly successful at enlisting majority support for new implementation measures to protect civil and political rights. In 1980 the Commission for the first time indirectly condemned an Eastern bloc ally by passing a resolution calling for withdrawal of foreign forces from Kampuchea. In the following two sessions, the Commission denounced foreign intervention in Afghanistan. The West also narrowly succeeded in getting Commission action on Poland and Iran in 1982. [There were also] several important Western-sponsored resolutions adopted by consensus—involving the appointment of special rapporteurs on mass exoduses and summary or arbitrary executions, and studies on the role of the individual in international law.[26]

The key to these and other developments within the commission was the role of Third World states that were truly nonaligned. They voted their concern for self-determination in Kampuchea and Afghanistan, and they also voted for economic rights and against racial discrimination.[27] Some Third World states like Senegal were vigorous and balanced in their attention to human rights violations. A number of Third World states were genuinely interested in human rights, even civil and political rights. Daniel Patrick Moynihan noted that one of the merits of framing issues in terms of human rights, rather than democracy pure and simple, was that a state did not have to be a democracy to pursue the subject with some real interest.[28] Of course, some Third World states, of various ideological stripes, sought to limit the activity of the commission. For example, Pakistan, India, and Ethiopia all took restrictive positions in commission debates at one time or another. And any state may seek to block attention to its own transgressions.

Yet it was Third World support for Western positions, and vice versa, that allowed the commission to do as much as it did. Since 1978 it has been publishing a black list of states that have been the subject of private complaints as noted confidentially by the subcommission. Over time this list has shown considerable balance.[29] To be sure, this black list is a very weak form of pressure; specifics are not provided. Also, a working group of the commission has been focusing in a balanced way on states in which persons "disappear" by forceful action.[30] A summary statement about the Commission on Human Rights seems accurate:

> Representatives continue to assert the principle of non-intervention when it suits their national interest, but in practice most members of the Commission have supported some initiatives to protect the human rights of citizens against violation by their own governments. . . . The Commission has systematically reviewed confidential communications alleging violations by members. . . . The commission has expanded its concern for violations far beyond the early narrow focus on South Africa and Israel and has reviewed allegations involving over thirty states. Members and NGOs now disregard the former taboo against attacking states by name in public debate and make sweeping public indictments. After thirty years, the Commission has become the world's first intergovernmental body that regularly challenges sovereign nations to explain abusive treatment of their own citizens.[31]

All of these trends should be solidified by the decline of the Stalinist bloc.

ECOSOC

The Economic and Social Council receives the reports of the Commission on Human Rights, as well as state reports under the U.N. Covenant on Economic, Social, and Cultural Rights, a treaty in legal force in about ninety states. In this part of the U.N. system, there does not at first glance seem to be striking change in the treatment of human rights. The conventional wisdom has been that on human rights, ECOSOC functions as a post office, carrying mandates from one body to another.[32] An analysis by an insider argued that ECOSOC was still giving "very superficial scrutiny" to state reports on socioeconomic rights and had failed to develop or borrow standards by which to evaluate violations.[33] Yet several further points can be noted, even if the ECOSOC votes on human rights reflect actions already covered in the Commission on Human Rights.

In the late 1960s, Third World states pushed for specific attention to human rights violations by South Africa and Israel in many parts of the U.S. system, including ECOSOC. That body, stimulated by reports not only from the Commission on Human Rights but also from the U.N. Special Committee on Decolonization, passed E/RES/1235 in 1967. This resolution—originally intended only for situations of racism, colonialism, and alien domination but amended by the West to include other human rights violations—authorized ECOSOC's suborgans to deal with specifics revealing a consistent pattern of gross violations of internationally recognized human rights. The following year, an effort to close the barn door failed; ECOSOC again refused to limit the scope of resolution 1235 to only some violations of human rights, and thus the Commission on Human Rights and its subcommission were authorized to take up specific patterns with full publicity.[34]

Three years after the passage of resolution 1235, ECOSOC adopted E/RES/1503, which permitted its suborgans to deal with private communications alleging violations of human rights. This resolution permitted NGOs as well as individuals—anyone with direct and reliable knowledge—to lodge an allegation confidentially with the Secretariat, which then passed on a sanitized version to the Human Rights Sub-Commission for possible future action.

The result of these two resolutions in ECOSOC was to make possible the expanded activity of the Human Rights Commission and Sub-Commission. Specifics could be pursued, and private information could be formally utilized. There was both a public and a confidential process, although the two did not always remain distinct. The point worth stressing is that certain Third World and Western states succeeded in getting authorized more serious attention to human rights. An effort by the East Europeans and other Third World states to keep the process limited to the international pariahs was not successful. The margin of success for the majority was very small on both resolutions. The key to the majority, in addition to Western states, was certain Third World states that sought a balanced approach to human rights protection.[35]

In 1986 ECOSOC created a new expert Committee on Economic, Social, and Cultural rights to monitor compliance with that covenant. This new uninstructed body replaced a moribund working group of government representatives, whose dilatory, if not disgraceful, performance fit with the judgment by a Secretariat official that the U.N.'s attention to socioeconomic rights was characterized by "hypocrisy and longwindedness."[36] Concern for those rights, for example, had never penetrated very deeply into U.N. efforts for economic development.[37] And relations between the instructed working group and the specialized agencies like the ILO and FAO had been antagonistic.[38] Although the new committee is definitely an improvement over the old working group, one cannot yet see a definite impact on state policy in this realm, although various private parties sought to assist the committee in assertive supervision of state policies.[39]

General Assembly

Much has been written, especially in the West, about human rights and the General Assembly (including its standing Third Committee on social affairs). There is no doubt but that the assembly has politicized human rights by employing double or otherwise unfair or unacceptable standards because of state foreign policy.[40] Israel was publicly and harshly criticized by a special committee made up of three states that did not even have formal diplomatic relations with the Jewish state. Yet the Soviet Union's gulag during its Stalinist period was never condemned by assembly vote. The assembly also never condemned the United States for blatant racial discrimination in the 1950s.

During the early days of the United Nations, when the U.S.-led West dominated assembly proceedings, a bias was evident as well. There was, for example, little attention to racial discrimination or the right to food. After the admission of numerous Third World states, the bias of the assembly shifted toward subject matter of concern to that coalition with dominant votes, and it is likely that the demise of the Stalinist representatives at the United Nations will cause some slight shift in assembly proceedings on human rights, even though fewer than ten votes are affected.

If the assembly has been mainly concerned with civil and political rights to the exclusion of serious attention to social, economic, and cultural rights, the focus on different civil-political rights, in different countries, has changed over time.[41] That focus is the result of a political process affected by reasons of state. Despite the priority given to reasons of state in assembly maneuvers, however, and despite the continuation of some bias, the 1980s saw considerable balance as well in the assembly's treatment of human rights.

For example, in 1982, the Third Committee held a doctrinal debate about the priority of rights. As the representatives of both New Zealand and Senegal noted, the debate was about the balance between individual and collective rights. An Irish resolution emphasized the former, a Cuban the latter. The crux of the matter came down to whether each resolutuion could be adopted without distorting amendments, thus signifying that each type of right had importance. The Cuban resolution was voted upon first and adopted by 104–1–24 (the single negative vote was cast by the United States; the abstainers were mostly Western). The Irish resolution was also finally adopted, 75–30–22. Voting with the West in the majority were forty-six nonaligned states.[42] A similar alignment carried the day on paragraph 12 of the Irish resolution, which authorized a study of the mandate of a possible high commissioner for human rights.

There is no one simple reason explaining a coalition. The list of those voting for the Irish resolution did not reflect a club of the pure on civil and political rights—witness the inclusion of Paraguay, then represented by an authoritarian government. Despite the fact that the Cuban resolution was assured passage and the Irish was not, the result was that individual civil and political rights received equal formal endorsement. This was made possible by the number of Third World states that were not prepared to endorse a one-sided approach to human rights, at least in principle. This debate and resulting resolutions were typical of the increased balance and agreement that progressively transpired in the assembly on human rights matters.[43]

Security Council

The Security Council has not been generally linked to the protection of human rights. This is not correct. Indeed on the two occasions prior to 1990 when the council reached a decision concerning enforcement action in relation to the charter's Chapter VII, the real issue at stake was human rights. The decision in the 1960s to consider Ian Smith's Unilateral Declaration of Independence in Rhodesia as a threat to peace meriting mandatory economic sanctions was a decision designed to implement the right to self-determination for the majority in what was to become Zimbabwe. That right is the first one listed in each of the two general U.N. covenants on human rights. The decision in the 1970s to consider arms traffic with South Africa a threat to the peace requiring a mandatory ban on such traffic was a camouflaged approach to the subject of apartheid as a gross violation of self-determination as well.

Of course, there is a bias at work here too, for it is only on the question of white minority rule that the council has been able to muster the votes to reach a decision in the legal sense and thus seek to enforce the exercise of human rights. Denial of self-determination and political participation unaffected by race has not drawn such authoritative council action.

Nevertheless, especially with regard to South Africa and Namibia, the council has called upon states to implement the principles contained in the Universal Declaration of Human Rights. As a member of the Secretariat has observed, in these actions the council "treated respect for the basic provision of the [1948 Universal] Declaration as a legal obligation of States as well as of their nations.[44]

The Dynamics: Five Factors

On human rights, the United Nations is not what it was. Promotion has increasingly been accompanied by protection attempts. Considerable diplomacy is expended at the United Nations on trying to implement rights, with rare enforcement efforts. What are the underlying reasons for this change? At least five sets of factors contributed to this modification.

States' Foreign Policies

A view that achieved some popularity in the 1980s was that events unfolded at the United Nations according to a struggle between the United States and the rest of the world.[45] It follows, then, that on human rights questions, any progress must be because of the quality of the diplomacy of the U.S.-led West. This view is overstated, although it is correct in one sense.

The old Soviet-led Stalinist bloc, joined by some Third World states, was consistently hostile to international civil-political rights and to any meaningful U.N. review process. The Stalinist interpretation of human rights under Marxism, one that is inhospitable to the prima facie meaning of U.N. instruments, was stated openly: "The political freedoms—freedom of the press, of expression, of assembly—are interpreted from class positions as conditions of the consolidation of the working people and the spread of socialist ideology which rules out the 'freedom' of anti-socialist propaganda, the freedom to organize counterrevolutionary forces against the fundamentals of socialism."[46] Thus the individual has the right to say and do what the party-state decrees is progressive for socialism. That being so, the Stalinist group tried to avoid real supervision of its rights policies by a non-Marxist review body.

The Stalinist Soviet Union was consistent in opposing real international standards and supervision. In 1947 it opposed having the U.N. Commission on Human Rights made up of uninstructed individuals. In 1948 it first tried to postpone and then finally abstained on the vote on the Universal Declaration. In the 1980s it argued that the U.N. Human Rights Committee should have no real control over states' interpretation of the civil-political covenant. The member of that committee from East Germany even argued that the committee had no right to take any action whatsoever when a state failed even to submit a required report.[47] On issue after issue during the first forty years of the United Nations, the Soviet Union and its allies, joined occasionally by such non-Marxist authoritarian states as Pakistan and the Philippines, tried to suppress attention to international civil-political rights and to vitiate real U.N. supervision of rights policies. The Soviet Union deviated from this orientation only when it had the opportunity to make difficulty for a strategic adversary—for example, supporting intrusive U.N. supervision of the rights situation in Pinochet's Chile.

The Stalinist Soviet Union and its shifting bedfellows on human rights did not always, or even fundamentally, triumph at the United Nations because of two factors. First, other states displayed an equally persistent interest in especially civil and political rights (as well as some interest in socioeconomic rights) and fought for a genuine review process at the United Nations. One thinks primarily of the Scandinavian states, but also at times of the United States, the rest of the Western coalition, and some Third World States. Second, a self-serving interpretation equal to that of the Soviets by some U.S. administrations offset the old Soviet position and, in a dialectical process, caused a number of states to seek a compromise leading to a certain type of progress. If the Soviet Union consistently displayed a double standard in favor of socialist states, so the United States at times manifested a double standard in favor of authoritarian and capitalistic states aligned with it. Whan a rapporteur for the Human Rights Sub-Commission authored a report criticizing economic relations supporting the governing junta in Chile after 1973, the United States helped suppress it.[48] When resolutions were introduced in various U.N. organs criticizing the gross violations of human rights in El Salvador and Guatemala, the United States voted against.[49] At one point the United States voted against a commission study on the right to food,[50] and the United States was the only government to vote against World Health Organization voluntary guidelines designed to protect mothers and infants from questionable marketing practices by the Nestle Corporation. It was especially obvious that the Reagan administration liked publicly to castigate leftist governments, such as Cuba's, while remaining silent about mass political murder by governments of the right, such as Argentina's. Ambassador Jeane Kirkpatrick wrote approvingly of such double standards.[51] Thus a U.S. double standard, an American self-serving bias, could be and was observed at the United Nations,[52] providing a counterpoint to the Soviet position.

In sum, because some states were genuinely interested in a cosmopolitan human rights program and because some sought a compromise between the self-serving positions of the superpowers, states' foreign policies contributed mightily to alteration of the United Nations' record on human rights. State hypocrisy, narrow self-interest, and blatant double standards, along with more cosmopolitan forces, combined to produce a certain progress over time.[53] Formally, there was a growing moral interdependence among governments, but frequently this was more formal than real.

Nongovernmental Organizations

One of the reasons the U.N. record on human rights is different in the 1990s from earlier days is the activity of nongovernmental international organizations. Groups such as Amnesty International, the International Commission of Jurists, the International League for Human Rights, and others have been creative and energetic in keeping the pressure on states to acknowledge and then implement human rights standards through their foreign policies.

It was NGO information that started various U.N. organs down the path of a slow but eventually interesting treatment of human rights violations in Equatorial Guinea in the 1970s. Confidential NGO information was provided to the Human Rights Sub-Commission, and eventually the commission sent a rapporteur for an in-country visit, which led to a public report critical not only of the fallen regime but of the sitting one as well. NGO pressure after the passage of E/RES/1235 quickly broadened the Human Rights Sub-Commission's focus beyond Israel and South Africa; information was submitted on Greece under military rule and also on Haiti. NGOs successfully pushed for passage of E/RES/1503 permitting confidential communiqués, again of broad scope. They kept the pressure on states to do something about the growing problem of torture, and Amnesty International played a key role in this regard. NGOs pushed successfully for a working group on disappeared persons. NGO reports are used openly by the Committee of Experts under the Racial Discrimination Convention. In the Commission on Human Rights, their information is referred to formally by Secretariat reports. In the Human Rights Committee, it is now acknowledged that members can informally use NGO reports as a basis for questioning the accuracy of state reports. The same is true in the new Expert Committee on Social, Economic, and Cultural Rights.[54]

NGOs have been so active on human rights at the United Nations that various states have threatened to curtail their activity—sometimes succeeding but more often failing. Some assertive NGOs on human rights have been denied the consultative status with ECOSOC that gives them official rights to speak in meetings and circulate documents,[55] although they can still contact state delegations outside meetings. The Stalinist Soviet Union tried unsuccessfully to exclude NGO reports from ECOSOC and its suborgans.[56] Other threats against NGOs have been made—by authoritarian Argentina and Iran, for example—to remove consultative status, but these have not been carried out. The very fact that NGOs are attacked by states suggests that these groups are taken seriously by states. Several observers believe that NGO activity is essential for continued efforts at protecting human rights.[57]

Secretariat

Members of the Secretariat have contributed to the changing United Nations record on human rights, from the secretary-general down through the directors (now under secretary-general) for human rights, to the Secretariat officials who service the various human rights working groups. The five secretaries—general have been supportive of human rights to varying degrees.

On a number of occasions, the secretary-general has used his good offices for quiet diplomacy designed to correct some human rights problem.[58] Publicly they have endorsed the human rights cause, as when Javier Perez de Cuéllar said in his 1983 annual report, "In the common quest to realize the ideals and objectives of the Charter, we must never lose sight of the quality of the world we are seeking to build and the ultimate raison d'etre for all our objectivities: the individual human being."[59] De Cuéllar appointed a personal representative, for example, to supervise the 1990 elections in Nicaragua.

The head of the Human Rights Division (now Centre) in the Secretariat has always been a Westerner: John P. Humphrey of Canada, Marc Schreiber of Belgium, Theo van Boven of the Netherlands, Kurt Herndl of Austria, and Jan Martenson of Sweden. Van Boven was perhaps the most assertive, so much so that he was dismissed by Perez de Cuéllar after conflicts with certain states like the Soviet Union and Argentina under military rule, the latter diplomatically supported by the United States.[60] Humphrey was highly active in a somewhat more diplomatic way, playing a key role in the drafting of the Universal Declaration, suggesting ideas to states that then pursued them through the U.N. system, and strongly defending civil and political rights as traditionally understood by the West.[61] Schreiber was perhaps less dynamic than van Boven or Humphrey, although these things are difficult to prove given the possibility of extensive quiet diplomacy. Herndl held his position for only a short time and made little impact, perhaps keeping a low profile after the dismissal of his predecessor. Martenson is also director of the Geneva office of the United Nations, which may diminish the time he devotes to human right activities, although it is difficult to judge the influence of a contemporary.

Uninstructed Bodies

Individuals on the Human Rights Sub-Commission and the Human Rights Committee must be given credit for contributing to increased efforts at specific protection. Mention should also be made of other uninstructed bodies: the Committee of Experts under the Racial Discrimination Convention, the Commission on Women, the Commission on Discrimination Against Women, the Committee of Experts and the Freedom of Association Commission of the International Labor Organization, the office of the UNHCR, and the relatively new Committee on Economic, Social, and Cultural Rights. The UNHCR is perhaps the uninstructed agency given the highest marks for its human rights work, although Thomas Farer also mentions UNICEF (United Nations International Children's Emergency Fund) in this regard.[62] (It is not clear why he fails to mention the ILO.)

On the Human Rights Sub-Commission and Committee under the Civil-Political Covenant and on similar bodies, there have been individuals keenly interested in the protection of human rights who have generated some influence, impossible to measure in the aggregate. A number of these persons have come from outside the Western political group.

World Public Opinion

One can overstate the importance of the idea of world public opinion, and it is certainly unwise to attribute much importance to something that cannot be precisely identified or clearly discerned in impact. Even so, I think it prudent to note what other scholars have observed. "National political leaders have to reckon with the possibility, and on occasion the reality, that powerful voices in their own societies will echo the words of the General Assembly, as they have done on issues of colonialism, human rights . . . and humanitarian assistance."[63] If this is what is meant by world public opinion, then there is probably a process at work that bears noting and merits more research attention in the future.

It seems highly probable, but not proved in all cases, that various public groups draw some of the inspiration and legitimacy for their human rights activity from U.N. resolutions, declarations, and conventions. Various groups in Eastern Europe referred to these documents as well as to others, such as the Helsinki Accord. Human rights groups in Argentina did the same, in addition to relying on human rights instruments under the OAS. Obviously there is some overlap between what is called world public opinion and the impact of NGOs, yet some groups and private citizens do not act directly on the U.N. system but are active at home in demanding that their governments abide by U.N. standards on human rights. In that sense, there is something that passes for world public opinion—weak and uneven in distribution but extant and possibly even growing. There is at least fragmentary evidence that even in closed societies, governments are asked by some of their citizens to observe the human rights standards endorsed at the United Nations.

One should not overlook the role of the communications media in focusing at least some popular attention on human rights. In the United States, for example, newspaper and television coverage of U.N. human rights proceedings may generate some domestic public opinion, at least from the attentive public, on executive and legislative branches. Attention from the *New York Times, Washington Post,* or television news programming could conceivably be considered part of world public opinion. Since this aspect of international human rights—the nature and extent of media coverage—has been grossly understudied, it is difficult to be precise about it.[64]

In the U.N. political process concerning human rights, coalitions frequently form to protect a particular right in a specific situation; these are made up of interested state delegates, uninstructed individuals, members of the Secretariat, and concerned officials of NGOs. They exchange information and coordinate tactics. Sometimes world public opinion operates indirectly as a background condition; participants in the U.N. system are aware of demonstrations, riots, or other actions by individuals not really represented in U.N. decisions—for example, Chileans or Lithuanians demanding democratic rights.

The Significance of U.N. Change

The significance of U.N. activity on human rights can be discussed in terms of immediate and long-term effects. The immediate impact is usually slight, for the United Nations has not been—and is not now—used primarily to bring about direct protection. All of its promotion efforts and most of its protection attempts entail considerable time to have an impact. Even the rare cases of attempted direct enforcement take considerable time. U.N. obligatory sanctions on the Ian Smith government of Rhodesia lasted from 1966–1968 to 1979. U.N. obligatory sanctions on South Africa have lasted since 1977.

There is not much evidence that implementation activity by the U.N. bodies discussed in this chapter has had much impact on target states, at least in the short run. In some cases, a critical and public approach has backfired, as in the 1970s when Pinochet used U.N. pressure about human rights violations in Chile to produce a national plebiscite endorsing his military regime. In situations in which change on human rights clearly occurs—for example, in South Africa or Eastern Europe and the Soviet Union—it is impossible to attribute change directly to the United Nations, since so many other possible causal factors exist, including unilateral and regional and private activity.

Furthermore, when a ruling group is determined to violate human rights, it is doubtful that any international arrangement short of armed intervention will bring an end to these violations in the short run. From Hitler through the Greek colonels (1967–1974) through the Argentine junta (1974–1982) to Rumania under Ceausescu (until 1989), fundamental violations of human rights ended only with the removal of the dictatorship or oligarchy. Some authoritarians may yield power more or less voluntarily (for example, the military in Brazil), but while they held power, no amount of international pressure was able to change the human rights situation. Until external military defeat or internal collapse (or a combination of both) occurred, international attempts at short-term protection of rights proved less than decisive in producing structural change.

Paradoxically, however, this failure to achieve clear success in the short term is not reason to terminate U.N. attempts to protect human rights. Such efforts, even if mostly indirect, feed into long-term efforts that may ultimately contribute to desired change.

The main goal of the United Nations in the field of human rights is beneficial change over time. The Human Rights Committee's main activity is to produce a record of patterns over time drawn from states' reports and members' questions. Under E/RES/1503, confidential communications and the Human Rights Sub-Commission's analysis are supposed to deal with patterns of gross violations of human rights over time. The Commission on Human Rights' publication of a black list about states, even though it is devoid of specifics, is designed to focus on certain states over time.

What would be required for successful immediate protection? The authority to command states to abandon practices that violate protected rights? The ability to apply such a command? Overwhelming political pressure directed at human rights violations to the exclusion of other interests? No U.N. human rights body has consistently exercised such authority and power. Only the Security Council comes close, and even its power to enforce is tenuous, as seen in the history of economic sanctions on Rhodesia or an arms embargo on South Africa. The council only rarely links enforcement action with human rights.

Those most familiar with U.N. human rights action understand that the organization does not normally utilize its authority and power for short-term protection.[65] As a general rule, only states and a few international agencies have the capacity to attempt direct, specific short-term protection: the European Court on Human Rights, the Inter-American Court on Human Rights, the International Committee of the Red Cross, the UNHCR, and a few others. Regional human rights courts issue judgments mandating immediate change dealing with specifics. Nonjudicial agencies such as the ICRC or UNHCR seek immediate change concerning specifics but through diplomacy (implementation) rather than command (enforcement). In summation, the United Nations's primary goal in the human rights field has become long-term implementation, against the background of promotion.

The sum total of U.N. activity is supposed to socialize or educate actors into changing their views and policies over time toward a cosmopolitan (universal) human rights standard as defined by U.N. instruments. Or, the sum total of U.N. activity is to dispose or withhold a stamp of legitimacy on member states according to their human rights record.

A version of the latter view gained some currency in U.S. circles in the 1970s and 1980s. Ambassadors Moynihan and Kirkpatrick, among others, charged that the United Nations was a dangerous place where a majority attempted to delegitimize the Western democracies while legitimizing its own violations of civil and political rights in the name of economic development or termination of exploitation.[66] The Moynihan-Kirkpatrick thesis was essentially correct when applied to the old Stalinist bloc and some Third World states, but it is not accurate as a description of the overall U.N. record on human rights.

It does seem correct to highlight the socialization process and the dispensing of legitimacy—two sides of the same coin—as an important ongoing development at the United Nations in the human rights area. From the sweeping away of Stalinist governments in Eastern Europe to the toppling of dictators in the Third World—for example, Somoza in Nicaragua, the shah in Iran, Marcos in the Philippines—the ruling regime lost its legitimacy in the eyes of important actors to considerable degree because of human rights violations. U.N. definitions of human rights, along with other international standards and actors, probably contributed to the process.[67] It remains impossible to disentangle the various causal factors precisely.

U.N. activity on human rights is most important for this long-term socialization process in which legitimacy is given or withheld because of the state's human rights performance. Any number of states are in need of the U.N. stamp of approval, or in need of avoiding its disapproval, although all have other sources of legitimacy, such as their own national traditions, performance, and internal procedures. U.N. impact is further attenuated because its human rights endeavors are poorly coordinated.

At some point, the long-term effects of the United Nations must become short term if the organization is to show improved impact on states and individuals. Socialization and manipulation of legitimacy must change specific behavior, must lead to direct protection by a national actor, if the United Nations is to have greater significance for human rights. In a few situations this linkage can be demonstrated.

In the case of *Filartiga v. Pena-Irala* in the United States, a federal court held torture to be prohibited by customary international law, using U.N. instruments and actions as part of its legal reasoning.[68] This case opened the possibility of specific prosecution for torturers of any nationality who appear in the jurisdiction of the United States. Other courts in the United States have also used U.N. instruments and activity on human rights as part of their decision.[69] The important U.S. case of *Forti v. Suarez-Mason,* stemming from the "dirty war" in Argentina, confirmed the significance of the *Filartiga* case and led to further important legal developments, partially based on U.N. developments.[70]

Other countries also show some influence from U.N. instruments in their legal and administrative decisions.[71] Politically it is clear that various groups and individuals refer to events at the United Nations to justify their existence and activity. And in situations like the 1990 elections in Nicaragua, the United Nations, in this case through an election supervision team, had a real, if partial and indirect, impact on human rights and even the structure of national politics.

Therefore a smattering of evidence suggests that U.N. activity on human rights over time can have some real impact in changing behavior by contributing to direct protection by national authorities. Other evidence suggests that in other situations, U.N. activity has very little, if any, impact.[72]

Conclusions

We do not lack for criticism of the United Nations when it comes to human rights. Ernst Haas wrote that U.N. efforts to implement human rights standards "do not work."[73] Richard Ullman concluded that "the U.N. human rights machinery has become so politicized as to be almost completely ineffective for either monitoring or for enforcement."[74] Moses Moskowitz argued that U.N. standards on human rights were vague and their supervision weak.[75]

A more balanced perspective is in order. Thomas Farer tried to summarize U.N. human rights developments by saying they constituted more than a whimper but less than a roar, while Jack Donnelly referred to them as constituting a strong promotional regime entailing political bias but a move in the 1980s "toward a much less partisan approach."[76] It is clear that U.N. action on human rights is better than it was but not what it could be.

The United Nations, narrowly defined, tries to promote and protect human rights in a process neither so streamlined nor so authoritative as that under the European Convention on Human Rights.[77] Its core procedures are less authoritative and probably less effective in the short run than those used by the ILO.[78] Some U.N. bodies have been less dynamic than the Inter-American Commission on Human Rights.[79] Information from NGOs is more formally employed in some European international regimes.[80] After all, even the League of Nations permitted private petitions and accorded NGOs a good deal of formal status on human rights.[81]

Yet it is well to recall, as Antonio Cassese remarked, that much criticism of the United Nations is "largely unfounded."[82] In the same vein Louis Henkin argued that "disappointment may reflect unwarranted expectations."[83] Both of these authors speak to the point stressed by John Gerard Ruggie: U.N. activity and "international human rights instruments are designed not to provide human rights or to enforce human rights provision, but to nudge states into permitting their vindication."[84] Or, in Henkin's words, "For the most part, human rights can only be promoted [and protected] indirectly" by the United Nations.[85] Indirect promotion and protection seems to be the métier of most international human rights agencies.[86]

This chapter has shown the reasons for a balanced view that recognizes the weaknesses of U.N. action on human rights but that also places those weaknesses in proper context. There has been political bias in the treatment of human rights in the General Assembly and Human Rights Commission, and there has been a notable lack of success in short-term implementation efforts. There has also been a marked trend across the U.N. system toward less partisan maneuvering in relative terms and also toward more implementation efforts rather than just promotion. This improved record, despite inherent weaknesses, holds the promise of a more equitable dispensation of legitimacy from the United Nations, as well as an improved socialization process.

A core U.N. human rights regime plus supplemental regimes exist, despite the interesting fact that the real expectations of important parties have not always converged in this issue area. There has been a formal convergence, in the sense that states members of the United Nations have formally endorsed human rights standards in the abstract or in general. There has thus been what might be called a growing global interdependence in formal morality. Formal morality is to be distinguished on occasion from real morality in the sense of a hidden political agenda. In short, what is formally endorsed as "good" has not always been the same as what states have really thought of as "good" in their concrete policies heavily influenced by reasons of state. It is well to recall that the European Stalinist coalition did not really accept an international standard on civil and political rights (and Stalinist China and Cuba still do not). The United States has never fully accepted the validity of socioeconomic rights, as I have shown elsewhere.[87] Formal global agreement has been accompanied by real and substantial disagreement.

Yet a coalition of states drawn historically from the industrialized democracies and from the truly nonaligned Third World, combined with other factors such as influence from the Secretariat, expert bodies, NGOs, and public opinion, has repeatedly converged to create and maintain U.N. human rights regimes and to try to embarrass states that violate their rules.[88] The various mechanisms of U.N. regimes remain somewhat chaotic, since not all supervising bodies or decision making organs act in concert.

It may be largely a matter of semantics whether one refers to the core U.N. regime as basically promotional or a "tutelage regime."[89] What deserves emphasizing is, first, that U.N. bodies increasingly seek not just to set human rights standards but to induce state compliance, and, second, that on occasion the sum total of U.N. action can help improve the exercise of human rights. While short-term protection of human rights is definitely not the U.N.'s forte, the *Filartiga* and *Suarez-Mason* cases, among other evidence, show clearly that international indirect promotion and protection can eventually have discernible direct effect.

Notes

1. David P. Forsythe, ed., *The United Nations in the World Political Economy* (London: Macmillan, 1989).

2. See David Forsythe, "The Political Economy of U.N. Refugee Programs," in ibid. for a comparison of the UNHCR and the ICRC.

3. Thomas J. Farer, "The United Nations and Human Rights," *Human Rights Quarterly* 9, 4 (November 1987): 550–86, writes of standard setting, promotion, and

protection. Jack Donnelly, "International Human Rights: A Regime Analysis," *International Organization* 40, 3 (Summer 1986): 599–642 presents a complex conception.

4. Rhoda Howard, "Human Rights, Development and Foreign Policy," in David P. Forsythe, ed., *Human Rights and Development* (London: Macmillan, and New York: St. Martin's, 1989), deals with human rights in terms of mind-sets and communities of obligation.

5. Howard Tolley, Jr., *The United Nations Commission on Human Rights* (Boulder, Colo.: Westview Press, 1987); Theo C. van Boven, "United Nations and Human Rights: A Critical Appraisal," in Antonio Cassese, ed., *U.N. Law/Fundamental Rights* (Alphen aan den Rijn: Sijthoff & Noordhoff, 1979), 119–36; Karel Vasek, ed., *The International Dimensions of Human Rights* (Paris: UNESCO, 1982).

6. James Frederick Green, an adviser to Mrs. Roosevelt, confirmed that the "Action Plan" was a diplomatic device to deflect criticism away from the U.S. policy shift. Interview, Atlanta, 1984. See also Robert E. Asher et al., *The United Nations and Promotion of the General Welfare* (Washington, D.C.: Brookings Institution, 1957), 699–705.

7. M.E. Tardu, "United Nations Response to Gross Violations of Human Rights: The 1503 Procedure," *Santa Clara Law Review* 20, 3 (Summer 1980): 559; and van Boven, "United Nations and Human Rights," 122. For a good overview of the early climate of opinion at the United Nations, see Leon Gordenker, "Development of the U.N. System," in Toby Trister Gati, ed., *The U.S., the U.N., and the Management of Global Change* (New York: New York University Press, 1983), 11–21.

8. The fight to save the subcommission was led by Chile, Mexico, and the Philippines. The Soviet bloc gave its support. Those voting to keep alive the subcommission were: Afghanistan, Argentina, Burma, Belorussia, Chile, Colombia, Czechoslovakia, Denmark, Dominican Republic, Ecuador, Egypt, Ethiopia, Haiti, Indonesia, Iran, Iraq, Liberia, Mexico, Pakistan, Paraguay, Peru, Philippines, Poland, Saudi Arabia, Syria, Ukraine, Soviet Union, Uruguay, Venezuela, Yemen, and Yugoslavia. *United National Yearbook, 1951* (New York: United Nations, 1954).

9. A/C.3/SR.89, September 30, 1948. See further A. Glenn Mower, Jr., *The United States, the United Nations, and Human Rights: The Eleanor Roosevelt and Jimmy Carter Eras,* (Westport, Conn.: Greenwood Press, 1979).

10. Thomas Buergenthal, "Implementing the Racial Convention," *Texas International Law Journal* 12, 2 and 3 (Spring–Summer 1977): 187–222. While this convention came into legal force in 1969 and now has over 120 adherences, it was not until 1982 that ten states permitted private petitions and thus brought that part of the treaty into legal force.

11. Danda D. Fischer, "Reporting under the Covenant on Civil and Political Rights: The First Five Years of the Human Rights Committee," *American Journal of International Law* 76, 1 (January 1982): 142–53. Under Article 41, states may declare that the committee is authorized to receive complaints from other states. Too much can be made of this. The history of other instruments—that is, the European Convention on Human Rights—shows that states are reluctant to make such legal claims. Similar political claims can already be made in the General Assembly or Commission on Human Rights.

12. Tom J. Zuijdwijk, *Petitioning the United Nations* (Aldershot, U.K.: Gower, 1982), 361, quoted in Donnelly, "International Human Rights," 160.

13. CCPR/C/SR.201, March 24, 1980; CCPR/C/SR.231, July 24, 1980; CCPR/C/SR.232, July 23, 1980; CCPR/C/SR.253, October 28, 1980; CCPR/C/SR.260, November 4, 1980.

14. *United Nations Chronicle* 20, 1 (January 1983): 105; 20, 7 (July 1983): 92–95; 20, 10 (November 1983): 57–64.

15. See further Tolley, *United Nations Commission on Human Rights,* chap. 8.

16. "Free" countries were Belgium, Costa Rica, France, Greece, India, Nigeria, Norway, Peru, the United Kingdom, and the United States. "Partly Free" were Bangladesh, Egypt, Mexico, Morocco, Panama, Sudan, and Zambia. "Not Free" were Argentina, Ethiopia, Ghana, Iraq, Pakistan, Rumania, Syria, the Soviet Union, and Yogoslavia. There is much controversy about the accuracy of this index.

17. Tolley, *United Nations Commission on Human Rights;* Douglas Sanders, "The U.N. Working Group on Indigenous Populations," *Human Rights Quarterly* 11, 3 (August 1989): 406–33.

18. Katherine Brennan et al., "The 40th Session of the U.N. Sub-Commission on Prevention of Discrimination and Protection of Minorities," *Human Rights Quarterly* 11, 2 (May 1989): 295–324.

19. *Human Rights Internet Reporter* 9, 1 and 2 (September–November 1983): 58–59.

20. Brennan et al., "40th Session"; David Weissbrodt, "Country-Related and Thematic Developments at the 1988 Session of the U.N. Commission on Human Rights," *Human Rights Quarterly* 10, 4 (November 1988): 544–58.

21. "Free": Australia, Canada, Costa Rica, Cyprus (Greek sector), France, West Germany, Greece, Italy, the Netherlands, the United Kingdom, Denmark, Fiji, India, Japan, Peru, and the United States. "Partly Free": Panama, Philippines, Uganda, Uruguay, Zimbabwe, Brazil, Gambia, Mexico, Senegal, and Zambia. "Not Free": Algeria, Bulgaria, Ethiopia, Jordan, Rwanda, Zaire, Argentina, Belorussia, China, Cuba, Ghana, Pakistan, Poland, Togo, the Soviet Union, and Yogoslavia. Again, this index is controversial.

22. Philip Alston, "The Alleged Demise of Political Human Rights at the U.N.: A Reply to Donnelly," *International Organization* 37, 3 (Summer 1983): 537–46; van Boven, "United Nations and Human Rights," 90.

23. Tolley, *United Nations Commission on Human Rights.*

24. Jack Donnelly, "Human Rights at the United Nations 1955–1985: The Question of Bias," *International Studies Quarterly* 32, 3 (Spring 1988): 275–303.

25. Weissbrodt, "Country-Related and Thematic Developments"; and *New York Times,* March 8, 1988, 6; March 7, 1989, 3; March 10, 1989, 4; March 11, 1989, 5; January 27, 1990, 3.

26. Tolley, *United Nations Commission on Human Rights.*

27. Ibid.

28. Daniel Patrick Moynihan, *A Dangerous Place* (Boston: Little, Brown, 1978), 281.

29. Through the spring of 1984, the following states had been targeted: Albania, Argentina, Benin, Bolivia, Burma, Chile, Equatorial Guinea, Ethiopia, Greece, Indonesia, Iran, Malawi, Nicaragua, Paraguay, South Korea (not a U.N. member), South Africa, Uganda, Uruguay, and the Soviet Union.

30. Through the spring of 1982, the following states had been targeted: Argentina, Bolivia, Brazil, Chile, Cyprus, El Salvador, Ethiopia, Guatemala, Guinea, Honduras, Indonesia, Iran, Lesotho, Mexico, Nicaragua, Philippines, Sri Lanka, Uganda, Uruguay, Zaire, South Africa, and Namibia. Interestingly, the working group was made up of three "Not Free" states (Ghana, Pakistan, and Yugoslavia) and two "Free" ones (Costa Rica and the United Kingdom).

31. Tolley, *United Nations Commission on Human Rights.*

32. James Frederick Green "Changing Approaches to Human Rights: The United Nations, 1954 and 1974," *Texas International Law Journal* 12, 2 and 3 (Spring–Summer 1979): 223.

33. Alston, "Alleged Demise." See also his "The United Nations' Specialized Agencies and Implementation of the International Covenant on Economics, Social and Cultural Rights," *Columbia Journal of Transnational Law* 18, 1 (1979): 79–118.

34. Tardu, "United Nations Response."

35. Ibid.

36. Quoted in Philip Alston, "Out of the Abyss: The Challenges Confronting the New U.N. Committee on Economic, Social and Cultural Rights," *Human Rights Quarterly* 9, 3 (August 1987): 379.

37. Theo Van Boven, "Human Rights and Development: The U.N. Experience," in Forsythe, ed., *Human Rights and Development.*

38. Alston, "Out of the Abyss."

39. Ibid.: Scott Leckie, "The U.N. Committee on Economic, Social and Cultural Rights and the Right to Adequate Housing: Towards an Appropriate Approach," *Human Rights Quarterly* 11, 4 (November 1989): 522–61; and "Symposium: The Iplementation of the International Covenant on Economic, Social, and Cultural Rights," *Human Rights Quarterly* 9, 2 (May 1987): 121–285.

40. Jack Donnelly, "Recent Trends in U.N. Human Rights Activity: Description and Polemic," *International Organization* 35, 4 (Autumn 1981): 633–55; but see also his more carefully considered "Human Rights."

41. Donnelly, "Human Rights."

42. Bahamas, Barbados, Botswana, Burma, Chad, Colombia, Costa Rica, Cyprus, Democratic Kampuchea (represented by the Pol Pot faction), Djibouti, Dominican Republic, Ecuador, Egypt, El Salvador, Fiji, Gabon, Guatemala, Ivory Coast, Jamaica, Kenya, Lesotho, Liberia, Malawi, Mali, Mexico, Morocco, Nepal, Niger, Papua New Guinea, Paraguay, Peru, Philippines, Senegal, Sierra Leone, Singapore, Somalia, Sri Lanka, Sudan, Tanzania, Thailand, Trinidad and Tobago, Upper Volta, Uruguay, Venezuela, Zambia, and Zimbabwe. Voting with the East Europeans in the minority were Afghanistan, Algeria, Angola, Argentina (under military rule), Congo, Cuba, Democratic Yemen, Laos, Libya, Madagascar, Mongolia, Pakistan, Syria, Vietnam. Other states abstained, including Ethiopia and Nicaragua. A/C.3/37/SR.60, December 1982, 7, 17–19.

43. Donnelly, "Human Rights."

44. Egon Schwelb and Philip Alston, "The Principal Institutions and Other Bodies Founded under the Charter," in Vasek, ed., *International Dimensions of Human Rights,* 262.

45. Richard Bernstein, "The United Nations vs. the United States," *New York Times Magazine,* January 22, 1984, 18ff. On human rights, see esp. 25–26.

46. Vladimir Kartashkin, "The Socialist Countries and Human Rights," in Vasek, ed., *International Dimensions of Human Rights,* 633.

47. CCPR/C/SR.201, March 24, 1980, 4–5.

48. Tolley, *United Nations Commission on Human Rights.*

49. *United Nations Chronicle* 20, 5 (June 1983): 28.

50. Ibid. 21, 7 (July 1983): 80.

51. Jeane Kirkpatrick, *Dictatorships and Double Standards* (Washington, D.C.: American Enterprise Institute, 1982).

52. If the U.S. double standard was particularly pronounced during the Reagan administration, in fairness it should be noted that in 1974 Rita Hauser, a former representative to the U.N. commission, testified that the United States frequently used a double standard at the United Nations. U.S. House of Representative, Committee on Foreign Affairs, "Human Rights in the World Community: A Call to Leadership," *Report of the Subcommittee on International Organizations* (Washington, D.C.: U.S. Government Printing Office, 1974), 10, 11. See also Tolley, *United Nations Commission on Human Rights.*

53. On the subject of how state hypocrisy can lead to beneficial change, see Louis Henkin, "The United Nations and Human Rights," *International Organization* 19, 3 (Summer 1965): 514.

54. The literature on NGOs has grown voluminously. Particularly enlightening are Virginia Leary, "A New Role for Non-Governmental Organizations in Human Rights," in Cassese, ed., *U.N. Law/Fundamental Rights,* 197–210; Nigel S. Rodley, "The Development of United Nations Activities in the Field of Human Rights and the Role of Non-Governmental Organizations," in Gati, ed., *The U.S., the U.N., and the Management of Global Change,* 263–82; and Chiang Pei-leng, *Non-Governmental Organizations at the United Nations: Identity, Role, and Function* (New York: Praeger, 1981). On the important role played by Amnesty International in helping negotiate the 1984 Convention on Torture, see Peter R. Baehr, "The General Assembly: Negotiating the Convention on Torture," in Forsythe, ed., *United Nations in the World Political Economy.*

55. "Rights Groups in Losing Battle for U.N. Role," *New York Times,* March 9, 1987, 5.

56. Philip Alston, "UNESCO Procedures for Dealing with Human Rights Violations," *Santa Clara Law Review* 20, 3 (Summer 1980): 669.

57. For example, David P. Forsythe, *Human Rights and World Politics,* 2d ed. (Lincoln: University of Nebraska Press, 1989).

58. B.G. Ramcharan, "The Good Offices of the United Nations Secretary-General in the Field of Human Rights," *American Journal of International Law* 76, 1 (January 1982): 130–41.

59. *United Nations Chronicle* 20, 9 (October 1983): 78.

60. Other reasons may have contributed to his dismissal. Some of his candid views are found in his book, *People Matter: Views on International Human Rights Policy* (Amsterdam: Meulenhoff, 1982).

61. John P. Humphrey, *Human Rights and the United Nations: The Great Adventure* (Dobbs Ferry, N.Y.: Transnational Publishers, 1983). Excerpts published as "The Memoirs of John P. Humphrey," *Human Rights Quarterly* 5, 4 (November 1983).

62. Farer, "United Nations and Human Rights."

63. Gordenker, "Development of the U.N. System," 33.

64. Students of international human rights are just now beginning to track the nature of newspaper and television coverage of this subject. Several general studies are in process at the time of writing, but none has been published. David P. Forsythe, in *Human Rights and U.S. Foreign Policy: Congress Reconsidered* (Gainesville: University Presses of Florida, 1989), shows that press coverage of the U.S. sale of shock batons to South Africa and South Korea led to a change in policy. For awareness of this gap in our knowledge about the impact of the communications media on human rights behavior, see William Shawcross, *The Quality of Mercy* (New York: Simon and Schuster, 1984), and Asbjorn Eide and Sigrun Skogly, eds., *Human Rights and the Media* (Oslo: Norwegian Institute of Human Rights, 1988).

65. See especially John Gerard Ruggie, "Human Rights and the Future International Community," *Daedalus* 112, 4 (Fall 1983): 93–110; and N.G. Onuf and V. Spike Peterson, "Human Rights and International Regimes," *Journal of International Affairs* 37, 2 (Winter 1984): 329ff. See also Henkin, "United Nations and Human Rights"; Tardu, "United Nations Response"; and Helge Ole Bergesen, "The Power to Embarrass: The U.N. Human Rights Regime between Realism and Utopia" (paper for the International Political Science Association World Congress, August 1982).

66. Moynihan, *A Dangerous Place,* 11 and passim; Jeane Kirkpatrick, *The Reagan Phenomenon* (Washington, D.C.: American Enterprise Institute, 1983).

67. Moynihan talks of the United Nations as a repository of "ideological authority," *A Dangerous Place,* 12. For a discussion of international human rights as a new standard of legitimacy with the potential to transcend debates over ideology, see Forsythe, *Human Rights and World Politics,* chap. 8.

68. U.S. Court of Appeals, 2d Circuit, June 30, 1980, no. 79-6090. 630 F.2d 876. A synopsis can be found in *American Journal of International Law* 75, 1 (January 1981): 149–53.

69. This has been especially true on refugee and immigration matters. See Gilburt D. Loescher and John A. Scanlan, "The Global Refugee Problem: U.S. and World Response," *Annals* 467 (May 1983). More generally see James C. Tuttle, ed., *International Human Rights Law and Practice* (Philadelphia: American Bar Association, 1978), and Richard B. Lillich, "The Constitution and International Human Rights," *American Journal of International Law* 83, 4 (October 1989): 851–62.

70. 762 F. Supp. 1531 (N.D. Cal.), 1987.

71. See especially Louis Henkin, ed., *The International Bill of Rights: The Covenant on Civil and Political Rights* (New York: Columbia University Press, 1981), chap. 13.

72. In an important study, Ernst Haas shows that ILO activity on behalf of freedom of association failed to alter the policies of a number of states, especially those in Eastern Europe: *Human Rights and International Action* (Stanford: Stanford University Press, 1970).

73. Ernst Haas, "Human Rights: To Act or Not to Act?" in *Eagle Entangled,* ed. Kenneth A. Oye et al. (New York: Longman, 1979), 188.

74. Richard Ullman, "Human Rights: Toward International Action," in *Enhancing Global Human Rights,* ed. Jorge I. Dominguez et al. (New York: McGraw-Hill, 1979), 10.

75. Moses Moskowitz, "Implementing Human Rights: Present Status and Future Prospects," in *Human Rights: Thirty Years After the Universal Declaration,* ed. B.G. Ramcharan (The Hague: Martinus Nijhoff, 1979), 109–30.

76. Farer, "United Nations and Human Rights": Donnelly, "International Human Rights" and "Human Rights."

77. Michael O'Boyle, "Practice and Procedure under the European Convention on Human Rights," *Santa Clara Law Review* 20, 3 (Summer 1980): 697–732.

78. Ernest A. Landy, "The Implementation Procedures of the International Labor Organization," *Santa Clara Law Review* 20, 3 (Summer 1980): 633–63; and Haas, *Human Rights and International Action.*

79. See chapter 4.

80. The review process, especially under the European Social Charter, makes extensive and formal use of NGO information. See further A.H. Robertson, *Human Rights in the World* 2d ed. (New York: St. Martin's Press, 1982), 197–211.

81. Chiang Pei-leng, *Non-Governmental Organizations,* chap. 2.

82. Antonio Cassese, "Progressive Transnational Promotion of Human Rights," in Ramcharan, ed., *Human Rights,* 249.

83. Henkin, "United Nations and Human Rights," 507.

84. Ruggie, "Human Rights," 106.

85. Henkin, "United Nations and Human Rights," 514.

86. See further Jack Donnelly, *Universal Human Rights In Theory and Practice* (Ithaca, N.Y.: Cornell University Press, 1989).

87. David P. Forsythe, "Socioeconomic Human Rights: The United Nations, the United States, and Beyond," *Human Rights Quarterly* 4, 4 (Fall 1982): 433–49.

88. On the role of the United Nations in embarrassing states, see especially Bergesen, "The Power to Embarrass," and Ruggie, "Human Rights."

89. See especially Onuf and Peterson, "Human Rights," Ruggie, "Human Rights," and Donnelly, "International Human Rights."

4

Human Rights and the Organization of American States: A Regime Analysis

A paradoxical situation obtains in the Western Hemisphere concerning internationally recognized human rights. Not a few hemispheric states have manifested over the years a systematic pattern of violation of universal human rights. These violations have been mostly major and wide-ranging, not trivial. Yet in this context, there has been, and still is, considerable regional attention to these same rights. There is, in fact, a functioning regime for the promotion and protection of international human rights in the Western Hemisphere, despite a milieu characterized by historical as well as contemporary gross violations of those rights.

How can it be that the same states that violate human rights (or are unable to control the violation of rights by private parties) have agreed on regional standards and even action for human rights? What explains the development of OAS human rights norms and agencies? In theoretical jargon, what are the regime dynamics? What impact has the regime had on its environment? In other words, how did it come to be that the OAS manifests the second-best regional regime for human rights (second only to the Council of Europe) but without the same underlying political commitment to implementing rights that characterizes Western Europe?[1]

Most authors writing about the OAS and/or hemispheric rights have not approached the subject in terms of regime dynamics. A formal-legal, descriptive approach was predominated. This may be partially because even regime theorists have treated regimes as an intellectual device for organizing policy outcomes. They have not been very precise in explaining why regimes are created as they were and evolve as they do.[2]

The Regime

The inter-American or pan-American system for hemispheric cooperation has existed for about a century; since 1948 the OAS has been its central institution. Impeding concise analysis is the fact that the OAS is a procedural and juridical jungle, with layers of legal and quasi-legal decisions constituting a crazy-quilt of organs and obligations.[3]

In focusing on the human rights sector of this system, some observers see two regimes: one based on the OAS Charter and one based on the American Convention on Human Rights.[4] The advantage to this approach is that it sharply delineates the presumably nonadjudicatory principles and processes revolving around the OAS Charter and the American Declaration on Human Rights, from the supposedly more enforceable provisions of the American Convention on Human Rights.

The view adopted here, however, is that there is one OAS human rights regime, with two implementation systems. There is one set of interlocking principles but two sets of rules and decision-making procedures designed to promote and protect human rights in the hemisphere.[5] The basic principles are set out in the OAS Charter, which mentions human rights and calls on member states to promote social development along with representative democracy. The core principles are also found in the American Declaration, which details not only civil and political rights but also social and economic rights derived from the charter, in a relatively more specific but still general form of thirty-eight articles, some being comprised of one short sentence. The charter was presumably legally binding as a treaty, although its human rights provisions may have been so general as to be unconstitutionally vague or part of a non-self–executing treaty when viewed from the national perspective.[6] The declaration was not intended to be legally binding immediately upon adoption in 1948, but it has acquired a special politico-legal status.

The more specific rules of the regime are found in both the statute and decisions of the Inter-American Commission on Human Rights and in the American Convention, as well as the subsequent statute and decisions by the Inter-American Court of Human Rights. The convention of eighty-two articles, like the declaration, deals mostly with civil, political, and procedural rights, although it does mention social and economic rights in a rather extended Article 26. The history of the commission, and the briefer history of the court, also show an overwhelming emphasis on civil, political, and procedural rights. There was some growing attention to social and economic rights by the commission in the 1980s.[7]

There is no doubt that the rules of the convention are binding on states parties (now numbering nineteen of thirty-three), especially as adjudicated by the compulsory jurisdiction of the court (now binding on eleven states). Whether the other rules are binding on OAS members is a matter of some debate.

The commission and court, as well as the organs of the OAS to which they may have a linkage (General Assembly, Permanent Council, and Organ of Consultation), are the monitoring agencies of the regime. The commission, an expert body that is now a principal organ of the OAS and elected by the

General Assembly, functions as a collective ombudsman in three ways usually: examining private petitions alleging human rights violations, compiling annual and country reports on the human rights situation, and promoting rights through general studies, seminars, fellowships, and the like. It carries out myriad specific duties such as supervising elections, visiting detention facilities, and submitting legal papers in national court cases. The commission also functions relative to the convention, in relation to the states obligated under it, as a quasi-juridical body of first recourse, similar to the European Commission on Human Rights.[8] Some of its promotional functions it shares with the Inter-American Institute; some of its monitoring functions it shares with the office of the OAS secretary-general or special bodies created to supervise elections.

The court, also an expert or uninstructed body, functions under the convention similarly to the European Court of Human Rights under the European Convention on Human Rights, with the added proviso that it can issue advisory opinions as requested by any OAS member. The three main political organs of the OAS (Assembly, Council, and Consultative Organ) may become involved in human rights matters either as part of a review mechanism related to the commission and/or court or if a human rights situation is viewed as linked to the peace and security of the region.

The unitary nature of the OAS human rights regime is confirmed by decisions taken by the OAS in the mid-1960s. Both the declaration and the statute of the commission were incorporated into the charter of the OAS, thus presumably acquiring binding force.[9] Hence the declaration (with the commission as ombudsman) and the convention (with commission and court as, respectively, first and second bodies of recourse) may not be as distinct as some lawyers have suggested. All of the principles may now be legally binding. Moreover, at times the commission has argued that the convention, or some part of it, is binding even on states that have not formally adhered to it.[10] The supporting interpretation is that the convention is an expression of regional customary law and thus the convention—or at least part of it—is binding on Chile or the United States, for example, even though such states are not full parties to it. They are said to be bound by customary law, notwithstanding their failure to ratify the treaty.

The use of regimes by scholars who study international relations has frequently raised questions of boundaries, nesting of regimes, and similar problems of definition and precision.[11] The view adopted here is that there is one, albeit complicated, regional regime for the protection and promotion of human rights associated with the OAS. A more important discussion, at least for the political theorist, entails attempting to explain the dynamics of the regime. Why do we see the creation of a formal regime based on general principles, then an activist monitoring agency, then a specific treaty, then a court with compulsory jurisdiction covering a third of the membership, with continuing changes at the time of writing?

On Hegemonic Leadership

The theory of hegemonic leadership has been popular with scholars explaining regime creation and change across international relations.[12] Especially for economic issue areas, the United States is pictured as the hegemon whose power and legitimacy of policy goals account for the creation of regimes. It is pictured as not only the most powerful actor in regime creation, whose leadership and resources create and sustain it, but also whose overall position is ultimately deferred to by other regime actors. Whether such regimes can continue in the context of the decline in power of the hegemonic leader (or whether the hegemon has actually declined in power) is a matter of some dispute.[13]

Problematical in this literature is the concept of hegemonic leader or leadership. It is not always clear what various authors mean when they write of hegemonic leadership in the construction and maintenance of regimes. In the original sense of Antonio Gramsci, a hegemonic leader leads because other actors who might wish to do otherwise eventually defer to the hegemon, either willingly or subconsciously. When based on rational calculation, others comply because they see both the leader's policy position and putative power as legitimate. Others willingly accept an inferior position, frequently in return for either public or particularistic goods provided by the leader.

Hegemonic leadership is not the same as dominance or convergence of policy. It implies necessarily a leader and followers, a superior and inferior relationship based on the hegemon's ability to influence others' into "voluntarily" accepting what the hegemon wants. If the leader compels compliance, it is dominance rather than hegemony. If there is agreement of policy views without some element of the lesser actors' initially wanting to do otherwise than comply, it is convergence rather than hegemony.

The United States became the leader of the Western alliance in large part because the other industrialized democracies eventually deferred to its superior position as the best arrangement for protecting their fundamental interests in the context of a perceived Soviet threat. This is most clear with regard to the North Atlantic Treaty Organization (NATO), in which the European members chafed under U.S. leadership and found aspects of it distasteful but still voluntarily stayed in the alliance as a collective junior partner. At times the United States had to induce or purchase deference from those inclined to do otherwise, as when it offered Strategic Defense Initiative (SDI) contracts to alliance partners who would "voluntarily" support SDI. Similarly, those who joined the World Bank and International Monetary Fund, including some outside the Western political grouping like Yugoslavia, did so with full knowledge of, and agreement to, U.S. hegemonic leadership.

Authors such as Robert Keohane are careful in trying to distinguish hegemonic leadership from other types of political behavior.[14] Nevertheless, the concept remains elusive and is bedeviled by fine lines between hegemony and dominance, leadership and convergence, successful and unsuccessful leadership, voluntary and coerced compliance. All of these complexities trace back to the elusiveness of influence in human relations.

A dominant—but not hegemonic—leader uses dominant power, manipulating material and psychological levers to obtain involuntary compliance from others. In this sense, political leadership is synonymous with successful exercise of political power (or influence). To be powerful, to be dominant is, ipso facto, to be a leader. The Soviet Union, for example, was the dominant power in Eastern Europe from 1947 to 1987, but it was not a hegemonic power—at least not in the eyes of most East European nationals, as proved by events during the 1980s. It led by exercising dominant power. One of Gramsci's primary objectives was to distinguish hegemonic from dominant leadership; only the latter was based on conscious coercion in the face of resistance.

Complicating the picture is the fact that, for example, some Eastern European ruling elites no doubt willingly deferred to the Soviet Union as part of their elite status. Thus the Soviet Union was a hegemonic power to some Eastern European rulers, but a dominant power to most of the peoples of Eastern Europe and to ruling elites in Yugoslavia and the West. One who exercises power may be seen as either hegemonic or dominant, depending on the values of those who defer (or dissent).

To refer to the exercise of dominant power as constituting hegemonic leadership is to confuse hegemony with dominance and thus to eradicate Gramsci's insights about the exercise of power and leadership. Robert Gilpin, for example, despite the usefulness of his works in other ways, makes precisely this error by referring to dominant powers as ipso facto hegemonic.[15] The United States, for example, was clearly a dominant power after World War II. It was a hegemonic power only to some states—i.e., its NATO allies. It remained a dominant power to the Stalinist bloc and parts of the Third World, since they frequently deferred to its power without accepting the legitimacy of its policy positions.

An analyst must also be careful to distinguish between hegemony and moral leadership. A moral leader leads because its policy position is widely seen as good; a moral leader, unlike the hegemonic leader, is not viewed in connection to especially military power.[16] The moral leader may not, in fact, control policy, since moral leadership may fail to persuade dominant or hegemonic power. Yet there is real meaning to the idea of moral leadership, in the sense of referring to those who take a leading and "good" position on some policy question. Lech Walesa and Nelson Mandela, for example, were widely regarded as leaders not so much by ability to coerce but by identification with "good" policy, even when imprisoned by others with dominant power. Likewise the Vatican or Costa Rica, to choose two actors in world politics almost at random, may exercise moral leadership on a policy question without much, if any, ability to coerce. They may or may not be decisively influential in terms of political power. An actor can be influential as a moral leader without being either a hegemonic or a dominant leader.

This conception of leadership is also not without problems of clarity. Moral leadership hinges on a subjective determination of "good" policy. Walesa may have been regarded as a moral leader in the West; he was regarded as an irresponsible troublemaker by some in the Stalinist East. Nevertheless, any treatment of leadership must make room for the type of leadership that is out in front in a "good" direction on policy questions. After all, the preferred definition of *lead* is to "show the way to." Only the second-ary definition is to "cause to follow."[17] Similarly, the preferred definition of *leadership* is "the position or guidance of a leader." Only the secondary defini-tion is "the ability to lead."[18] One can be a leader, at least in moral terms, without exercising controlling or decisive influence.

Moral leadership combined with putative dominant leadership yields hegemonic leadership. The hegemonic leader leads by a combination of puta-tive dominant power and legitimacy of policy. Because the hegemon's policy position is seen as good and because the hegemon is seen as having the power to compel implementation of policy if necessary, or at least the power to induce compliance through payments, there is "voluntary" deference from others. But moral leadership can exist as a distinct type of influence in and of itself, including attempted leadership that fails.

The theory of hegemonic leadership, with its combination of stimulating but problematical content, has been offered in explanation of the OAS human rights regime. According to Jack Donnelly, if one inquires into the dynamics of the OAS and human rights, "Much of the explanation lies in power, partic-ularly the dominant power of the United States. . . . The Inter-American human rights regime is probably best understood in these terms. The United States, for whatever reasons, decided that a regional regime with relatively strong monitoring powers was desirable, then exercised its hegemonic power to ensure its creation and support its operation."[19]

Donnelly has written an excellent overall analysis of human rights regimes, the best in the political literature to date. His assertions about the OAS, however, lack supporting evidence, and he mixes dominant with hege-monic power. Moreover, while it is sometimes correct to emphasize U.S. power in the creation and evolution of the OAS regime, U.S. influence can be overestimated.

I argue that the OAS human rights regime came into being and evolved not primarily because of U.S. hegemonic leadership but because of a conflu-ence of factors entailing supportive and limiting factors. The supportive fac-tors include moral interdependence among hemispheric elites; moral leader-ship by OAS agencies and a shifting coalition of hemispheric states; and periodic assertions of power (influence) by the United States that may be characterized at times as dominant (but rarely as hegemonic) and at times as moral leadership (but mostly not).

Permeating the creation and evolution of the OAS human rights regime are three limiting factors. The first of these is the widespread hemispheric resistance to U.S. influence on many questions, which takes the diplomatic-legal form of an emphasis on traditional national sovereignty and is the result of repeated U.S. interventions in the internal affairs of hemispheric states. These persistent claims to national sovereignty help explain both the absence—in most cases—of U.S. hegemonic power, as well as an important reason why the regime has been less effective than the West European human rights regime. This factor operates to make most (but not all) U.S. successful exertions of power dominant rather than hegemonic and to limit the effectiveness of the regime's protection of human rights. National sovereignty is thrown up as a barrier not only against the United States but against the regime itself. Complicating and strengthening the use of claims to national sovereignty is the fact that the United States itself has championed such claims at times.

The second factor is that many hemispheric elites historically have accepted human rights only as abstract values and have not genuinely desired to see them applied to the masses, especially indigenous Indians. Hence moral interdependence of elites has been historically accompanied by a severe limitation on the scope of practice of rights. The reigning hemispheric political culture south of the Rio Grande has been a conflicted one, with principles of autonomy and equality of individuals contradicted by claims to elite privilege. (The United States, too, had a conflicted political culture, at least until the 1960s, because equal human rights were legally denied to racial minorities.)

The third limiting factor curtailing the evolution and effectiveness of the regime is the hemispheric preoccupation historically with communism or, more precisely, Cuban model states tied closely to the Soviet Union. This preoccupation has at times caused the deemphasis of human rights protection as defined by the regime. At the same time, it has led to situations of genuine if periodic hegemonic leadership by the United States in which lesser states have reluctantly but eventually deferred voluntarily to U.S. policy positions and exercises of power. While this situation has obtained primarily on security (and economic) issues, its ramifications have been mostly limiting for the regional human rights regime. One should note that the United States could be a hegemonic leader in security and economic issue areas but not in human rights.

While U.S. positions on hemispheric human rights questions were (and are) periodically important, a number of regime developments came about despite U.S. opposition or passivity. This is not leadership in any sense of the word. On other questions, the United States used its power to support steps toward a weak regime while blocking steps toward a more effective one. This may be considered political leadership if the United States successfully employed dominant power, but such situations may only reflect convergence of views rather than U.S. dominant power. To the extent that one finds U.S. dominant power in opposing a strong regime, it may not be considered successful moral leadership if one believes that regional action on human rights is good policy. On a very few occasions, the United States exercised moral leadership by pushing for regional action on human rights but ultimately was unable to influence others (or very many) to follow.

Whether the United States is correctly viewed as a leader with regard to the OAS and human rights depends partly on which conception of leadership is employed and sometimes whether its position—win or lose—is viewed as moral. (Those who subscribed to the Kirkpatrick doctrine and believed it was good to deemphasize human rights violations by anticommunist allies of the United States in order to focus on the larger evil of communism arrived at different judgments about morality and legitimacy.) It is not easy to prove U.S. hegemonic leadership in relation to the OAS human rights regime. U.S. policy positions and exercises of influence are difficult to characterize as hegemonic, dominant, or moral.

Donnelly correctly noted the absence of hegemonic leadership in the creation and maintenance of the European regional human rights regime.[20] Among other interesting examples is the U.N. refugee regime, which was not created by U.S. leadership and which the United States came to influence significantly only after creation.[21] Similarly, the United States played only a marginal role in the creation of the U.N. antitorture regime, which owed much more to Sweden, the Netherlands, and Amnesty International.[22] It is patently clear that not all international human rights regimes depend on hegemonic leadership in creation and functioning.

One should be cautious in generalizing about the U.S. complicated role in OAS human rights activity over time and make allowance for complexity that resists simple categorization, even if reality makes the task of the political theorist more difficult.

Regime Creation

The creation of the OAS human rights regime stemmed first from moral interdependence among the elites of the hemispheric states. When, in the 1940s, members of the OAS adopted human rights principles in both the OAS Charter and the American Declaration on Human Rights, these principles reflected values held widely, albeit at a high level of abstraction, throughout the region. Rights were recognized and endorsed internationally because of culture (or, if one prefers, morality). Latin elites no less than North American ones accepted in the abstract the validity of democratic and human rights principles. This is clear enough in the national constitutions adopted by OAS members over the past century and a half. Such vague (albeit contradicted) principles were as much a part of neo-Iberian as Anglo-Saxon culture.[23]

It was not as if U.S. power had to compel or purchase acceptance of human rights values on resisting neo-Iberian elites. Rather, Spanish and Portuguese descendants, constituting independent elites since the 1820s, also accepted human rights as abstract principles. In 1826 Simon Bolivar, on behalf of Peru and without any U.S. leadership on the issue, called for a regional confederation to undergird democracy.[24] And in 1946 Uruguay took the lead in pushing the Larreta Doctrine in favor of democratic intervention in Argentina.[25] There has been widespread acceptance of human rights principles in the hemisphere over time, and this was certainly true in the 1940s when the foundations of the OAS human rights regime were laid.

Against this background, a small number of Latin states in the 1940s tried to exert moral leadership in behalf of precise legal obligations and a capacity for regional action by the OAS on human rights. (A basic value judgment in this work is that what is termed moral is that which seeks effective protection of human rights.) This handful of Latin states (Panama, Uruguay, Brazil, Mexico, the Dominican Republic, Cuba, Venezuela) also pushed for binding human rights commitments at the San Francisco Conference that led to the establishment of the United Nations.[26] In both diplomatic arenas, they were defeated by the United States and other major states. The United States, like most other states in the Western Hemisphere, was prepared to endorse human rights principles in international documents but not to accept precise legal obligations leading to international action. This view carried the day.

Whether the U.S. position represents leadership is open to interpretation. Certainly the United States was influential in helping to acknowledge vague principles and in defeating something stronger. There was continuing opposition to U.S. policy, which made its power less than hegemonic, but there was also support and/or convergence. Sometimes the United States followed the initiatives of others—which may be support, or perhaps dominant power if that support proved decisive (can support be leadership?). In 1946 the United States supported Uruguay in wanting regional action on human rights in Argentina, but this example of moral leadership-support led to failure.

What is indisputable is that in 1948, only six of twenty-one states, not including the United States, wanted the American Declaration to be part of the OAS Charter and hence binding in international law. And only eight of twenty voting states, not including the United States, wanted a binding convention on human rights at that time.[27] At this same time, the United States successfully opposed the creation of any OAS agency specifically charged with human rights action. Hemispheric moral interdependence led to endorsement of human rights principles; small states' moral leadership in favor of a strong regime failed; U.S. power helped create a weak regime that declared human rights but was unable for a time to promote or protect them through international action.[28] It is very difficult to say with precision about each issue of regime creation whether U.S. policy equated with hegemonic leadership, dominant leadership, or simply a convergence of policy views among many states.

From the beginnings of the OAS human rights regime, limiting factors contradicted supportive ones. In the events of the 1940s, the Latin preoccupation with national sovereignty was evident by the terms they wrote into the OAS Charter. Language the Latins introduced and pushed repeatedly stressed regional endorsement of national sovereignty and nonintervention in domestic affairs, by which the majority hoped to restrain the dominant United States with its history of regional gunboat diplomacy.

The charter repeatedly emphasized sovereign rights. After endorsing human rights and democracy, the lesser hemispheric powers insisted on such meaningless statements as: "The fundamental rights of States may not be impaired in any manner whatsoever" (Art. 8). Having pledged to uphold individual rights and democracy, the Latins then added the contradictory statement that the state has the right "to organize itself as it sees fit" (Art. 9). To make sure the contradiction was not missed, they repeated it in Article 13: "Each State has the right to develop its cultural, political and economic life freely and naturally. In this free development, the State shall respect the rights of the individual and the principles of universal morality."

The contradiction between international endorsement of human rights and democracy, and equal endorsement of national freedom of decision, so clearly evident in the charter, is an old one in the hemisphere. Bolivar's nineteenth-century push for an international federation of democrats failed since his scheme infringed on national prerogatives. Uruguay's concern for democracy in Argentina in 1946 failed for the same reason; most hemispheric states did not support regional action on human rights.

Strengthening the hemispheric claims to national sovereignty was the fact that the United States, for most of the 1940s and 1950s, also objected to OAS action on human rights. There is evidence of U.S. sensitivity to the question of minority treatment within the United States, and thus its opposition to international action on rights, whether from the United Nations or OAS.[29] There is also the fact that after 1952 the Eisenhower administration agreed to defer multilateral diplomacy for human rights in order to defeat Brickerism within the United States.[30] Thus on hemispheric human rights issues, the United States in effect joined most of the Latin states in elevating national sovereignty over international authority and competence. It strains credulity to refer to U.S. policy at this time as either moral or hegemonic leadership. Others exercised moral leadership that the United States opposed. Others emphasized national sovereignty that the United States supported. (An alternative interpretation is that the United States led in both the creation of a declaratory regime and blocking a protective one, with many other member states falling in behind the U.S. position. I believe, conversely, on the basis of a perusal of the documents covering which state introduced which proposal and verbally supported it with certain arguments, that the Latins led in emphasizing national sovereignty and the United States supported their position, but for different reasons.)

A second limiting factor was equally important. The practice of rights within their states gave hemispheric governments pause, even as they asserted the universal validity of human rights principles. In the 1940s and 1950s much of the United States was still characterized by its version of apartheid. In much of the rest of the hemisphere, it could hardly be argued that lower classes in general and especially indigenous populations were treated with equal respect. Hemispheric political morality or culture was mostly a contradicted one: human rights values were accepted in principle and widely violated in practice.

Some might be inclined to say that, given the widespread violation of human rights throughout much of the hemisphere in the 1940s—in the United States and elsewhere—the enactment of human rights provisions in the OAS Charter and American Declaration on Human Rights was hypocritical. This moral hypocrisy, however, was essential in the sense of producing the necessary diplomatic and legal basis for concrete human rights action later. This is not the only example of state hypocrisy in the human rights domain leading to beneficial results over time, for much of the same process has transpired at the United Nations.[31] There can be a formal convergence of views that is not verified by practice; the formal convergence can help bring about more congruent practice over time.

A third limiting factor was that during the early days of the OAS, the United States saw the organization more as an anticommunist security arrangement than as an actor for human rights. Just as the United States had sought to exclude European colonial powers from exercising hemispheric influence from the time of the Monroe Doctrine, so it saw the OAS primarily as an anticommunist and specifically anti-Soviet organization.[32] Some authors spoke of the OAS as multilateralizing the Monroe Doctrine, and Fidel Castro was supposed to have referred to the OAS as the U.S. colonial office.[33]

In the 1940s and 1950s, the United States was not interested in exercising moral leadership through the OAS for human rights, even if it had the putative power to do so. The clearest evidence for this is the record of highly authoritarian and repressive governments that it either created or supported, in Guatemala, Nicaragua, and elsewhere, with negligible diplomatic attention to their human rights record. U.S. preoccupation with the cold war, combined with an international defense of its own domestic human rights violations, plus an executive desire to defeat Brickerism, all led into the same policy toward the OAS human rights regime. Only a weak, declaratory regime was endorsed. This might be termed leadership in the sense of the successful exercise of political influence but not leadership in the sense of striving for the effective protection of human rights. Since this policy position was similar to that of most other hemispheric states, it is difficult to say how much the United States had to influence these other states and how much its policy simply converged with theirs.

This analysis suggests that the OAS human rights regime was created less through clear hegemonic leadership and more through a genuine convergence of majority views reflecting a combination of somewhat unique factors that were both supportive and limiting for the regime. Supportive factors were elite moral interdependence (although highly abstract), moral leadership mostly by small Latin states (like Uruguay, Panama, and Venezuela), and the influence of the United States in accepting at least a declaratory regime. Limiting factors were Latin claims to national sovereignty (which were supported by the United States on human rights matters in this era), the widespread violation of rights in practice (including the United States), and the U.S. emphasis on the OAS as an anticommunist alliance rather than a social actor. The clearest case for U.S. hegemonic leadership pertains to this last factor, involving U.S. putative military and economic resources unmatched by other hemispheric states, which provided the public good of a noncommunist regional order in the interest of all ruling elites prior to 1959. Thus the United States was a hegemonic leader in creating and maintaining an OAS security regime, which interacted with, and weakened, the OAS human rights regime. The situation was indeed paradoxical. The United States emphasized anticommunism, which in and of itself constituted a defense of civil and political rights, at least in the abstract. But this emphasis, combined with other factors, undercut efforts in behalf of precise international obligations and actions in behalf of human rights.

Regime Evolution

From the creation of the OAS human rights regime until about 1959, there was no significant evolution in its principles, rules, or decision-making procedures. Virtually all elites were content with or resigned to the status quo. From 1959, changes took place that eventually transformed that regime into a strong-promotional and weak-protective regime. The same set of six factors remained at work (three supportive and three limiting) but in a different mix. U.S. policy was sometimes influential but rarely in hegemonic fashion.

Attempted U.S. hegemonic leadership within the hemisphere on the basis of anticommunism was rarely successful. At the time of the Cuban revolution in 1959, for example, most hemispheric states resisted U.S. attempts to pressure or coerce Castro from power.[34] It was only after Castro developed closer ties with the Soviet Union that the OAS voted to expel Cuba from membership and voted unanimously in 1962 to endorse the U.S. naval "quarantine" in the Cuban missile crisis. Absent the question of Soviet intrusion into the hemisphere, most OAS states defended the right of a state to its own internal development. (Later most OAS states opposed U.S. "covert" coercion against the Sandinista government in Nicaragua, and not only most OAS states but also most state members of the Caribbean Community opposed the U.S. invasion of Grenada that was rationalized partially in the name of anticommunism.)[35]

Thus the United States could exercise true hegemonic leadership at times like Cuban missile crisis when hemispheric states had no doubts about the dangers posed by the Soviet Union. At other times, U.S. successful anticommunism came not through hegemonic but rather dominant power, as when it overthrew the Arbenz government in Guatemala or helped to destabilize the Allende government in Chile. (The 1989 U.S. invasion of Panama fit the pattern almost precisely; it was an exercise of dominant U.S. power unanimously condemned by other OAS members. The deviant point was that the principal U.S. rationale had little to do with communism.)

Significant regime evolution started about a decade after its creation because of a mix of factors, not because of hegemonic leadership. In 1959 Venezuela sought OAS action against the Trujillo government in the Dominican Republic, which it charged with fomenting unrest in Venezuela.[36] Cuba made similar complaints. These charges were couched not only in terms of Trujillo's violations of national sovereignty, territorial integrity, and nonintervention in domestic jurisdiction but also in terms of violations of human rights by Trujillo at home. At this same time there was a growing, if mixed, concern about the drift of events in Cuba and thus a willingness among a few OAS members to breach the walls of absolute sovereignty by looking into human rights issues in countries as well as the ramifications of them abroad.

The Eisenhower administration, despite its informal agreement with Congress not to push human rights in international fora, and probably looking at Cuba as much as at the Dominican Republic, supported regional action on human rights in the Dominican Republic. Most OAS members, however, preferred the traditional view that action on human rights was a domestic matter—whatever the principles of the charter and American Declaration might imply.

Given this diplomatic logjam comprising moral leadership by Venezuela and the United States but widespread resistance by others, the OAS finally agreed on a compromise, one part of which was the creation of the Inter-American Commission on Human Rights to promote human rights. The commission was not to, and did not, immediately take up the problem of human rights in the Dominican Republic, and it was not to deal with other specifics. (Mediation on the Dominican matter was given to another OAS agency.) The commission was to make general studies and promote human rights education.

Even this mandate was too much for the United States, which abstained on the vote creating the commission. While it apparently was willing to tolerate grudgingly what it had opposed before—an OAS human rights agency—it objected to parts of its terms of reference, which were viewed as going too far. The United States tried to emasculate the new commission in several ways, such as voting to reduce the length of its sessions and to disallow its handling of individual complaints. These limiting positions carried the day as far as formal mandate was concerned. The overall U.S. position was complex: favoring action on human rights in the Dominican Republic (and by implication in Cuba), barely tolerating a new commission, and opposing a dynamic or authoritative commission.

It is not too much of an overstatement to say that the commission was created out of specific crisis in a political compromise to give the impression of doing something, given Venezuelan demands about the Dominican Republic and U.S. concern about Cuba, while most member states wanted to ensure that the OAS did not breach the walls of national sovereignty very much. (Trujillo was removed from the scene by political events, and only later did the commission inquire into events in the Dominican Republic.)

Out of the regional crisis of 1959 emerged the commission in a small but crucial step toward a stronger regime. The trigger was a crisis leading to an unclear general willingness, if not to do exactly what Venezuela wanted, at least to do something. There seemed to be a widespread belief that human rights violations were related to the peace and security of the hemisphere and that in that formulation human rights might be a legitimate area of at least general action by the OAS.[37] The United States was only one among several important actors, and its policy was inconsistent. It championed action on human rights for a time, probably with an eye more on Cuba than the Dominican Republic. But when the issue became systematic regional action on human rights, it grew more cautious. It was willing to tolerate a weak commission but clearly opposed one with any significant activities—not foreseeing that it was going to wind up with a very dynamic one.

In these events circa 1959, which were to turn out to be important for the evolution of the regime, moral leadership—in the sense of proposing and lobbying for more effective human rights action—came primarily from states like Venezuela. The United States exercised influence in the sense of supporting some second-choice or fallback positions. This might be considered dominant power in the sense that these positions were eventually adopted. Whether the U.S. role can be properly seen as involving the exercise of hegemonic leadership is highly problematical, since it is not clear how much it had to lead others and how much its policy simply converged with similar policy independently arrived at.

The consolidation of the OAS human rights regime into a promotional-protective one centering on the commission came about immediately after the 1959 crisis, and the leadership was exercised not by the United States but by commission members.[38] The individual members of the commission, elected in their personal capacity by the General Assembly, and despite their formal mandate, began to inquire into human rights conditions in specific countries, starting with Cuba, Haiti, and the Dominican Republic, whose post-Trujillo government gave its cooperation. They also began to process private petitions alleging human rights abuses, despite a previous vote in the assembly denying them this authority. The initiative of these uninstructed individuals was thus paramount in the expansion of OAS human rights action.

Eventually practice was established under the commission's aegis that individuals did have a right of private petition linked to the American Declaration on Human Rights, and if governments did not respond within 180 days, the commission could presume the veracity of the complaint; in-country visits by the commission were normal, with the consent of the state, both regarding petitions and more general reports and with regard to crises; both annual reports and special reports could be specific about problems and remedies. Eventually the commission played an important role in a number of difficult situations, including in the Dominican Republic (1965), Nicaragua (1978), and Colombia (1980), as well as throughout Central America. Its concerted action in Argentina under military rule (1976–1982) did much to confirm its active stance and more systematic approach toward gross violations of rights. The role of the commission as collective ombudsman, working to implement the human rights principles of the OAS Charter and American Declaration on Human Rights, primarily through diplomacy, thus came about largely through its own seizing of initiatives, some of them clearly beyond its 1959 statute.

An assertive commission, however, could not have endured without state support, and some support proved forthcoming over time. (Other active OAS agencies have been reined in by states members.)[39] The evidence of growing state support in general for the commission's activities is ample. Its statute was revised to conform to its actual practice, the revised statute was made part of the OAS Charter, and the commission was elevated to a principal OAS organ. This evolution was not linear. There was some effort to undercut the commission's activities in the early 1970s.[40] In general, the commission mantained enough state support to continue its highly active profile but not enough support to translate its active diplomacy into decisive pressure or enforcement.

Developments in the policy of the United States toward the commission as the center of OAS action on human rights were complex. The first era of commission activity started during the waning years of the Eisenhower administration, and no doubt the commission's early focus on Cuba generated some U.S. acquiescence to an active commission. Clearer U.S. acquiescence came during the short-lived Kennedy administration. Kennedy's Alliance for Progress intended to make at least democracy, if not a broader range of human rights, central to the peace, security, and economic growth of the hemisphere. Anticommunism was pursued through socioeconomic reform, including greater attention to human rights. The first two years of the Kennedy period were therefore sympathetic to OAS action on at least some human rights.[41] U.S. policy thus supported the early expansion of commission activity but did not cause it. Supporting influence is not normally the same as hegemonic leadership.

Lyndon Johnson's presidency is difficult to categorize concerning the OAS human rights regime:[42] The Johnson administration gave support and prominence to important human rights events such as upgrading the commission's status and was only too happy to have an active commission help it extract itself from its Dominican intervention, but overall the Vietnam War pushed other foreign policy concerns aside.[43] By the end of the 1960s, much of the earlier U.S. interest in regional civil rights and socioeconomic reform had been dissipated.

The trend of neglect intensified during the Republican presidents of 1969–1976. President Nixon and Secretary of State Kissinger initially believed that the introduction of human rights factors into foreign policy considerations undesirably complicated that calculus.[44] Later, while one could document Kissinger's speeches in favor of the OAS human rights regime, particularly with regard to Chile in the 1970s, careful research could also document Kissinger's messages to the Chilean government, as well as to U.S. diplomats, to disregard those speeches since they were intended only to placate congressional elements.[45] The dominant strain in Republican foreign policy thus remained hostile to genuine regional action on human rights. To complicate matters, however, Congress voted a special appropriation in 1976 intended for the OAS Human Rights Commission.

President Carter changed the prevailing neglect and negativism for a brief four years by signing the American Convention on Human Rights; supporting a diplomatic offensive to obtain other signatures and ratifications; publicly castigating human rights violators such as Brazil, Guatemala, Uruguay, and Argentina; supporting increased appropriations for the commission; working closely with the American activist president of the commission, Thomas J. Farer; manipulating some U.S. bilateral foreign assistance in the name of rights; taking human rights into account in voting in the Inter-American Development Bank and other multilateral banks; engaging in quiet diplomacy in behalf of the victims of politics; and utilizing the OAS commission, among other OAS organs, in an attempt to rid Nicaragua of Somoza.[46] While the

United States under Carter did not channel all of its regional human rights concerns through the OAS, it did give greater attention to the regime than past administrations.

This Carter policy of emphasizing human rights, especially in the Western Hemisphere, was altered drastically by the first Reagan administration. Implementing the Kirkpatrick doctrine of sympathy for noncommunist authoritarian allies, the U.S. government tried to renew military maneuvers with Chile, to maximize arms transfers to Guatemala and El Salvador, and to normalize relations with the Argentine junta, among other policies.[47] The policy of deemphasizing noncommunist human rights violations was accompanied by a skepticism, if not hostility, toward multilateral institutions that was so ideological that attacks were made even on those international organizations like the World Bank and the International Monetary Fund that reflected significant U.S. advantage in them.[48]

However much the second Reagan administration may have inched toward a more balanced interest in human rights violations in places like Chile and Paraguay, as well as toward less hostility toward multilateralism, generally both Reagan administrations were unsympathetic to the OAS in general and its human rights regime in particular.[49] Not only was the OAS ignored on security issues touching Nicaragua, El Salvador, and Grenada, but also the OAS human rights regime functioned without major U.S. leadership or support during this period. Only when the commission cited Castro's Cuba or the Sandinistas' Nicaragua for human rights violations did the Reagan administration lend support. Reagan's withholding of funds to the OAS greatly damaged the organization in general and its human rights program in particular.[50]

Thus if one looks at the Inter-American Commission on Human Rights as the chief monitor and diplomatic hub of the OAS human rights regime, its evolution clearly cannot be explained by U.S. hegemonic power. At times U.S. policy was supportive of the moral leadership exercised by the commission. At other times it was neglectful or clearly negative. At best, U.S. policy was combined with other state policy, and with the activism of the commission itself, to explain the fitful starts, expansion, and retrenchments of the regime. Exercises of supporting or converging influence are not normally hegemonic leadership.

What best explains the evolution of the regime is the moral leadership by the independent commission, in the context of the moral interdependence of the region (as expressed in abstract human rights principles). But the commission and larger regime were still severely limited by widespread commitment to national sovereignty, by state fear of regional authoritative action against widespread human rights violations, and particularly during Republican governments in Washington by preoccupation with anticommunism rather than human rights violations.[51]

This same pattern obtains for other parts of the regime as well. It was not the United States but rather other OAS members that pushed for a binding human rights convention cum court. From the 1940s to the mid-1970s, U.S. administrations indicated repeatedly they were opposed to such developments. The convention was nevertheless negotiated, with some U.S. participation but not much leadership, and sufficient adherences were obtained by 1978 to bring it into legal force. The court began to operate in 1980. Carter broke the U.S. pattern of negativism by signing the convention and submitting it to the Senate for advice and consent to ratification, although he allowed State Department lawyers to gut it with reservations and understandings, and he never seriously lobbied for consent.[52] The Human Rights Bureau and Patricia Derian did lobby in its behalf in regional affairs.[53] The Reagan administration was hostile toward the convention and court. The United States is not one of the nineteen states bound by the convention, it is not one of the eleven states accepting obligatory adjudication by the court, and there is no prospect that it will become a party to either. An American national does sit as a judge on the court but by nomination of Costa Rica. Clearly with regard to this part of the regime, matters have developed largely in spite of the United States, not because of it.

The most influential role that the United States has played concerning the convention and court was, under Carter, to urge others to ratify the treaty and accept the compulsory jurisdiction of the court. This may be a case of strange and limited hegemonic leadership: limited because the larger hemispheric states refused to accept U.S. preaching, strange because the United States never practiced what it preached.

Finally with regard to regime evolution, we should note developments in the OAS General Assembly, Permanent Council, and Organ of Consultation. State action here can be taken as one measure of interest in regional management of human rights issues.[54] The first and most significant point is that member states have never used these bodies for systematic and significant diplomatic pressure on human rights violations, much less voted sanctions.[55] The Latin commitment to national sovereignty and sensitivity about domestic human rights record is too great. The United States largely deferred to this reigning consensus.

Second, there has been some erratic but increased review of the commission's activities since the mid-1970s. Until that time there was no assembly debate about the work of the commission. After that time and starting with Chile as a target, there was some assembly attention to specific countries because of the situation of human rights. At least it can be said that the annual report of the commission triggers some attention to human rights problems within OAS meetings. The specificity and seriousness of this attention, however, seem to vary.[56]

The U.S. record concerning human rights in the main OAS organs has varied with administrations in Washington, but overall one cannot find a pattern that would support an interpretation of hegemonic leadership. The United States was primarily concerned with the cold war, and—except during the Carter era—Washington's anticommunist allies knew that their human rights violations would not become targets of concerted action, in the OAS or outside. U.S. representatives occasionally made speeches in behalf of human rights, but on such issues, the United States has consistently displayed neither moral leadership nor successful influence. Without those ingredients, one cannot have hegemonic leadership.

Regime Impact

The human rights regime of the OAS has evolved far beyond its start as simply a declaratory regime, but its impact on its political environment has been less than profound. The principles and rules have been clarified and expanded, and the monitoring agencies have become more active and important relative to the past, yet gross violations of fundamental human rights persist. Periodic improvements in democratic and other human rights have usually been followed by periods of renewed repression, which the regime in the past has been unable to prevent or even mitigate. By the early 1990s, the OAS in general was on the point of collapse. On most issues, it was marginalized by most member states, although it had a limited renaissance in regional peace plans for Central America. (The OAS played a large but not exclusive role in supervising elections in Nicaragua in February 1990 and subsequently in helping to disarm the contras.) While human rights activities might fairly be considered the bright spot on OAS history,[57] a close examination reveals the "modest"[58] and limited impact of that regime.

The Commission as Ombudsman

As the diplomatic hub of the regime, the commission is the proper point of departure for an inquiry into impact. First we examine its extraconventional role. The subject is complex and elusive, with exceptions to generalizations. As a first-order generalization, however, the commission has marched to its own beat, largely cut off from the support of member states in concrete terms that could make its recommendations influential.[59] The commission has exercised moral leadership but not controlling political influence. This condition stems mostly from the absence of sustained public and elite opinion in its behalf, which could generate pressure on target states.[60]

It is as if the politics of the region were a soccer game in which the commission were the referee. The referee tries to implement the rule book, blowing the whistle at infractions and cautioning players and coaches about impermissible behavior. But the participants, and even the fans, despite having agreed to have one, pay only the slightest attention to the referee and play the game mostly without attention to the rules. This analogy accords with events in the mid-1970s. The commission took a strong stand against Pinochet's violations of human rights; states members of the OAS refused to take follow-up action; and several members of the commission resigned in protest against state indifference.[61] The United States supported Pinochet.

While the commission has obtained general state support in the form of a rather passive toleration of its activities, a review of its different activities indicates severe limitations on its influence. First, its diplomatic consideration of individual petitions in its extraconventional role (unrelated to the court) has not led to many solutions of the problem raised. Most of its positions on these questions have generated little discernible impact.

The impact of its country reports and annual reports may have been slightly greater, if only because these have led to some follow-up in the General Assembly, whereas its stand on individual petitions has not. On occasion a particular country report has become an important element in subsequent diplomacy and politics. For example, the commission's scathing report on Somoza's policies in the late 1970s appears to have contributed to a call by the Organ of Consultation for his resignation, and that call seems to have had a major impact on the dictator's decision to leave Managua.[62] For example, the commissioner's tough report on Pinochet's early policies seems to have been cited with some effectiveness in congressional hearings on Chile, with the State Department's attempt to disregard human rights abuses having to be modified, although the executive maintained support for the Chilean dictator.[63] But mostly there is an absence of that type of discernible influence. While more study is needed on the impact of commission annual and country reports, the few attempts to track them thus far show mainly negligible impact in the short term.[64]

Lest we become too negative, the commission engages in more public diplomacy on an in-country basis than any other human rights agency sanctioned by intergovernmental agreement.[65] Some of this activity has been extremely important, as when the commission became involved in the Dominican Republic in 1965 and in Colombia in 1980. In both cases, many lives were saved and other rights protected by the skillful diplomacy of the commission's members. Also, the cumulative impact of all of these commission activities may yet prove important in the long term. The commission battles established governmental policy, as well as majority opinion, in many instances, such as in its effort to curtail the use of the death penalty in the United States. One should perhaps not expect many short-term victories in these situations, but the long-term gains for human rights may be different. Success in the human rights domain may consist most fundamentally of advancing and entrenching the idea of human rights. Cumulative commission decisions, if supported by democratic states, may have this effect over time. The commission engages in quiet diplomacy to correct human rights violations. This is difficult to track and its impact over time elusive.

Overall, the commission as an ombudsman for the rights in the American Declaration has been dynamic far beyond the expectations of 1959. As one observer said of the commission, "This is no pussyfooting or white-washing organization."[66] But its impact has been decidedly modest thus far because of the absence of governmental, intraelite, and public support for its specific policy positions. This condition stems from the same three limiting factors that have been present from the beginning of the regime: a predominantly Latin emphasis on national sovereignty (which the United States mostly supports in the human rights domain), the related national concern not to become a focus for regional action in the face of clear violations of regional human rights standards, and the U.S. preoccupation with perceived security concerns linked to the cold war.[67]

The fact that the convention is now in legal force, however, and even more so the fact that eleven states have consented to automatic jurisdiction by the court, indicates the potential for change in basic dynamics, at least for part of the OAS membership.

The Adjudicatory System

The application of the American Convention on Human Rights covers only about a decade, too short a period of time to make a decisive impact on regional politics. Forty percent of the OAS membership has not explicitly consented to be bound by the treaty, and 65 percent has not consented to the compulsory jurisdiction of the court. (There was a previous regional court around the turn of the century that handled human rights cases among other types, but it floundered on the hard rocks of regional politics—most decisively when the United States undercut its pronouncements with regard to Nicaragua, which it was then trying to control.)[68]

Nevertheless, the court is off to an interesting start under the convention, having rendered several advisory opinions that have generated some influence. In one notable case, it ruled that a Costa Rican draft law requiring that journalists attend particular training programs was an illegal restriction on freedom of the press; this case pertaining to licensing of journalists was given important press coverage and was widely seen as having a broad impact.[69] In its only binding judgment to date, the court, acting on petition from the commission, which itself was responding to an individual complaint, ruled that Honduras was responsible for the operation of death squads and was obligated to pay monetary compensation to the family of a disappeared person. In this extremely sensitive case, the court secured the initial cooperation of the government in question, and at the time of writing was negotiating the amount of compensation.[70] This case, if successfully concluded, could set precedent impinging on other governments tolerating death squad activity, some of which have accepted the court's compulsory jurisdiction.

Thus the commission and court, operating in relation to the convention, are beginning to make a small impact on hemispheric politics. The case load of the court is obviously much less than that of the European Court of Human Rights. We can only guess at the transformation that would occur should the United States become a party to the treaty and accept the court's compulsory jurisdiction. But there is no indication that any such historic change by the United States is imminent. The Reagan administration even withdrew its qualified consent to compulsory jurisdiction from the International Court of Justice in the wake of losing, then ignoring, the case of *Nicaragua v. United States*.[71] There was no hue and cry from the American body politic when this historic change of position toward the World Court was announced. While the Bush administration has taken some small steps to repair relations with the World Court, it has mostly ignored the OAS human rights regime. There is no indication that it will consider ratification of the American Convention, much less accept the compulsory jurisdiction of the court.

Conclusions

Of the British Parliament it has been written:

> Constitutional changes are hardly ever the result of deliberations by legal experts in search of an ideal blueprint. They are conditioned by the compromises of power-seeking politicians involved in particular circumstances. . . . Powers acquired could easily be lost. Much depended upon the accident of personalities and events, upon the fortunes of war, which are seldom predictable and the characters of monarchs and magnates, which are even less easy to forecast.[72]

A similar interpretation about the unplanned and circumstantial evolution of institutions has been applied persuasively to the changing United Nations and its charter.[73] U.N. norms and policies have changed in response to a series of shifting political crises and changing state priorities, with some influence generated by Secretariat officials and private parties. There has been no single causal factor accounting for change, either for the United Nations as a whole or for its core human rights regime.[74] Something similar can be said about the creation and evolution of the OAS human rights regime, however distressing this may be to the political theorist looking for a simple model to explain change.

On human rights issues across international relations, not just within the OAS, the United States has not always been a moral leader. One must distinguish between national self-image and reality. Just as the United States actively opposed some of the international action designed to end slavery and the slave trade in the past, so it has acted in the contemporary era to block or retard some international measures designed to improve the implementation of human rights.[75] This has been true within the U.N. framework and within the OAS framework.[76] I have noted the U.S. initial opposition to a protective regime in the 1940s, to an authoritative commission circa 1959, to the American Convention, and to the American court. Because key changes in norms and agencies transpired despite active U.S. opposition sometimes, and just passivity sometimes, one cannot accurately conceive of the United States as a moral leader for the OAS human rights regime.

There can be no hegemonic leadership without moral leadership as a component. The United States cannot lead on a policy question in hegemonic fashion without broad agreement that its policy position is good or legitimate. The United States has not consistently exercised hegemonic leadership on human rights issues within the OAS. Because of such factors as executive preoccupation with Soviet-led communism, not to mention congressional opposition to U.S. attention to internationally recognized human rights during the 1950s, the United States has frequently chosen not to apply the power at its disposal in behalf of rights.[77]

On rare occasion the United States has joined an unsuccessful moral leader in this domain—in 1946 in joining Uruguay for democratic intervention in Argentina, 1959 in joining Venezuela for democratic intervention in the Dominican Republic, circa 1962 in devising the Alliance for Progress (and in early 1989 in supporting OAS action to implement the results of democratic elections in Panama). On occasion it has been a quasi-moral leader with partial success, constituting quasi-hegemonic leadership, as when it pushed, with some success, for ratification of the convention and acceptance of the court's compulsory jurisdiction during the Carter administration—without accepting these measures itself.

Absent, for the most part, moral and hegemonic leadership, this leaves the possibility of either U.S. leadership through dominant power or just convergence of policy positions. It is true that at certain junctures in the creation and evolution of the OAS human rights regime, the U.S. policy position was essentially the same as that adopted finally by the OAS. This was the case in the late 1940s with the creation of a declaratory regime and concomitant rejection of something stronger, from 1948 to 1959 concerning drifting with the status quo, in 1959 with the creation of a formally weak commission (although the United States abstained on the authorizing resolution), and in a few other situations.

Here the crucial question is whether the United States led by exercise of power (influence) or whether its policy position simply fit with the policies of most other OAS members. Congruence is not leadership. Convergence of policy is not the same as persuading or manipulating others to follow one's lead. In Western Europe, there has been congruence on regional human rights policy but not hegemonic leadership by any one state. I believe the evidence indicates—in the late 1940s when the regime was created, in the late 1950s when the commission was created, and later when OAS member states tolerated a commission acting beyond its formal mandate—multilateral convergence rather than U.S. dominant power. Sometimes the United States supported what others initiated. In either case, it is difficult to show U.S. leadership, even if one acknowledges some U.S. influence in a supporting or converging sense. But not all exercises of influence qualify for hegemonic leadership.

The best argument for U.S. hegemonic leadership in relation to the OAS human rights regime is the following: the United States led in emphasizing the OAS as a security alliance, not as a social actor; this implied declaring human rights principles but not engaging in regional action; and when others initiated changes in the regime after 1958, the United States threw its decisive support to what others wanted. In the last case support became political leadership. This line of interpretation increasingly loses its plausibility as one closely looks at events after 1958, when the United States continued barely to tolerate, if not oppose, various developments that were consolidated despite U.S. lack of enthusiasm. Progressively into contemporary times, with limited exceptions, the United States is more reluctant follower than leader with regard to the OAS human rights regime.

Rather than because of some form of U.S. leadership, the OAS human rights regime was created and evolved because of the changing interplay of the six variables explicated already. Moral interdependence of neo-Iberian as well as Anglo-Saxon elites, moral leadership mostly by commission and court officials plus the representatives of certain smaller states, and occasional U.S. influence all pushed the declaratory regime into one that was simultaneously strong-promotional and weak-protective. The regime failed to become as strongly protective as the regional regime in Western Europe because of widespread Latin emphasis on national sovereignty (which the United States sometimes emphasized also), widespread violation of rights (which the United States overcame to a relatively greater extent than many of its authoritarian neighbors), and U.S. preoccupation with perceived security interests defined as anticommunism.

This combination of factors provides a richer and more convincing explanation of the dynamics and impact of the OAS human rights regime than the theory of hegemonic leadership. The latter prism is too monocausal to explain the complexity of regional action for human rights in the Western

Hemisphere. The interpretation presented here is a useful intermediary position between the cumbersome description of each event and an oversimplification that sacrifices too much of reality.

This explanation of the creation and evolution of the OAS human rights regime cannot completely explain the fate of other human rights regimes. There may be, however, some causal factors in OAS developments that are of importance in other regimes, even if they have an impact on different ways in different regimes. One thinks of such possibly universal factors as the depth of moral interdependence or the commitment to national sovereignty. But no one has explained OAS developments very well by using a model based on the West European experience, so why should we expect an explanation of the OAS human rights regime to fit other rights regimes, much less economic, security, and environmental regimes?

Can the six variables lead to a reliable probability analysis shedding light on the future of the OAS regime? The key word in the question is *reliable,* and the answer has to remain conditional. One can conceive of certain if-then scenarios derived from the six variables that might prove useful in charting the future in a general way. If moral interdependence deepened (became less abstract), which is to say if national elites "learned" a further commitment to human rights values;[78] if moral leadership continued to be exercised not only by small states and OAS agencies but also by other parties such as the Catholic church and the press;[79] if the end of the superpower cold war was institutionalized and the United States became less preoccupied with Soviet influence in the hemisphere, one could predict an increase in the protective capability of the regime.

But the pull of the past remains strong. Most OAS members continue to fear the power of the Yankee colossus. Hence, claims to national sovereignty are not likely to diminish soon. The end of the cold war may only free the United States to intrude more in Latin domestic affairs, perhaps in the name of fighting a drug war. Moreover, the United States shows few signs of abandoning its historic unilateralism across international relations and few signs of accepting an international definition of human rights as supervised by international agencies.[80] Thus certain hemispheric factors that limit OAS action for human rights are likely to remain, continuing to distinguish the OAS from the Council of Europe in human rights matters. (The introduction of East European states into that Council would complicate the comparison tremendously.)

The Inter-American Commission and Court have made a modest impact on regional politics through invocation of the human rights principles and rules formally endorsed by states. Building on a combination of state hypocritical lip-service to, and moral-cultural affinity for, human rights principles, the guardians of the regime show modest success in indirectly protecting rights in the sense of pressing or commanding states to directly implement what they endorsed in principle.[81] That they had not been able to do more was the result of the conflicted compromises between supporting and limiting forces that allowed them to operate in the first place.

Notes

1. For one comparison of the European and OAS human rights regimes, see Burns H. Weston, Robin Ann Lukens, and Kelly M. Hnatt, "Regional Human Rights Regimes: A Comparison and Appraisal," *Vanderbilt Journal of Transnational Law* 20, 4 (1987): 585–637. For background information on the European regime, see Council of Europe, *Yearbook of the European Convention on Human Rights* (Strasbourg: Council of Europe, annual); Jacob Sundberg, ed., *Laws, Rights and the European Convention on Human Rights* Littleton, Colo.: F.B. Rothman, 1986); Vincent Berger, *A Casebook on the European Court of Human Rights* (Savage, Md.: Rowman and Littlefield, 1989); and Ralph Beddard, *Human Rights and Europe: A Study of the Machinery of Human Rights Protection of the Council of Europe,* 2d ed. (London: Sweet and Mazwell, 1980).

2. Robert O. Koehane and Joseph S. Nye, Jr., "Power and Interdependence Revisited," *International Organization* 41, 4 (Autumn 1987): 725–53.

3. Tad Szulc, "The Inter-American Regional Organization," in William Manger, ed., *The Alliance for Progress: A Critical Appraisal* (Washington, D.C.: Public Affairs Press, 1963), 127.

4. Thomas Buergenthal and Harold G. Maier, *Public International Law,* 2d ed. (St. Paul, Minn.: West Publishing Co., 1990), 132–39.

5. This has evolved as the standard definition of a regime, as used in Stephen D. Krasner, ed., "International Regimes," *International Organization* 36, 2 (Spring 1982): special issue.

6. A.V.W. Thomas and A.J. Thomas, Jr., *The Organization of American States* (Dallas: SMU Press, 1963), at 221, hold that mention of democratic principles in the charter is not legally enforcable. I know of no national court cases that have used the OAS Charter's provisions on human rights directly as controlling law. Compare the academic perspectives in Charles G. Fenwick, "The Charter of the Organization of American States as the Law of the Land," *American Journal of International Law* 47 (April 1953): 281–84, and M.O. Hudson, "Charter Provisions on Human Rights in American Law," *American Journal of International Law* 44 (July 1950): 543–48. By analogy, mention of human rights in the U.N. Charter has had a checkered history in the courts in North America. As a generalization, U.S. courts have not used the charter as hard law. See further Bert B. Lockwood, Jr., "The United Nations Charter and United States Civil Rights Litigation," *Iowa Law Review* 69, 4 (May 1984): 901–56.

7. Larry LeBlanc reviews the attention given to various categories of rights by various OAS organs in "The Inter-American Commission on Human Rights and Economic, Social, and Cultural Rights" (paper presented at the thirtieth annual convention of the International Studies Association, London, March 28–April 1, 1989).

See also his earlier "Economic, Social, and Cultural Rights and the Inter-American System," *Journal of Interamerican Studies and World Affairs* 19 (1977): 61–82.

8. For an analytical review of commission tasks, see Tom J. Farer, *The Grand Strategy of the United States in Latin America* (New Brunswick, N.J.: Transaction Books, 1988), 72–75.

9. Ibid., 70–71; Thomas Buergenthal, "The Inter-American Court of Human Rights," *American Journal of International Law* 76, 2 (April 1982): 231–45, esp. 243.

10. Larry LeBlanc, "Problems in Interpreting and Applying Inter-American Human Rights Regime Norms" (unpublished paper, 1989).

11. Keohane and Nye, "Power and Interdependence Revisited," esp. 741–42, nn. 32, 33.

12. See, for example, several of the essays in William P. Avery and David P. Rapkin, *America in a Changing World Political Economy* (New York: Longman, 1982); and Rapkin, ed., *World Leadership and Hegemony* (Boulder, Colo.: Lynne Rienner Publishers, 1990).

13. On regimes and declining hegemony, see Robert Keohane, *After Hegemony: Cooperation and Discord in the World Political Economy* (Princeton: Princeton University Press, 1984). On whether the United States has actually declined in power resources or whether it has just arrived at policies that fail to maximize its power potential, see Susan Strange, "The Persistent Myth of Lost Hegemony," *International Organization* 41, 4 (Autumn 1987): 551–74. For reasons that will become clear, this last thesis is relevant to this chapter.

14. Keohane, in *After Hegemony,* tries to stay true to the Gramscian sense of hegemonic leadership. See further John Hoffman, *The Gramscian Challenge: Coercion and Consent in Marxist Political Theory* (Oxford: Blackwell, 1984); Joseph V. Femia, *Gramsci's Political Thought: Hegemony, Consciousness, and the Revolutionary Process* (Oxford: Clarendon, 1981); and Roger Simon, *Gramsci's Political Thought* (London: Lawrence and Wishart, 1982).

15. Robert Gilpin, *War and Change in World Politics* (New York: Cambridge University Press, 1981). I am grateful to my graduate assistant, Kelly-Kate Pease, for an analysis of those equating hegemony with dominance. Her unpublished paper (fall 1989) argues that many writers use the concept of hegemony ambiguously and inconsistently: "As a result, the utility of hegemony as a tool for understanding international relations has been significantly impaired."

16. See further G. John Ikenberry and Charles A. Kupchan, "Socialization and Hegemonic Power," *International Organization* 44, 3 (Summer 1990): 283–316, for a discussion of the relationship between hegemonic leadership and coercion.

17. *Webster's New World Dictionary of the American Language,* college edition (Cleveland and New York: World Publishing Co., 1960), 830.

18. Ibid., 831.

19. Jack Donnelly, "International Human Rights: A Regime Analysis," *International Organization* 40, 3 (Summer 1986): 625.

20. Ibid., 620–24.

21. David P. Forsythe, "The Political Economy of U.N. Refugee Programs," in Forsythe, ed., *The United Nations in the World Political Economy* (London: Macmillan, 1989), 131–43, among other sources.

42. Peter Baehr, "The General Assembly: Negotiating the Convention on Torture," in Forsythe *United Nations in the World Political Economy,* 36–53.

23. On acceptance of human rights values widely but in limited form, see Margaret E. Crahan, ed., *Human Rights and Basic Needs in the Americas* (Washington, D.C.: Georgetown University Press, 1982), chap. 1, among other sources.

24. Thomas and Thomas, *Organization of American States* 214–15.

25. Ibid.

26. See, among others, Paul Gordon Lauren, *Power and Prejudice: The Politics and Diplomacy of Racial Discrimination* (Boulder, Colo.: Westview Press, 1988), 151–58.

27. Larry LeBlanc, *The OAS and the Protection and Promotion of Human Rights* (The Hague: Martinus Nijhoff, 1977), 46–51; Thomas and Thomas, *Organization of American States,* 212–33; Cecilla Medina Quiroga, *The Battle of Human Rights: Gross, Systematic Violations and the Inter-American System* (Dordrecht: Martinus Nijhoff, 1988), esp. 38, 54; John C. Drier, *The Organization of American States and the Hemisphere Crisis* (New York: Harper & Row, 1962), 103–4; Hector Gros Espiell, "The Organization of American States (OAS)," in K. Vasak and P. Alston, *The International Dimension of Human Rights* (Westport, Conn.: Greenwood Press, 1982), 2: 543–74.

28. Donnelly, "International Human Right," writes of declaratory, promotional, and protective regimes.

29. Lauren, *Power and Prejudice.*

30. Attempts at a more accurate understanding of the decidedly modest U.S. contributions to internationally recognized human rights can be found in David P. Forsythe, "The United States, Human Rights, and the United Nations," in Margaret Karns and Karen Mingst, eds., *The United States and Multilateral Institutions: Patterns of Changing Instrumentality and Influence* (Boston: Unwin Hyman, 1990), 261–88. The effects of Brickerism are reviewed there. See also the following chapter.

31. Thomas Buergenthal, "International Human Rights Law and Institutions: Accomplishments and Prospects," *Washington Law Review* 63, 1 (January 1988): 6, 15. Louis Henkin, "The United Nations and Human Rights," *International Organization* 19, 3 (Summer 1965): 514: "Even governments that suppress individual rights feel compelled to pay them the homage of hypocrisy, and those who preach, even if they do not yet practice, inevitably keep alive the aspirations and hopes and demands of their citizens."

32. Thomas and Thomas, *Organization of American States,* 219; Jerome Slater, *The OAS and United States Foreign Policy* (Columbus: Ohio State University Press, 1967), 7, 240–43; M. Margaret Ball, *The OAS in Transition* (Durham: Duke University Press, 1969), 373 and passim; J. Lloyd Mecham, *The United States and Inter-American Security 1889–1960* (Austin: University of Texas Press, 1961); Gordon Connell-Smith, *The Inter-American System* (London: Oxford University Press, 1966). John D. Mertz and Lars Schoultz, eds., *Latin America, the United States, and the Inter-American System* (Boulder, Colo.: Westview, 1980).

33. Farer, *Grand Strategy,* p. 25, refers to the U.S. view of the OAS as a continuation of the mind-set of the Monroe Doctrine. For the supposed remark by Castro, see Richard J. Bloomfield, "The Inter-American System: Does It Have a Future," in Tom J. Farer, ed., *The Future of the Inter American System* (New York: Praeger, 1979), 3.

34. Supra, note 31.

35. The pattern was personified by an adviser to the Jamaican government who said privately to me at a conference in 1989: "We don't like U.S. intervention, but we like international communism even less. So we supported the U.S. intervention in Grenada, because of the Cuban and Soviet-bloc advisers. But we opposed U.S. interventions in places like Nicaragua and Panama. It's not entirely consistent, but that's the way we feel."

36. This version draws on Thomas and Thomas, *The Organization of American States*, 235–40; LeBlanc, *The OAS*, 46–51; Anna P. Schreiber, *The Inter-American Commission on Human Rights* (Leyden: A.W. Sijthoff, 1970), 27–35; José A. Colranes, "Human Rights and Non-Intervention in the Latin American System," *Michigan Law Review* 65, 6 (April 1967): 1147–82.

37. On the distinction between human rights per se and human rights related to international peace and security, see Thomas and Thomas, *Organization of American States*, 236; Slater, *OAS and United States Foreign Policy*, 192–93; Schreiber, *Inter-American Commission*, 28.

38. Quiroga, *Battle of Human Rights*, 74–75; Schreiber, *Inter-American Commission*, 45–50; Jane D. Peddicord, "The American Convention on Human Rights: Potential Defect and Remedies," *Texas International Law Journal* 19, 1 (Winter 1984): 141.

39. The Inter-American Peace Committee is cited in this regard by Bryce Wood, "Human Rights Issues in Latin America," in Jorge I. Dominguez et al., *Enhancing Global Human Rights* (New York: McGraw-Hill, for the Council on Foreign Relations, 1980), 192.

40. Ibid., 175.

41. Robert A. Packenham, *Liberal America and the Third World* (Princeton: Princeton University Press, 1973). The United States tried to bring down the Duvalier government in Haiti during 1963; Slater, *OAS and United States Foreign Policy*, 12.

42. See further Carlos Garcia Bauer, "The Observance of Human Rights and the Structure of the System for Their Protection in the Western Hemisphere," *American University Law Review* 30, 1 (Fall 1980): 5–20: protection activities by the commission expanded about 1965, but credit is given not to the United States but to Chile, Uruguay, Guatemala, and Ecuador. Other observers (Farer) see no concrete expansion during this time, while still others (Schreiber) see not only expansion but also U.S. leadership.

43. "United States Ratifies OAS Charter Amendments: Statement by President Johnson," *Department of State Bulletin*, May 13, 1968, 614.

44. Forsythe, "Human Rights in U.S. Foreign Policy," 105, no. 2 *Political Science Quarterly* (Fall 1990): 435–454.

45. Too many authors have taken Kissinger's favorable speeches about the OAS and human rights at face value. More analytical is the treatment in Farer, *Grand Strategy*, 88. See also David P. Forsythe, *Human Rights and World Politics*, 2d ed. (Lincoln: University of Nebraska Press, 1989), chap. 5. Clearly Kissinger was saying one thing publicly and another privately.

46. From a vast literature, see Lars Schoultz, *Human Rights and United States Policy toward Latin America* (Princeton: Princeton University Press, 1981); Joshua Muravchik, *The Uncertain Crusade: Jimmy Carter and the Dilemmas of Human Rights Policy* (Latham, Md.: Hamilton Press, 1986); Sandra Vogelgesang, *American*

Dream, Global Nightmare: The Dilemma of U.S. Human Rights Policy (New York: Norton, 1980); A Glenn Mower, Jr., *Human Rights and American Foreign Policy: The Carter and Reagan Experience* (Westport, Conn.: Greenwood Press, 1987); Richard D. Fagen, "The Carter Administration and Latin America: Business as Usual?" *Foreign Affairs* 57, 3 (America and the World, 1978): 652–69.

47. David P. Forsythe, *Human Rights and U.S. Foreign Policy: Congress Reconsidered* (Gainesville: University Presses of Florida, 1989); David Heaps, *Human Rights and U.S. Foreign Policy: The First Decade* (New York: American Association for the International Commission of Jurists, 1984); Mower; Farer, *Grand Strategy.*

48. Robert L. Ayres, "Breaking the Bank," *Foreign Policy,* no. 43 (Summer 1981): 104–20. The journal entitled this section of articles "Retreat from Multilateralism." A series of Reagan attacks on international organizations led to the designation of a "crisis of multilateralism."

49. Tamar Jacoby, "Reagan's Turnaround on Human Rights," *Foreign Affairs,* 64, 5 (Summer 1986): 1066–86; but compare Forsythe, "Human Rights in U.S. Foreign Policy."

50. *New York Times,* October 26, 1987, 18.

51. Jacoby, "Reagan's Turnaround." Reagan's supposed turnaround on human rights was not a shift on human rights per se but rather a belated recognition that attention to human rights could fit with an anticommunist security policy. Hegemonic leadership on security policy might or might not favorably affect a human rights regime, depending on the types of factors analyzed in this chapter. In its anticommunism, the Reagan administration showed egregious disdain for international law and organization in its hemispheric policy. See further Robert A. Pastor, "The Reagan Administration and Latin America: Eagle Resurgent," in Kenneth A. Oye et al., *Eagle Resurgent? The Reagan Era in American Foreign Policy* (Boston: Little, Brown, 1983), 359–92. In fact, the Reagan administration had such tunnel vision about "Cuban model states" that it violated or ignored all sorts of international standards, human rights or otherwise.

52. Richard B. Lillich, *U.S. Ratification of the Human Rights Treaties* (Charlottesville: University Press of Virginia, 1981).

53. Wood, "Human Rights Issues," 174. But it is well to keep in mind that under Carter, the Human Rights Bureau was not well coordinated with the regional bureaus. Derian's interest were not always reflected in the Latin American Bureau. See further Caleb Rossiter, "Human Rights: The Carter Record, the Reagan Reaction," *Report* of the Center for International Policy (Washington, D.C., 1984).

54. See further Thomas Buergenthal and Robert E. Norris, *Human Rights: The Inter-American System* (Dobbs Ferry, N.Y.: Oceana Publications, 1988), booklets 6, 7.

55. Wood, "Human Rights Issues," 190; LeBlanc, *The OAS,* 171; Quiroga, *Battle of Human Rights,* 159.

56. Buergenthal and Norris, *Human Rights;* Quiroga, *Battle of Human Rights,* 157–89; Wood, "Human Rights Issues" 175–78; Thomas Buergenthal, "The Inter-American System for the Protection of Human Rights," in T. Meron, ed., *Human Rights in International Law* (Oxford: Clarendon, 1984), 2: chap. 12. Tom J. Farer, "The OAS at the Crossroads: Human Rights," *Iowa Law Review* 72, 2 (January 1987): 405; Margaret E. Crahan, "Human Rights and U.S. Foreign Policy: Realism

versus Stereotypes," in K. Middlebrook and C. Ries, eds., *The United States and Latin America in the 1980s* (Pittsburgh: University of Pittsburgh Press, 1986), 424–39.

57. LeBlanc, *The OAS*, 169; Farer, "OAS," 406. The seven-member commission, with a staff of five to ten, accounted for about 1 or 2 percent of the overall OAS budget, two-thirds of it paid by the United States. Wood, "Human Rights Issues," 191.

58. Farer, "The OAS," 403; Farer, *Grand Strategy*, 77–78.

59. Ibid.

60. I could find only one brief and partial discussion of this point in all the literature on the OAS; see Farer, "The OAS," 413, for mention of the effects of a large, uneducated, imporverished, repressed lower class in many OAS member-states.

61. See especially LeBlanc, *The OAS*, 61.

62. See especially Farer, *Grand Strategy*, 194–97. His suggestion of possible commission influence in El Salvador in 1977 is provocative, even if lacking hard proof.

63. The situation is difficult to summarize. The commission's pressure on Chile seems to have affected congressional debates, U.S. voting in the international banks, and State Department rhetoric, but key U.S. support for the dictator remained unchanged until after about 1983. See Forsythe, *Human Rights and U.S. Foreign Policy*, 101–6; Bryce Wood, "Human Rights and the Inter-American System," in Farer, ed., *Future of the Inter-American System*, 140–41. Wood, "Human Rights Issues" 181–83; LeBlanc, *The OAS*, 162. This case would appear to be typical. There was some commission influence in some circles but not decisive or structural influence overall.

64. Attempts to evaluate the impact of commission reports are found in Farer, *Grand Strategy*, 89–97; Wood, "Human Rights Issues," 181–91; Schreiber, *Inter-American Commission*, chaps. 7–8; LeBlanc, *The OAS*, passim; Quiroga, *Battle of Human Rights*, passim. In the 1980s, the *New York Times* usually reported the publication of the U.S. Country Reports on Human Rights on p. 1, while covering the Annual Report of Amnesty International on inside pages, usually pp. 3–6. It usually did not cover at all the annual or country reports of the commission, which is also noted by Schreiber, *Inter-American Commission*, 68, who observed some coverage by Miami papers, especially when Cuba was targeted. Commission headquarters are in Washington, D.C. For a rare *New York Times* coverage of the commission, see June 4, 1990, 4: "O.A.S. Human Rights Report Warns Mexicans on Election Fraud."

65. Farer, *Grand Strategy*, 76; Robert E. Norris, "Observations *In Loco:* Practice and Procedure of the Inter-American Commission on Human Rights," *Texas International Law Journal* 19, 2 (Spring 1984): 285–318. The only other human rights agency to act extensively in-country, and at least sometimes on the basis of intergovernmental agreement, is the ICRC, which normally does not publicize the details of its delegates' observations. David P. Forsythe, "Human Rights and the Red Cross: The International Committee of the Red Cross," *Human Rights Quarterly* 12, 2 (May 1990): 265–89.

66. Wood, "Human Rights in the Inter-American System," 128.

67. A number of observers have emphasized the strong Latin commitment, especially by the military, to a national security doctrine or an all-dominating national security state. The United States, too, has overstated national security concerns. See esp. Lars Schoultz, *National Security and United States Policy Toward Latin America* (Princeton: Princeton University Press, 1987).

68. General developments are traced in H. Lauterpacht, *International Law and Human Rights* (n.p. Archon Books, 1968).

69. *New York Times,* November 29, 1985, 8; Leonard H. Marks, "A Gain for the Latin Media," *New York Times,* December 14, 1985, 15.

70. *Valesques Rodriguez Case,* Series C, No. 4 28, *International Legal Materials* 291, 1989. See further *New York Times,* July 30, 1988, 2.

71. *Military and Paramilitary Activities in and against Nicaragua,* 1984 ICJ Reports 392, and 1986 ICJ Reports 14. See further David P. Forsythe, *The Politics of International Law: U.S. Foreign Policy Reconsidered* (Boulder, Colo.: Lynne Rienner Publishers, 1990), chap. 3.

72. Robert Blake, "Forming a Robust Constitution," *London Sunday Times,* April 2, 1989, G–3.

73. John G. Stoessinger, *The United Nations and the Superpowers: China, Russia, and America* (New York: Random House, 1977), chap. 10.

74. On the dynamics behind the core human rights regime, compare Donnelly, "International Human Rights," with Forsythe, "Human Rights and the United Nations, 1945–1985," *Political Science Quarterly* 100, 2 (Summer 1985): 249–69.

75. Lauren, *Power and Prejudice,* 28–31.

76. Supra, notes 74 and 29.

77. This recalls Susan Strange's differentiation between U.S. power resources, which in her view remain potentially predominant, and U.S. policies, which through mistaken judgments or choice lead to lack of influence in the world. The United States could clearly have been a moral leader for human rights and might have been a hegemonic leader for human rights, but is was not because of the factors analyzed here, such as preoccupation with anticommunism, which paradoxically led to deemphasizing human rights.

78. The concept of learning may soon rival that of hegemonic leadership and regimes as a focal point for scholars of international relations. See George Modelski, "Is World Politics Evolutionary Learning," *International Organization* 44, 1 (Winter 1990): 1–24, and Ernst B. Haas, *When Knowledge Is Power: Three Models of Change in International Organizations* (Berkeley: University of California Press, 1989).

79. Among many sources documenting the Catholic church's splintered but increasing attention to human rights in Western Hemisphere, see Penny Lernoux, *Cry of the People* (New York: Penguin, 1982).

80. That part of American political culture called American exceptionalism, which leads to the view that the United States has nothing to learn from others about human rights and that the United States should act unilaterally because of its moral superiority, is nicely revisited in Tammi R. Davis and Sean M. Lynn-Jones, "City upon a Hill," *Foreign Policy* 66 (Spring 1987): 20–38.

81. Schreiber, *Inter-American Commission,* 157, notes not only that most OAS members pay lip-service to human rights as part of their heritage but also that they do not like to have pointed out their wide gaps between theory and practice on this subject, which gives some leverage to the commission and court. For the clear point that international action for human rights provides at best indirect protection, with states being called upon to provide direct protection, see not only the literature cited by Forsythe in "Human Rights and the United Nations," but by Donnelly in the excellent *Universal Human Rights in Theory and Practice* (Ithaca, N.Y.: Cornell University Press, 1989), 266–69.

5
Human Rights and the United States: Exceptionalism and International Society

Despite the development of a considerable corpus of international law on human rights and despite the growing proportion of time that public international organizations devote to human rights, nation-states remain the key to promoting and protecting human rights. International law is derived from states. Public international organizations are constructed by states. International law must be activated and used by states. International organizations are highly, but not completely, dependent on state policy for resources and direction. The world is no longer characterized by a pure nation-state system. States must share the world scene with other actors, public and private, but they retain considerable authority and power.

Virtually all the important states of the world are increasingly expected, by their citizens and others, to have a human rights component to their foreign policy. David D. Newsom, an experienced U.S. diplomat, suggests that the origins of human rights in foreign policy stem from various factors: ideology played out abroad, concern for rights at home, the division of power within the central government, pressure groups, past mistakes in foreign policy, and so forth.[1] Even authors like R.J. Vincent, who are initially inclined to see human rights in foreign policy as a type of imperialism and thus a way for one state to try to project its values abroad, increasingly come to the conclusion that a more cosmopolitan definition of human rights exists and plays a larger role in international relations than in the past.[2] Evan Luard agrees that most states, for whatever reason, find it difficult to avoid addressing human rights issues in their contemporary foreign policies.[3]

U.S. citizens may tend to think that human rights and foreign policy is a peculiarly U.S. subject. That is not the case. The French government has sometimes played a large role in correcting human rights gross violations in former French colonies. Spain has been active on human rights issues in its former colonies in the Western Hemisphere. The contemporary Soviet Union has created what is essentially a bureau of human rights in its Foreign Ministry, somewhat similar to the one in the U.S. Department of State. West Germany and Japan temporarily suspended their foreign assistance programs to Asian states like Burma because of human rights violations. Sweden and the

Netherlands took the lead in the U.N. General Assembly in pushing for the 1984 treaty against torture. The black African states have repeatedly called for tough international action against apartheid in South Africa. We now know a good bit about the place of human rights in Canadian foreign policy.[4] We also know that the Scandinavian states have been closely monitoring their development assistance and human rights conditions in recipient developing nations.[5] These and many more examples reinforce the point that most states are expected to have, and do have (in varying degrees), an active human rights component to their foreign policies.

Nevertheless, national diplomats are periodically reluctant to push the human rights issue.[6] Attention to internationally recognized human rights can circumscribe the nation-state's freedom of maneuver in the long run. Expectations about proper values, and means of implementing them through international action, may be directed against South Africa today. Those same expectations and international steps may be directed against a close ally or even oneself tomorrow. Thus attention to human rights may mesh only uneasily with short-term security, economic, and other expediential interests. Pressures can build for equal or equitable treatment of human rights in all states, a situation that may prove inconvenient for the state pursuing arms control, economic, or other agreements with a state manifesting serious violations of human rights. When President Carter seemed to direct more of his human rights policy toward anticommunist authoritarians in the Western Hemisphere than to communist states, he came under vigorous attack, especially from conservative critics.[7] Given such complexities, some diplomats and even some governments may be inclined to downgrade human rights in their bilateral foreign policies, however much they might pay lip-service to the notion of human rights in multilateral organizations. Japan in particular seems to be reluctant to jeopardize, significantly and over time, economic interests because of human rights considerations. It became increasingly involved in the economy of South Africa as other states withdrew and was quick to resume a business-as-usual approach to the People's Republic of China after the 1989 massacre in Tiananmen Square.

Yet the evolution of international relations is definitely in the direction of more international attention to the human rights situations in nation-states. Only with the greatest of difficulty can a state avoid taking a position on major human rights questions around the world. Frequently a state feels compelled by internal pressures or the proddings of allies to do more than pontificate and record votes in international organizations; frequently it takes action itself of a political, economic, or (rarely) military nature. This chapter examines the record of the United States in these matters across recent administrations.

As Arthur Schlesinger, Jr., wrote, "The United States was founded on the proclamation of 'unalienable' rights, and human rights ever since have had a peculiar resonance in the American tradition."[8] But this fondness for human rights rhetoric has presented two fundamental problems in foreign policy. As first a reluctant great power and then a more willing superpower, the United States has faced the traditional conflict between commitment to human values and exercise of power for other interests. Equally important in an interdependent and nonhegemonic world, the United States has painfully discovered that its version of human rights is not the same as that of the rest of the world. This chapter traces the workings of these twin dialectics (rights rhetoric and national interests, and rights rhetoric and community standards) from 1945 to the present in order to suggest that the United States, despite its dominant power, has not been the major shaper of community standards or international regimes on human rights; in its bilateral diplomacy, it is still struggling to locate precisely human rights on its foreign policy agenda; and the Congress, while it still does not codetermine human rights in foreign policy, is ignored and bypassed only at peril for an administration. I finally suggest that some painful political socialization is in store for the United States when it deals with human rights in foreign policy, especially since human rights in its many and complex forms will remain on both the U.S. and global agendas.

Multilateral Diplomacy

While the United States pictures itself as the leader of the free world and a city on a hill to be emulated by others, U.S. multilateral diplomacy has been far from the forefront of efforts to create international regimes on human rights.[9] Indeed, if one views U.S. policy on this subject in terms of four periods, three of them have been characterized by various forms of foot-dragging on human rights in multilateral diplomacy.[10]

Limited Support (1945–1952)

It is true that the United States was sympathetic to some mention of human rights in the U.N. Charter, but this first era of U.S. foreign policy on human rights should be labeled one of limited support only. The United States was determined to keep charter language limited to vague generalities, resisting most of the efforts of smaller states and private groups in favor of more specific and demanding obligations.[11] The United States, in professing support for international standards of human rights, did not go far enough in that support to guarantee decisive action.

The same orientation held for the Universal Declaration of Human Rights. Although Eleanor Roosevelt and her State Department advisers supported strongly the declaration, they were at great pains to emphasize its nonbinding and aspirational character.[12] The declaration is almost certainly more important politically and legally than was foreseen in 1948, and states that sought to move beyond charter provisions in some way should be given credit for achievements over time. But that does not change the historical fact that in the 1940s and early 1950s, the United States was opposed to precise and binding obligations in the issue area of human rights. Fear of international scrutiny of its domestic practices, in the south and elsewhere, loomed large in U.S. calculations.

The United States was not silent on human rights issues at the United Nations, but there is ample evidence that its support for a core international regime, and for other rights regimes, was limited. The United States endorsed the self-denying ordinance of the U.N. Human Rights Commission, which ruled out specific review of states' human rights policies, and ironically it successfully sought the demise of the U.N. agency on freedom of information because of budgetary concerns. It did not even support the effort to create an international regime for refugees until later, after the Office of the U.N. High Commissioner for Refugees had demonstrated its utility in the East-West struggle in the aftermath of Hungarian events in 1956.[13]

Neglect (1953–1974)

The limited U.S. support for internationally recognized human rights turned to outright neglect given Brickerism at home and Dullesism in foreign policy by 1953. Brickerism—that movement for a constitutional amendment limiting the treaty prerogatives of the executive—caused the Eisenhower administration to eschew leadership on and participation in the development of formal human rights regimes.[14] Whatever the merits of arguments for and against adherence to human rights treaties, Brickerism plus the debate on the genocide treaty left a lasting impression in the U.S. policy that human rights treaties were so controversial that they were better left alone.[15] Thus the genocide treaty languished in the Senate until 1986, and the U.N. Covenants on Civil-Political and Social, Economic, and Cultural Rights were not even submitted until 1977 (where they have languished since). Most other human rights treaties suffered the same fate of neglect; the United States has become a party to only a half-dozen human rights treaties over the years, none of major importance save the Geneva Conventions of August 12, 1949, pertaining to victims of armed conflict (some would add U.S. acceptance of the U.N. Convention on Political Rights of Women).

Dullesism, the self-righteous preoccupation with Soviet-led communism, solidified the notion that by contesting the Soviet Union, one was contributing to human rights. While true enough when speaking of U.S. support for constitutional democracy in Western Europe, containment of the Soviet bear did not lead always or even frequently to similar liberal regimes in places like South Korea and Iran, not to mention Nicaragua and Guatemala. When applied strictly to multilateral diplomacy, Dullesism meant that fora like the United States were seen almost exclusively as places to score debating points against communists adversaries—as on the subject of forced labor in the Soviet Union.

Thus, starting with the Eisenhower administration, which was under intense pressure by Brickerite forces in Congress, one saw the demise of human rights as a separate issue on the national foreign policy agenda and the collapse of U.S. human rights policy into its strategic policy. It was a merger credible and hence untroubling when applied to European affairs. It was a merger incredible when examined more closely, as it eventually was under traumatic events, in parts of the Third World.

To be sure, in the interim, the Kennedy and Johnson administrations spoke of the need to promote democracy, especially in the Western Hemisphere. The Alliance for Progress, technically not under the OAS but billed as the hemisphere's answer to poverty and repression, continued the merger of human rights as a means to containment of communism.[16] Yet this approach, fashioned by U.S. liberal state capitalism, floundered on the illiberal state capitalism that dominated Latin America at the time.[17]

In larger perspective, the Kennedy administration was too short-lived to have much of an impact, and the Johnson administration was consumed by the Vietnam War, which estranged the United States from the United Nations in particular, where U.S. policies were under attack not only from the majority of states but also from Secretary-General U Thant. When others took the lead to improve the functioning of the U.N. Human Rights Commission or to get U.N. action on private petitions about human rights violations, the United States was supportive, but it did not play a leadership role in the 1960s on multilateral human rights.[18]

The Nixon-Kissinger team downgraded both human rights as a separate issue and multilateral diplomacy still further. Kissinger in particular has left a written record arguing against the intrusion of human rights into the calculus of geostrategy,[19] even if he tried to reformulate his views later in the face of considerable criticism.[20] The record showed, however, that when Kissinger went through the motions of speaking to an OAS gathering on human rights, he later informed the target country (Chile) that the speech was for domestic consumption only.[21] Also, the origins of Basket Three on human rights in the Helsinki Accord lay not with Kissinger and the United States but with the West European democracies.

Given such views by top U.S. officials and given their private reprimands of State Department officials who broached the subject of human rights violations with foreign officials, it was not by accident that Daniel Patrick Moynihan was made ambassador to the United Nations, which he then characterized as a dangerous place where totalitarian regimes sought to use the language of human rights to delegitimize the West.[22] He and others like

Senator Henry Jackson (D–Washington) were clear in their views that the human rights issue should be used as a weapon in the East-West struggle, at the United Nations as elsewhere.

The twin impacts of Watergate and Vietnam brought the Nixon-Kissinger team into disrepute, as much for their substantive policies as for their duplicity. The trauma of Vietnam brought home to the American polity, among other things, the disturbing truth that resisting communism was not always the same as protecting human rights. That tragic war helped produce a decoupling of human rights and security policy in U.S. foreign policy, thus leading to the third era. In other words, the collapse of global containment of communism as the cornerstone of U.S. foreign policy had human rights implications.

Renewed Interest (1974–1980)

The trauma of Vietnam, when added to Watergate, caused the Congress to assert itself on foreign policy. The result for human rights was a renewed interest in internationally recognized human rights as a relatively separate issue. When Congressman Donald M. Fraser (D–MN), chair of the obscure Subcommittee of International Organizations and Movements, began his systematic hearings in 1973 on human rights, which were to have major impact on the agenda of U.S. foreign policy, he and his principal assistant, John Salzburg, gave a clear international framework to the concept of human rights. It was articulated that human rights meant rights defined by the International Bill of Rights (the charter provisions, the Universal Declaration, and the two U.N. covenants). They argued that both on international definition and multilateral diplomacy were important for an effective U.S. policy on the question.[23]

When, in the next stage of congressional action, legislation was approved on the subject of human rights, much of it referred to "internationally recognized human rights." This was true of three general statutes linking human rights to U.S. security assistance, U.S. economic assistance, and U.S. voting in the international financial institutions. All three acts from the 1970s contained the stipulation that U.S. foreign policy was to be affected by a "consistent pattern of gross violations of internationally recognized human rights" in recipient states. This language was incorporated into other legislative acts as well. By the late 1970s, the Congress had reacted to a perceived amoral or immoral U.S. foreign policy by legislating human rights into foreign policy by general, country-specific, and function-specific statutes.[24] Although the United States was not a party to most human rights treaties, U.N. developments on human rights affected Congress as it tried to compel the executive to consider human rights apart from a basically unilateral approach to anticommunism.

Kissinger resisted these congressional pressures to the end of his tenure under President Ford.[25] The Carter administration did move somewhat in the direction desired by Congress. Human rights was given great rhetorical prominence as a separate issue, and at least some Carter policies were supportive of multilateral diplomacy on the subject. Examples are the administration's opposition to the Byrd amendment permitting trade with Rhodesia and the concomitant support for U.N. mandatory sanctions on the Ian Smith government; its vote in the Security Council for a mandatory arms embargo on South Africa; its acceptance in principle of socioeconomic human rights; its utilization of the OAS to help rid Nicaragua of Somoza; and its submission to the Senate of four signed human rights treaties (the two U.N. covenants, the American Convention on Human Rights, and the Convention on Racial Discrimination).[26]

This executive attention to human rights apart from what the president termed an "inordinate" fear of communism on the nation's part, whether stemming from congressional pressures, personal commitment, or campaign rhetoric,[27] was most assuredly not a simple adoption of multilateral standards. It was not as if the Carter administration learned, or internalized, international standards and then applied them across the board in U.S. foreign policy. That administration had to be pushed by Congress into economic pressure on Uganda because of human rights violations. Carter allowed executive lawyers to gut his signature on the two U.N. covenants with extensive reservations and understandings.[28] He resisted congressional efforts to introduce consideration of internationally recognized human rights into the workings of the international financial institutions, such as the World Bank. Thus, much U.S. foreign policy was not at all, or only begrudgingly, affected by multilateral standards on human rights.

Yet on balance the Carter administration, building on the foundations set by Congress, did show—however erratically—renewed attention to internationally recognized human rights. This was less a global crusade based on the International Bill of Rights and more an unsystematic series of piecemeal efforts to help individuals when U.S. strategic and economic interests were not perceived as overwhelming.[29] But it gained sufficient notoriety to yield to a fourth period.

Exceptionalism Triumphant (1981–1988)

The Reagan administration's policies on human rights were initially almost a caricature of U.S. exceptionalism cum cold war politics. Truth on human rights had been discovered in the enlightenment and implemented primarily through the American Revolution. Hence the U.S. commitment to civil and political rights constituted an example to others. That being the case, the United States had no need for international standards, which in any event were so broad as to permit the cover-up of communist violations of civil and political rights—the only true rights. The United Nations, and most other international organizations not under significant U.S. influence, were seen as best as unimportant and at worst as under the control of the Second and Third Worlds.[30] (In fact, initial Reagan foreign policies were so unilateralist that they attacked even the international organizations that were under significant U.S. influence and were important to many U.S. interests, such as the World Bank and International Monetary Fund.)[31]

The early Reagan orientation toward rights was personified by Ernest Lefever, nominated to be assistant secretary of state for human rights and humanitarian affairs. Lefever had criticized Carter for "trivializing" human rights by not seeing the subject as part of the cold war; he had further stated, before recanting during his confirmation hearings, that he was in favor of rolling back human rights legislation passed by Congress because of the same reasoning. His research institute had circulated views favorable to white minority rule in South Africa.[32] The withdrawal of his nomination in the face of bipartisan opposition led to the confirmation of Elliott Abrams, which in turn led to a more polished version of much of what Lefever stood for.

At the United Nations, the Reagan team was outspoken in its attacks on human rights violations by communist nations and outspoken as well in its defense of authoritarian allies like Chile, Argentina, and Guatemala. The Reagan administration engaged in a prolonged "review" of the human rights treaties submitted to the Senate by Carter. Similarly negative views were directed to human rights developments in the OAS. The Kirkpatrick doctrine on dictatorships and double standards guided human rights policy, at the United Nations as elsewhere, between 1981 and 1988.[33] Unlike the Nixon-Kissinger team, the Reagan forces wanted to raise the human rights issue loudly and clearly when competing with the Soviet Union and its clients but not when working with anticommunist allies.

There was some measure of change on these policies toward international standards and multilateral diplomacy during the second Reagan administration, especially after 1985. For example, the United States introduced and lobbied for a resolution in the U.N. Human Rights Commission critical of the Pinochet regime in Chile, and Reagan also came to support ratification of the Genocide Convention. I remain unpersuaded, however, that the second Reagan administration took community standards or international regimes on human rights very seriously.[34] The administration still manifested at the United Nations a clear preference for discussing communist violations, notably Cuba's,[35] and remained largely indifferent to many other international rights developments (for example, it was largely passive in the long struggle to approve a new U.N. convention on torture).[36]

During this era of pronounced U.S. exceptionalism, a bipartisan majority in Congress frequently challenged administration human rights policies through both general and specific legislation. It altered some aspects of U.S.

foreign policy in places like South Africa, Chile, and Guatemala, and where it did not control policy, it nevertheless was an important influence on human rights policy in places like El Salvador, the Philippines, and Liberia. The Reagan administration proceeded on the basis of exceptionalism and cold war politics, but Congress maintained some balanced implementation of international human rights standards, however tenuously in the face of executive power.

Summary

The United States, clearly the dominant power in the early postwar period, for a time perhaps even a hegemonic power, and then by the 1980s still primus inter pares, was nevertheless not a global leader in the development and functioning of most international human rights regimes. Initially it was too concerned to shield its own human rights record in race relations, and then it was caught up in the hysteria of Brickerism (and McCarthyism). Thus domestic politics prevented a leadership role in this issue area of international affairs. The residue of domestic politics, plus preoccupation with the global competition with the Soviet Union, negated U.S. leadership until first the Congress and then the Carter administration tried to reorient foreign policy in the 1970s. This renaissance in U.S. interest in internationally recognized human rights and multilateral diplomacy was dealt a severe blow by the exceptionalism and cold war orientation of the Reagan administration. To a certain extent, Congress persisted in its effort to define and influence the U.S. foreign policy agenda in the light of international developments on human rights, even as the Carter team was retired to the sidelines.

Bilateral Diplomacy

Close observers of the international human rights scene know well that international regimes beyond Western Europe are weak. As Jack Donnelly has written, most are declaratory or promotional rather than enforcement oriented.[37] Even the human rights regime associated with the Council of Europe cannot handle all human rights problems in the region. Consequently it is important to inquire into the place of human rights in bilateral policies. This is especially true of the United States, which is not fully a part of most human rights regimes.

The Carter Period

With the advantage of some years' distance, the Carter administration's bilateral human rights policies are simple to summarize. That administration never developed a central concept or overall strategy to guide its human rights policies, adopting a case-by-case approach with little thought to the overall impression that was being created.[38] It sought to act where major strategic or economic interests were not at stake. It thus wound up focusing on some Latin American authoritarian regimes like Uruguay, Nicaragua, Chile, and others, while deferring strong action against comparable violators such as El Salvador, the Philippines, Saudi Arabia, and South Korea. Other cases like Iran constituted a melange of human rights and other concerns. If immediate policies seemed to require it, the president appeared to have no difficulty in praising serious rights violators, such as the Polish government. The overall impression created was one of great confusion and inconsistency.

The United States intervened frequently in behalf of individuals but was not so clear in its commitment to structural or fundamental change. It often appeared to emphasize negative approaches such as public condemnation or reduction of foreign assistance, although the president himself emphasized more positive approaches at least on occasion.[39] The United States sought to interfere with market forces as little as possible, believing that economic sanctions should not be a major tool of human rights policy.[40]

The overall result of Carter human rights policies were decidedly mixed and decidedly difficult to judge with precision. In some situations, immediate goals were achieved: Somoza was removed from power in Nicaragua, Jacobo Timerman was released by Argentina, the military in the Dominican Republic was deterred from seizing power. Perhaps even more important, the salience of human rights issues gave impetus to individuals and groups around the world to push for more attention to their rights. It is impossible to determine, however, the extent to which the Carter administration is responsible for the strengthened rights movements in the Western Hemisphere, the Philippines, and other places.

It is less problematical to assess the extent to which the administration's emphasis on human rights undermined U.S. power in relation to Soviet-led communism, as charged by the Reagan camp. Certainly in places like Iran, Nicaragua, El Salvador, and elsewhere, U.S. ignoring of human rights problems contributed to the political instability that erupted during the Carter administration's watch. Thus it was not the Carter emphasis on human rights that undermined these U.S. allies as much as it was the oppressive domestic conditions that had been festering unattended for decades. The prominence of foreign human rights rhetoric does not produce instability unless the domestic conditions are ripe for instability. And it should be noted that Carter, too, contributed to this unfortunate U.S. tendency on occasion; his administration increased foreign assistance to Marcos in the Philippines during the time of martial law and gross violations of human rights.[41]

Carter policies varied considerably on the question of how to cope with instability. One searches in vain for the supposed emphasis on human rights that purportedly undermined the shah.[42] On the other hand, Carter worked extensively to oust Somoza and then tried intermittently and despite congressional complications to co-opt his successors with a sizable foreign assistance program. In El Salvador he followed still a third course, providing extensive economic assistance to the shaky government but increasing military assistance only slightly in the quest of pressure for human rights reforms. Whatever the record of Carter policies in the midst of social revolution, it remains true that the neglect of human rights issues by Nixon and Kissinger was ultimately more damaging to U.S. interests in the world than the uneven renewed interest in those rights by the Carter team, especially when one is aware of how difficult it is for a foreign power to impose its will on a nationalistic ruling elite.

Moreover, it is highly likely that the U.S. rhetorical emphasis on rights made its communist competitors uneasy, even if the Carter team did not focus on communist violations as much as candidate Reagan and his supporters wanted. Parts of the Carter administration, however, represented by Zbigniew Brzezinski, did maintain precisely that focus.[43]

The Reagan Period

Attacking the Carter record, the Reagan administration initially intended to collapse human rights policy back into its strategic (and moral) anticommunism. Particularly after the demise of the less than eloquent secretary of state, Alexander Haig, and after the rise of the intelligent and assertive Abrams, the early Reagan team composed a clear policy on human rights in foreign policy.[44]

Beyond the usual lip-service to an even-handed approach to human rights issues, the Reagan forces did not take public or forceful action against authoritarian violations of human rights as a general rule. Neither military nor economic assistance was reduced to these regimes, regardless of their gross and persistent violations of human rights. (Nor were their loan applications opposed in the international financial institutions, U.S. law notwithstanding.) Indeed, it was Reagan policy to work as closely as possible with governments like Chile and Argentina, and with South Africa, unless prevented from doing so by Congress. While "constructive engagement" was used officially in U.S. relations with South Africa, it accurately explained the Reagan approach to all authoritarian allies. The positive approach and reinforcement, in the supposed quest of friendly persuasion and change, was explicitly argued with reference to a few countries like Guatemala. Most of these friendly approaches were without benefit for the human rights situation. The clearly positive changes that occurred in places like Guatemala were more the result of congressional restrictions on foreign assistance than of friendly persuasion by the administration.

Deteriorating rights situations went unopposed in the Philippines, Haiti, and, for a time, South Korea, despite congressional attempts to focus on such situations. And in salient trouble spots like El Salvador and Nicaragua, administration spokesmen, as well as the president, made clear that nothing could be worse than a communist government; noncommunist violations of human rights (whether by the contras in Nicaragua or the military and related death squads in El Salvador) would be seen in that light.[45]

The Reagan administration preferred to emphasize the power struggle with the Soviet Union, viewed to be sure as part of a moral struggle as well, rather than to implement either international or more strictly U.S. standards on human rights in a wide-ranging effort. The exceptions to this generalization are three. The administration did intervene with authoritarian allies in behalf of individuals, such as Kim Dae Jung in South Korea. It did restrict the transfer of crime control equipment to certain authoritarian violators of human rights in a quiet process as required by U.S. law (with the notable exceptions of transfer of electric shock batons to South Africa and South Korea, eventually terminated under negative publicity, and the transfer of equipment that could be used for torture to Turkey). The administration did, through the Agency for International Development and as required by U.S. law, redirect some U.S. economic assistance away from general economic development projects and toward basic human needs projects and did require special supervision of the distribution of assistance because of human rights violations in certain countries.[46] In these three aspects, the Reagan administration followed precedents set by the Carter team. Otherwise, as David Heaps observed, Reagan's human rights policies were clear but exceedingly narrow, focusing on communist violations of human rights.

The Reagan team ran up against the perennial problem of how to exercise influence on regimes that did not receive foreign assistance from or trade extensively with the United States. Aside from implementing the Jackson-Vanik amendment denying most-favored-nation status in trade for communist countries with unreasonable emigration procedures, and aside from economic sanctions on Poland, which did not change the legal banning of Solidarity, the administration fell back on Carter policies of publicly embarrassing communist countries in the Helsinki Follow-up Conferences and in other international meetings.

The Reagan team did differ from the Carter team in at least two further—and controversial—respects. It forcefully raised the question of coercive birth control in the People's Republic of China and for this and other reasons terminated funding to international agencies active in family planning. Also, it revived an old idea that had first been aired by Dante Fascell (D–Fla.) and other congressional Democrats in order to push for the Endowment for Democracy. But then at one point, the Reagan team interpreted this positive support for democratic private groups to mean that conservative and perhaps even nondemocratic entities in both France and Panama would be the recipients of secret U.S. largesse—at least until Congress and the press forced a change in policy.

Ironically the Reagan administration, having made the same mistake of earlier U.S. governments in effectively ignoring noncommunist violations of human rights in the name of strategic competition with the Soviet Union, but having elevated this mistake to the level of (the Kirkpatrick) doctrine, suddenly found itself during its second term with a series of rebellions on its hands that jeopardized its security arrangements. In the Philippines, Haiti, South Africa, South Korea, and Panama, not to mention the continuing problems in El Salvador, domestic rebellions erupted or intensified against governmental repression, oppression, and corruption. In the Philippines, Haiti, and South Africa, events outpaced a U.S. policy wedded to the status quo. Particularly in the Philippines, the president tried to explain away the realities of the impending revolution against Marcos, and only at the eleventh hour and under the friendly pressure of fellow Republicans Senator Paul Laxalt (Nevada) and Senatory Richard Lugar (Indiana), did he shift policies and support the forces for democracy and change. The same outlines of policy pertained equally well to Haiti and to the ongoing revolt in South Africa.

Stung by these events, which called into question the fundamental basis of U.S. strategic policy (with human rights policy as an appendage), officials of the administration after 1985 began to exert pressure on friendly authoritarians to try to head off other building revolts. This was the case in Chile, Paraguay, and, more belatedly, South Korea.

Some observers saw these changes as a shift in Reagan human rights policies.[47] From a narrow point of view, it was, but more fundamentally it was a shift in strategic thinking that secondarily entailed a shift in human rights policies. What still preoccupied the Reagan administration was communism in places like Chile, Panama, and South Korea—or at least a virulent anti-Americanism that could disrupt strategic calculations. U.S. concern about the resurgence of the Left in Chile, the stability of the Panama Canal, and a change in the balance of power on the Korean peninsular chiefly motivated the Reagan administration. It was this type of concern that motivated overall U.S. policy toward these countries, a concern that necessitated some pressure on the strongman to make concessions to democratic forces. In Paraguay, being of little strategic significance, a genuine shift in strictly human rights policy seems to have occurred on the part of the United States. (In Liberia and Zaire, the traditional policy of sweeping human rights abuses under the diplomatic carpet continued unabated.)

A full accounting of the reasons for these shifts in policy has yet to be provided. No doubt the obvious deficiencies of past Reagan policies in particularly the Philippines and Haiti played a role. Congressional pressures were also at work. Moreover there were changes in administration personnel. Kirk-patrick and some of the other ultraconservatives had departed, and the more moderate Richard Schifter had replaced Abrams in the Human Rights Bureau.

In summary, while the outset of the Reagan administration showed clear differences from the Carter approach to human rights, by the end of the second Reagan administration, there were a number of similarities between the two.

The Congress

It is traditional as well as convenient to speak of U.S. foreign policy and human rights strictly in terms of an administration and its multilateral and bilateral policies. But a fuller understanding of U.S. foreign policy necessitates considerable attention to the congressional impact, certainly in the 1980s.[48] (The courts, on the other hand, can still be treated as a marginal consideration when examining human rights in the U.S. foreign policy. In the 1980s there have been a few cases affecting how the political branches approach human rights in foreign policy. Worthy of mention are *Filartiga v. Pena, Forti v. Suarez-Mason,* and *INS v. Cardoza-Fonesca,* among others. Still other recent and interesting U.S. cases that touch on a question of the international law of human rights have more to do with internal U.S. administrative decisions than with U.S. foreign policy—for example, *Rodriguez-Fernandez v. Wilkinson.*)[49]

It was the Congress that compelled the executive to retreat from a leading position in the development of international human rights regimes in the late 1940s and early 1950s. In this matter, the Congress did indeed codetermine foreign policy, and thus it bears coresponsibility with the Eisenhower administration for the debilitating collapse of human rights policy into the strategic policy of anticommunism.

After congressional somnolence and the development of the imperial presidency, it was the Congress, not Jimmy Carter, that sought to place internationally recognized human righs as a relatively distinct issue back on the U.S. foreign policy agenda and sought to coordinate U.S. bilateral with multilateral diplomacy. Even when the Carter administration sought to take the lead on human rights matters, and even if some Democratic members of Congress tended to deter to executive leadership on the question, Congress as a whole remained active. It passed Section 701 of the International Financial Institutions Act, requiring the introduction of human rights considerations into IFI transactions, against the wishes of the Carter team. It forced Carter to support an economic embargo on Uganda and to take action to protect human rights in countries like the Philippines and South Korea. Section 502B of the Foreign Assistance Act, supposedly governing provision of security assistance, was made legally clear and binding despite the usual executive pleas for flexibility in diplomacy. A number of bans on direct or indirect provision of assistance to particular countries (Cambodia, Vietnam, Laos, Cuba, and Uganda) were voted for apparent or partial human rights reasons, despite Carter's opposition.

More striking was the continued congressional assertiveness on human rights matters from 1981, when the popular Reagan was in the White House and when the Republicans controlled the Senate, until 1987. This period can be summarized somewhat unexpectedly as a time when a relatively cosmopolitan and internationally aware Congress fought a running series of battles with a parochial and unilateralist administration. Starting with the battle over the Lefever nomination and continuing in debates over El Salvador, Chile, South Africa, the Philippines, and others, at least a significant part of, if not a clear majority in, the Congress tried to get the Reagan team to focus on internationally recognized human rights, either because it was morally correct or because in the long run it was in the U.S. national interest.[50] (Ironically, this was the same Congress that was following Reagan's lead in bashing the United Nations on numerous subjects, including debilitating cutbacks in funding U.N. programs including the regular budget.)

That the Reagan administration was able to persist in its initial orientations as long as it did with some self-defined success can be attributed not only to the firmness of its convictions but also to the existence of two stages in the congressional process. In the first stage of subcommittee government in Congress, various subcommittees, on human rights matters especially on the House side where the Democrats were in control and where a human rights subcommittee existed, the administration was badgered more or less constantly. But in the second stage of congressional proceedings where voting no the floor occurred, Congress was too fragmented by party, house, and faction to be able to hold the administration's feet to the fire. Thus while earlier Congresses had been able to put human rights legislation on the books, later Congresses had great trouble in effectuating effective oversight because of party and ideological divisions in voting.[51]

On some issues, however, there was majority sentiment at this second stage of voting, and thus the Reagan administration was restricted in its policies toward such countries as South Africa, Chile, Argentina, Guatemala—and periodically and erratically in El Salvador and Nicaragua. The Reagan administration was also overwhelmingly censured in Congress for its vote in the World Health Organization against humane standards for the marketing of infant formula.

There is no doubt but that problems arise because of this continuing congressional assertiveness on human rights. Congressional concern is highly personalized rather than institutionalized, especially in the Senate. This means that Congress focuses on some human rights issue not because that is the most egregious situation, that is where the United States has most influence, or that is where other interests are most adversely affected by human rights problems. Rather, Congress acts because some member of Congress or a staff person becomes concerned with a situation and successfully builds a coalition to do something about it. Moreover, different parts of Congress frequently ride their human rights horses in different directions, leading to much confusion. This problem was particularly evident in the late 1970s. Additionally, there are the standard problems in congressional action: slowness in action, necessity for action by compromise, and playing to the gallery.

Whatever the balance sheet concerning congressional action on human rights in foreign policy, Congress is still determined to play a major role in this aspect of foreign policy. In fact, the general decline in respect for Reagan's foreign policy in the wake of the Iran-contra scandal, and the other information gleaned through the Iranian-contra hearings in 1987 about the chaotic process of Reagan foreign policy making, certainly had the effect of reinforcing congressional assertiveness on foreign policy matters, including human rights. If true that in the history of the Republic congressional assertiveness on foreign policy ran in cycles of about a generation, the end of this cycle is not yet in sight.

Conclusions

It is easier to write analytic description than to compile axioms on human rights and foreign policy that will be accepted as true by a variety of people of different historical experiences and political persuasions. According to Crabb and Holt, the issue of human rights became "possibly the most tangled web in American foreign policy."[52] Lincoln Bloomfield wrote, "What can be doubted is whether the U.S. government will ever be able to express those [human rights] values in its foreign policies in any form that is either coherent or sustained."[53] According to Sandra Vogelgesang, "There is no simple or enduring domestic consensus behind concern for human rights in U.S. foreign policy—by the executive branch, the Congress, or the American people."[54] And according to Abrams, normally the personification of self-assurance, "The human rights problem is so complex that mistakes will inevitably be made."[55]

Are we then to conclude that there are no lessons from the history of the past forty years of U.S. foreign policy and human rights? I suggest that there are.

First, it is clear that international regimes exist on human rights, will continue to exist, and are in fact and in general growing more effective relative to their own past.[56] (Whether they are effective enough, now or in the future, to prevent a consistent pattern of gross violations of rights is another question.) If the United States keeps itself apart from these regimes, as it has done on the core human rights regime, it will not be able to exercise much leadership on the multilateral dimension of global human rights. Even other democratic states, which normally cooperate with or defer to U.S. leadership, like Sweden and the Netherlands, will learn to act without the United States, as they did with regard to the convention on torture. With the demise of European Stalinism and the rise of new democratic states traumatized by past human rights violations, we can expect states like Czechoslovakia and Hungary to push ahead with their own policies in supporting human rights regimes, leaving an ultracautious U.S. government lagging behind. This is precisely what happened at the U.N. Human Rights Commission in 1989, when democratic Hungary took the lead (with Sweden) in condemning violation of minority rights in Ceausescu's Rumania.

Both Brickerism by the Congress and a jingoistic view of U.S. exceptionalism by the Reagan administration, to cite two obvious examples, led to the giving up of influence in multilateral affairs on human rights. To use an oft-cited example, the United States cannot shape the functioning of the U.N. Human Rights Committee if it is not party to the Civil and Political Rights Covenant.

Hence future U.S. administrations will need to struggle to convince the Senate that consent to ratification of human rights treaties is in the broad U.S. national interest. This should not be an insurmountable hurdle given existing views in the Senate, the changed position of the American Bar Association, the readiness of other private groups and expert witnesses to support ratification, and if necessary the use of the argument that U.S. ratification will provide another channel to use against Cuban violations of rights. The Reagan administration's support for ratification of the Genocide Treaty may turn out to be a benchmark in making progress. Reagan also signed the Torture Convention (even if he did gut its implementing machinery). Moreover, where the United States has participated more fully in rights regimes, as on refugees, it is clear that it has considerable influence on the functioning of such regimes.

If the United States genuinely desires an international environment conducive to human rights, it should become a full participant in international human rights regimes. This will entail struggle with the more parochial and jingoistic elements in the Senate, but to act otherwise is to abandon at the multilateral level democratic allies and moderates in the Third World and to give extraordinary influence to those who would use the language of rights for their own repressive ends. Since rights regimes are here to stay, which is another way of saying that human rights will remain on the global agenda, and since the United States lacks the power to force its views unilaterally on most parties (the invasion of Panama in 1989 is more an exception than a rule), to hold the United States apart from these regimes is to throw away both influence and impact. And it can be shown empirically that international rights regimes can be improved, albeit slowly and through struggle.

Second, human rights as a relatively distinct issue has become a permanent part of the U.S. foreign policy agenda. The Nixon-Kissinger preference for a policy of pure geostrategy, with human rights either as a strictly domestic issue or as window dressing, has been repudiated—as much by Republicans as by Democrats. Equally important, the attempt by the first Reagan administration to return to cold war politics by collapsing human rights into anticommunism has also been rejected, again as much by Republican members of Congress as by their Democratic colleagues.

Indeed, in the final years of the second Reagan administration, any number of staunch anticommunists discovered that an active and even-handed attention to human rights contributed to the national interest. One does not fight radical movements by ignoring the reasons for growth of the New Peoples army in the Philippines, the reasons for widespread opposition to Somoza, or the reasons for the resurgence of the violent left in Chile. (There is, admittedly, still the problem of how to encourage an orderly process of change away from repression toward stable protection of rights in different political, cultural, and economic conditions.)

The Reagan administration made valuable contributions to strengthening the position of human rights in U.S. foreign policy by first demonstrating the bankruptcy of the effort to erase the subject as a distinct issue and then by showing the importance of human rights to containing extremist influence. No future government will be in a position to repeat the first Reagan administration's initial desires, and in any event Congress has placed numerous human rights statutes on the books—and holds at least the threat of oversight, which it sometimes does exercise, although in somewhat unpredictable ways.

It is also important to observe that the congressional legislation requiring State Department reports on human rights conditions, and later reports on department overtures concerning torture, has had a political socialization effort within the Foreign Service and larger State Department culture.[57] Compared with the mid-1970s, that community of foreign affairs managers is now much more sensitive to human rights issues. It tends, as a group, to accept more readily human rights as part of the legitimate agenda. At a minimum, the top echelon of the State Department, under both Democrats and Republicans, has recognized that if the department does not act on human rights concerns, Congress will proceed without it. Secretary of State James Baker has shown considerable concern for congressional and other domestic opinion.

It has been said, at least by theorists, that human rights are trumps, that they override other policy considerations.[58] This may be true in stable domestic polities, where the central government monopolizes legitimate use of force, and where independent courts exist to pronounce on conflict of policies and conflict of rights. In the nation-state system, however, human rights can probably rarely be trumps when pursued in foreign policy. As an empirical matter, national security will be trump, but it does matter to what extent, and how, human rights considerations are folded in with security policy. In much past U.S. policy, specific human rights have not been folded in but rather have been ignored. In many situations, concern for human rights can be compatible with U.S. security interests. There is likely to remain, however, a good deal of inconsistency on the matter. The subject of economic interests also needs to be addressed.[59]

Third, the Congress for the foreseeable future will remain attentive to human rights. Having contested Kissinger, Carter, and Reagan on the subject, the Congress shows no signs of growing weary of the fray. Human rights is frequently a high-visibility issue bringing political rewards to members of Congress. Stephen Solarz (D–NY) and Richard Lugar did not hurt themselves politically by having high profiles on human rights in the Philippines. Senators Christopher Dodd (D–Connecticut) and Nancy Kassebaum (R–Kansas) have not hurt themselves politically by sponsoring legislation on South Africa or Liberia. And the disarray of Reagan policies in the mid- and late 1980s invites further behavior of similar nature. Questions of individual self-interest aside, Congress as a whole does get exercised over human rights violations. It did so not only concerning South Africa, where it overrode a presidential veto to implement economoc sanctions, but also concerning the People's Republic of China, where it narrowly failed to override a veto in an effort to legalize and strengthen the sanctions already adopted by the executive (but also effectively undercut by President Bush who signaled through secret diplomacy that the pressure was reduced).

With a statutory basis for attention to human rights having been laid, with a human rights subcommittee on the House side, with publicity to be gained by members of both parties through attention to human rights, with private secular and church groups prepared to work with attentive members, with expanded congressional staff with expertise on the subject, and with an elite press also more attentive to rights issues, it is inconceivable that Congress will turn away from the subject in the near future. Short of an administration that comes up with a near-perfect human rights policy, which the Bush administration certainly has not, and especially given the political socialization that has occurred within Congress on human rights since 1973, Congress will remain an important maker of policy (and sometimes taker of influence from international rights regimes). When during the Bush administration El Salvador was the scene of the murder of several important civilians by elements linked to the governmental side in that continuing civil war, Congress immediately took up debate on the wisdom of reducing or suspending U.S. foreign assistance to the government. Congress also tried to institute economic punishments against Saddam Hussein's Iraq before his invasion of Kuwait, in part for human rights reasons.

Finally, the U.S. historical difficulty in relating to human rights on the global plane is part of the U.S. difficulty in adjusting to an interdependent, nonhegemonic world in which U.S. exceptionalism is widely regarded as a jingoistic myth, much like the Monroe Doctrine, that can be, and is, ignored by others. At times the United States is estranged from the rest of the world, in part (and only in part) because it sees itself as a shining city on a hill when very few other governments do. This estrangement did not arise because the United States is the only nation with citizens who demand political and civil rights. Others do, as witnessed from Peking to Panama. This estrangement did not arise because helpful lessons cannot be learned from the U.S. experience with rights. There is much evidence that many other peoples around the world, in places like China and Eastern Europe, look to the United States at least for lessons in prosperity and perhaps even in freedom.

But others demand rights that go beyond the U.S. tradition. They demand entitlements to adequate food, clothing, shelter, health care, and education. To argue that these demands on public authorities are not as essential to human dignity and welfare as demands for civil and political rights is to fail to understand and relate to less affluent, less individualistic societies. Such a U.S. posture of denial also creates another split with democratic allies, all of whom accept a broader conception of rights than the United States. The United States should take socioeconomic rights more seriously and should join with its democratic allies and others in striving to make those standards more specific and more important in international diplomacy.[60]

If the United States were to move further away from exceptionalism, it might learn some important lessons from international standards on human rights, and from rights practices of other countries, that would improve its own society. On the subject of access to higher education, provision of health care to the nonaffluent, implementation of the death penalty on juvenile offenders, provision of child care for working citizens, or any number of other subjects, there are not many others around the world who look to the United States for positive examples.

In some circles of U.S. society, it is provocative enough to suggest that international standards on human rights could teach the United States something important on traditional foreign policy subjects pertaining to containment of adversaries, maintenance of reliable allies, and promoting economic development with dignity. But could it be that those international standards might actually teach the United States something important about itself? That, too, may fairly be considered a foreign policy issue, or at least an intermestic one.

Notes

1. David D. Newsom, ed., *The Diplomacy of Human Rights* (Lanham, Md.: University Press of America, 1986), esp. 1–13.

2. R.J. Vincent, ed., *Foreign Policy and Human Rights* (Cambridge: Cambridge University Press, 1986), esp. 1–7.

3. Evan Luard, *Human Rights and Foreign Policy* (Oxford: Pergamon Press, 1981).

4. Robert O. Mathews and Cranford Pratt, eds., *Human Rights in Canadian Foreign Policy* (Toronto: McGill-Queens, 1988).

5. Various editors, *Human Rights in Developing Countries* (Copenhagen: Special-Trykkeriet Viborg, annual). This is a publication compiled by private experts commissioned by the Norwegian authorities.

6. R.J. Vincent, *Human Rights and International Relations* (Cambridge: Cambridge University Press, 1986), esp. the final chapter, "Human Rights in Foreign Policy."

7. Joseph Muravchik, *The Uncertain Crusade: Jimmy Carter and the Dilemmas of Human Rights Policy* (Lanham, Md: Hamilton Press, 1986).

8. Arthur Schlesinger, Jr., "Human Rights and the American Tradition," *Foreign Affairs* 57, 3 (America and the World, 1978): 503–26.

9. See especially Tammi R. Davis and Sean M. Lynn-Jones, "City upon a Hill," *Foreign Policy* 66 (Spring, 1987): 20–38.

10. A fuller argument can be found in David P. Forsythe, "The United States, the United Nations, and Human Rights," in Margaret Karns and Karen Mingst, eds., *The United States and Multilateral Institutions: Patterns of Changing Instrumentality and Influence* (Boston: Unwin Hyman, 1990).

11. A. Glenn Mower, Jr., *The United States, the United Nations, and Human Rights* (Westport, Conn.: Greenwood Press, 1979), 5. Paul Gorden Lauren, "First Principles of Racial Equality: History and the Politics and Diplomacy of Human Rights Provisions in the United Nations Charter," *Human Rights Quarterly* 5, 1 (Winter 1983): 1–26. John P. Humphrey, *Human Rights and the United Nations: A Great Adventure* (Dobbs Ferry, N.Y.: Transnational, 1984).

12. In addition to the works cited in note 4, see M. Glen Johnson, "The Contributions of Eleanor and Franklin Roosevelt to the Development of International Protection of Human Rights," *Human Rights Quarterly* 9, 1 (February 1987): 19–48.

13. David P. Forsythe, "The Political Economy of U.N. Refugee Programs," in Forsythe, ed., *The United Nations in the World Political Economy* (London: Macmillan, 1989).

14. One of the best treatments remains Vernon Van Dyke, *Human Rights, the United States, and World Community* (New York: Oxford University Press, 1970).

15. Natalie Kaufman Hevener and David Whiteman, "Opposition to Human Rights Treaties in the United States Senate: The Legacy of the Bricker Amendment," *Human Rights Quarterly* 10, 3 (August 1988): 309–38.

16. An excellent analysis of the U.S. (weak) emphasis on democratic values as part of containment in the Third World is provided by Robert A. Packenham, *Liberal America and the Third World* (Princeton: Princeton University Press, 1973).

17. See especially Richard Fagen, "The Carter Administration and Latin America: Business as Usual?" *Foreign Affairs* 57, 3 (American and the World, 1978): 652–69, for the concept of illiberal state capitalism in Latin America.

18. For an overview of change in human rights developments at the United Nations and an analysis of the several reasons for that change, see David P. Forsythe, "The United Nations and Human Rights, 1945–1985," *Political Science Quarterly* 100, 2 (Summer 1985): 249–70.

19. In *American Foreign Policy: Three Essays* (New York: Norton, 1969), pt. 2, Kissinger argued that the traditional U.S. approach to foreign policy resisted concepts of power, equilibrium, and stability in favor of debilitating moral and legal principles. Human rights fit under these latter principles.

20. Henry Kissinger, "Continuity and Change in American Foreign Policy," in Abdul A. Said, ed., *Human Rights and World Order* (New Brunswick, N.J.: Transaction, 1978), 154–67.

21. *Washington Post,* February 27, 1977, C-1; see also *New York Times,* September 27, 1974, 18.

22. Daniel P. Moynihan, *A Dangerous Place* (Boston: Little, Brown, 1984). It is not that Moynihan is totally wrong, only that there was considerably more to U.N. human rights activity than a Soviet effort to delegitimize "bourgeois" regimes.

23. According to a letter from Salzburg to me, the emphasis on international human rights stemmed from the mandate of the subcommittee that Fraser chaired, the chairman's "strong belief" in the United Nations and international law, and the assistant's background in U.N. human rights affairs. See further Donald M. Fraser, "Freedom and Foreign Policy," *Foreign Policy* 26 (Spring 1977): 152; Congressional Research Service, "Human Rights in the International Community and in U.S. Foreign Policy, 1945–76," *Report,* prepared for the Subcommittee on International Organizations, House Foreign Affairs Committee, July 24, 1977, and "Human Rights in the World Community: A Call for U.S. Leadership," *Report,* Subcommittee on International Organizations, House Foreign Affairs Committee, March 27, 1974.

24. A more complete account can be found in David P. Forsythe, *Human Rights and U.S. Foreign Policy: Congress Reconsidered* (Gainesville: University Presses of Florida, 1988).

25. For example, U.S. law required the State Department to submit reports on human rights conditions in countries receiving U.S. security assistance. Kissinger refused to release these reports to the Congress until just before leaving office, when he released several short and superficial ones.

26. For one overview, see David P. Forsythe, *Human Rights and World Politics* (Lincoln: University of Nebraska Press, 1989).

27. In addition to Carter's *Keeping Faith* (New York: Bantam, 1982), esp. 144, see Elizabeth Drew, "Reporter at Large: Human Rights," *New Yorker,* July 18, 1977, 36.

28. See further Richard B. Lillich, ed., *U.S. Ratification of the Human Rights Treaties* (Charlottesville: University Press of Virginia, 1981).

29. Compare Joshua Muravchik, *The Uncertain Crusade,* with David P. Forsythe's review of this book in the *American Political Science Review* (September 1987).

30. In addition to Muravchik, *Uncertain Crusade,* see the Introduction to *Country Reports on Human Rights Practices for 1981,* Report submitted to Committees on Foreign Affairs and Foreign Relations, Joint Committee Print, February 1982 (Washington, D.C.: Government Printing Office, 1982), 1–11. See further Jeane Kirkpatrick, *The Reagan Phenomenon and Other Species on Foreign Policy* (Washington, D.C.: American Enterprise Institute, 1983).

31. In *Foreign Policy* 43 (Summer 1981), under the title of "Retreat from Multilateralism," see Robert L. Ayres, "Breaking the Bank," 104–20, and Richard A. Frank, "Jumping Ship," 121–38.

32. "Nomination of Ernest W. Lefeaver," *Hearings,* Senate Committee on Foreign Relations, 97th Cong., 1st sess., May 18, 19, June 4, 5, 1981.

33. Forsythe, *Congress Reconsidered.*

34. The fuller argument is presented in ibid.

35. *New York Times,* March 24, 1987, 12.

36. Peter R. Baehr, "The General Assembly as Negotiating Forum: The Treaty on Torture," in Forsythe, ed., *The United Nations.*

37. Jack Donnelly, "International Human Rights: A Regime Approach," *International Organization* 40, 3 (Summer 1986): 599–642. See also his *Universal Human Rights in Theory and Practice* (Ithaca, N.Y.: Cornell University Press, 1989).

38. See especially Caleb Rossiter, "Human Rights: The Carter Record, the Reagan Reaction," *Report,* Center for International Policy (Washington, D.C., September 1984), and Lincoln P. Bloomfield, "From Ideology to Program to Policy: Tracking the Carter Human Rights Policy," *Journal of Policy Analysis and Management* 2, 1 (Fall 1982): 1–12. See further Sandra Vogelgesang, *American Dream, Global Nightmare: The Dilemma of U.S. Human Rights Policy* (New York: Norton, 1980), and Muravchik, *Uncertain Crusade,* 39. The Carter Library in Atlanta has on display a presidential memo directing subordinates to use positive approaches to human rights issues whenever possible. It is not clear to date what further information might be contained in presidential papers on these subjects.

40. Vogelgesang, *American Dream, Global Nightmare.*

41. Among several sources, see Raymond Bonner, *Waltzing with a Dictator: The Marcoses and the Making of American Policy* (New York: Vintage, 1988), passim.

42. The laying to rest of this popular myth is attempted not only by Iranian scholars such as James A. Bill in his *The Eagle and the Lion: The Tragedy of American-Iranial Relations* (New York: Yale University Press, 1988), but also by critics of Carter's policies like Muravchik, *Uncertain Crusade.*

43. Zbigniew Brzezinski, *Power and Principle: Memoirs of the National Security Adviser 1977–1981* (New York: Farrar, Straus, Giroux, 1983).

44. David Heaps, *Human Rights and U.S. Foreign Policy: The First Decade 1973–1983,* for the American Association for the International Commission on Jurists (n.p., 1984).

45. The evidence is marshaled in Forsythe, *Congress Reconsidered.*

46. See ibid.

47. Tamar Jacoby, "Reagan's Turnaround on Human Rights," *Foreign Affairs* 64, 5 (Summer 1986): 1066–86.

48. For the full argument, see Forsythe, *Congress Reconsidered.*

49. For a concise summary, see Richard B. Lillich, "The Constitution and International Human Rights," *American Journal of International Law* 83, 4 (October 1989): 851–62; Richard B. Lillich and Hurst Hannum, "Linkages between International Human Rights and U.S. Constitutional Law," *American Journal of International Law* 79, 1 (January 1985): 158–63; Farooq Hassan, "The Doctrine of Incorporation," *Human Rights Quarterly* 5, 1 (Winter 1983): 68–86. And see Howard Tolley, Jr., "International Human Rights Law in U.S. Courts" (paper prepared for the annual convention of the American Political Science Association, Chicago, 1987).

50. Forsythe, *Congress Reconsidered.*

51. For a detailed examination, see David P. Forsythe and Susan Welch,

"Human Rights Voting in Congress," *Policy Studies Journal* 15, 1 (September, 1986): 173–88.

52. Cecil V. Crabb, Jr., and Pat M. Holt, *Invitation to Struggle: Congress, the President, and Foreign Policy,* 2d ed. (Washington, D.C.: Congressional Quarterly Press, 1984), 187.

53. Bloomfield, "From Ideology," 54; Vogelgesang, *American Dream, Global Nightmare,* 111–12.

55. Abrams, speech, Georgetown University, October 12, 1983, quoted in Forsythe, *Congress Reconsidered.*

56. See, for example, Donnelly, "International Human Rights," and Forsythe, "The U.N. and Human Rights."

57. Judith Innes de Neufville, "Human Rights Reporting as a Policy Tool: An Examination of the State Department Country Reports," *Human Rights Quarterly* 8, 4 (November 1986): 681–99.

58. Ronald Dworkin, *Taking Rights Seriously* (Cambridge: Harvard University Press, 1977).

59. I subscribe to the argument that business should not be above mortality, human rights, or politics. See further Stanley Hoffmann, *Duties beyond Borders* (Syracuse, N.Y.: Syracuse University Press, 1981), chap. 3. Most U.S. administrations, including Carter's, were reluctant to interrupt for-profit activities in the name of human rights unless communism was involved.

60. In addition to the well-argued book by Henry Shue, *Basic Rights: Subsistence, Affluence, and U.S. Foreign Policy,* (Princeton: Princeton University Press, 1980), see Cyrus Vance, "The Human Rights Imperative," *Foreign Policy* 63 (Summer 1986): 3–19. See also David P. Forsythe, "Socioeconomic Human Rights: The United Nations, the United States, and Beyond," *Human Rights Quarterly* 4, 4 (Fall 1982): 433–49, and Donnelly, *Universal Human Rights in Theory and Practice.*

6
Human Rights and Private Transnational Action: The International Committee of the Red Cross

For a considerable time observers of world politics have charted the growth in numbers, and perhaps in influence, of private organizations that act across international boundaries.[1] Some of these are profit seeking and are widely referred to as multinational or transnational corporations, although their membership or board of directors is mononational.[2] Other NGOs with a transnational scope to their activities may be political in the sense that they comprise political parties, such as the Socialist International, or they act as traditional interest groups trying to advance the particular and immediate self-interests of their members, such as the International Chambers of Commerce.

One of the characteristics of the human rights issue area of world politics is the intense activity of human rights NGOs. They may be roughly considered analogous to public interest groups in the United States, in the sense that they lobby not for particular and expediential interests of their members but rather for the public good of greater attention to internationally recognized human rights.[3] The activity of such groups produces no direct and immediate benefit to the members of the group (save for psychic satisfaction), hence the idea of their producing a public or collective good.

Very few of these human rights groups are organized internationally or have an international membership. One source lists the following human rights groups with international membership: Amnesty International (London), Anti-Slavery Society (London), Inter-American Press Association (Miami) (probably not primarily a human right group), International Commission of Jurists (Geneva), International Confederation of Free Trade Unions (Brussels) (probably not primarily a human rights group), International League for Human Rights (New York), International PEN (London), French League for the Defense of the Rights of Man and of the Citizen (Paris), Minority Rights Group (London), Survival International (London), World Federation of United Nations Associations (Geneva) (probably not primarily a human rights group), World Conference on Religion and Peace (New York) (probably not primarily a human rights group), World Council of Churches (Geneva), and World Jewish Congress (Geneva).[4]

In addition, a multitude of basically national groups move in and out of the domain of internationally recognized human rights. These private groups with a national membership may be religious or secular. They may define their primary goals in terms other than advancement of internationally recognized human rights. This is certainly the case for the Americans for Democratic Action, the American Federation of Labor, the American Association for the Advancement of Science, or the Joint Baltic American Committee, to choose just a few at random. But these groups, too, become active from time to time on selected issues having to do with internationally recognized human rights. For example, the AFL-CIO, even if its primary concern is the socioeconomic self-interest of its membership, has been active on such issues as suppression of labor rights in Poland and Chile. And the annual meeting of the U.N. Human Rights Commission in Geneva attracts hundreds of private groups lobbying for various causes, most of which neither have international membership nor derive their raison d'être from the International Bill of Rights.

It is almost always impossible to analyze precisely the influence of any one group or coalition of groups on a given situation. First, many possible causal factors are at work at a given time. If we take the situation of human rights violations in the Soviet Union and Eastern Europe in the early 1980s, we can identify numerous efforts to ameliorate those violations: debates and questions in various U.N. bodies, finger pointing in the follow-up conferences to the Helsinki Accord, unilateral state decisions, worldwide press and television and radio coverage, and the activity of human rights NGOs. Important changes in the region after 1985 may have been stimulated by all, or none, of this international action for human rights. It is scientifically impossible to factor out the precise contributions of the NGOs, at least by way of general analysis. Even on a specific question like the use of political psychiatry against dissidents, the private action of the World Psychiatric Association was meshed with governmental pressures.[5]

On a few occasions it may be possible to identify some fairly precise influence by human rights NGOs on public policy. One source has identified some laws passed by the U.S. Congress on human rights abroad that resulted at least in part from private group activity.[6] Other sources have documented the work of Amnesty International (AI) in such a way that certain prisoners of conscience almost surely benefited from its action.[7]

Yet even in these types of analyses, NGO activity would have been unavailing were it not for sympathetic public officials. Successful interest group activity always depends on sympathetic public officials who have the authority—and the power—to do what NGOs want done. Thus even when private groups claim, with reason, to have influenced public policy, their influence is always meshed with the influence of public authorities. Interest groups do not so much convince opponents of the rightness of their cause; rather, they find sympathetic public officials and give them the information that galvanizes them to act in ways they are prone to anyway.[8] This means that group influence is merged with other factors.

I have noted the extensive and sometimes important activity of human rights NGOs functioning within the U.N. system. In other places, there are excellent treatments of the activity of these private groups in Washington, for example, with regard to U.S. foreign policy toward the Western Hemisphere.[9] In this chapter, we look at a private group that over 130 years has evolved into a unique and respected actor, so much so that although private, it has been given some recognition in public international law. That actor is the International Committee of the Red Cross, whose mandate encompasses victims of war and detained victims of politics.

The ICRC has become a unique actor for human rights since the early 1860s. It is in essence a private or nongovernmental organization, although it has received formal status in public international law. Despite this recognition, the ICRC remains mostly private for three reasons: it makes its own policy as a Swiss private association rather than taking instructions from public bodies; its presents itself frequently to public authorities as a private actor, sometimes even when operating in an armed conflict supposedly governed by public international law; and it gives its detailed reports privately to the authority in question rather than publicizing them, although other information is released.

Not all observers have been prone to think of the ICRC as a human rights actor. It has been traditional to view the agency as a charitable organization, perhaps even as a humanitarian do-gooder. The agency itself has historically preferred terminology related to charity and humanitarianism rather than human rights. But the ICRC has now acknowledged what others have been saying for some time:

> There is . . . a field in which the Red Cross—and particularly the ICRC—has been greatly concerned about human rights, but without in fact saying so in so many words. That field is the protection of man against the absolute power of an enemy, particularly in the event of international and non-international armed conflicts, and also in situations occurring in internal disturbances and tension.[10]

It is therefore correct to view the ICRC as a human rights actor concentrating on certain human rights related to war and political detention. It operates against the background of public international law, especially the law of war, but it frequently eschews arguments based on law.

While the ICRC as a human rights actor has attained a unique and generally respected position in international relations, three types of criticism have repeatedly surfaced about its activities: some believe the agency is not vigorous enough in trying to accomplish its mandate, some believe that mandate is too much affected by tradition and amateurism, and some believe the agency has major organizational problems, starting with its all-Swiss membership. But since the ICRC is still not well known outside of specialized circles, we first review some basic information.

Some Basics

The ICRC arose out of the war between Italy and Austria in the mid-1860s. Henry Dunant, a Swiss national shocked by the cavalier way those states left their wounded soldiers to die on the battlefield of Solferino (not totally unlike in Chad in the 1980s), resolved to start a private humanitarian society to care for sick and wounded combatants. Having created what was to become the ICRC, he and his colleagues in Geneva sought to guarantee a role for these auxiliary medical societies by having them acknowledged and endorsed in public international law. Thus arose the first Geneva Convention for war victims in 1864. Out of these events emerged over time the International Red Cross made up of the ICRC, national Red Cross (or Red Crescent) societies (now numbering 146), and their federation, the League of Red Cross and Red Crescent Societies, plus other assemblies, commissions, and joint bodies.[11] (In the rest of this chapter, the term *Red Cross* is shorthand for *Red Cross* and *Red Crescent*.)

Also emerging from these beginnings was a series of treaties on victims of war that came be to known as the core law of war, or humanitarian law, or Red Cross law, or human rights law in armed conflict. Nine treaties from 1864 to 1977 comprise the conventional law, which has given rise to sizable libraries for analysis and supporting documentation.[12]

Thus the original ICRC, ignoring the adage that "moderation in war is an imbecility,"[13] set out to do nothing less than to humanize war. In certain respects it succeeded and indeed has seen a spillover effect from war to related situations (such as political or security detention).

The modern ICRC has held itself somewhat apart from the rest of the International Red Cross. Historians can debate whether this pattern emerged because of self-pride or some other reason.[14] The results of the attitude are not in doubt, however. For some seven decades, the International Red Cross has been less a cohesive organization and more a loosely joined communications network.[15] There is an ICRC and also a Swiss Red Cross. The ICRC is the agency that formally recognizes national Red Cross societies, but after that point, the ICRC has little formal or informal control over them. The

League of Red Cross Societies arose after World War I when the ICRC clearly lost control of the network. The ICRC failed to respond to the desires of active and powerful national societies such as the American Red Cross, so they and others formed their own federation, which has subsequently and periodically competed for leadership of the movement. (Since World War I was thought to be the war that ended wars and since the League of Nations Covenant seemed to bar war, perhaps some thought there was no further need of the ICRC to deal with war victims; hence one should create a new agency, the League of Red Cross Societies.)

As if this were not at times confusing enough, the Red Cross Conference, which meets every four years, also entails governments that are parties to the Geneva Conventions and Protocols for victims of war. Thus the fox of raison d'être is introduced directly into the humanitarian hen house. (Reasons of state are sometimes introduced indirectly by national Red Cross societies that do the bidding of their governments.) In 1986 the Red Cross Conference, led by African states, voted to suspend the government of the Republic of South Africa (but not the South African Red Cross, which is racially integrated) from participation in that conference. The ICRC, as both a matter of principle and foreseeing difficulties for its fieldwork, refused to support the movement for suspension. The South African government, in reaction to the conference suspension, demanded that the ICRC suspend its activities within South Africa. (After some weeks the ICRC was allowed partially to resume its prison visits and other tasks. Later the ICRC itself decided to suspend its activities for a time, given the lack of cooperation from South African authorities.)[16]

The 1986 conference also approved new wording pertaining to the Statutes and Rules of Procedure of the International Red Cross, which in its entirety was optimistically renamed a movement. Fortunately for the ICRC, and despite much commentary about a more tightly integrated Red Cross, movement cohesion was not in fact achieved. As before, the ICRC was acknowledged as "having a status of its own."[17] It is true that the ICRC was "to carry out mandates entrusted to it by the International Conference." But such instructions to the ICRC and league had to be "within the limits of their statutes. Thus the ICRC could resist a conference mandate that fell outside tasks defined by the ICRC's own statutes, despite wording that gave the final decision on all these matters to the conference. As before, the rules of the movement constituted a crazy quilt of inconsistent statements, and as before, the ICRC ran its own show—although inevitably linked to other agencies utilizing the Red Cross–Red Crescent symbol.

And as before the ICRC was only delicately linked to the League of Red Cross Societies. A plethora of words in the new statutes of the movement sought to give the impression of unity but in fact confirmed independent agencies. "[T]he International Committee and the League shall maintain frequent regular contact with each other at all appropriate levels so as to coordinate their activities in the best interest of those who require their protection and assistance." "[T]he International Committee and the League shall conclude with each other any agreements required to harmonize the conduct of their respective activities."

But in 1988 the situation in Ethiopia showed the fragility of Red Cross integration. The ICRC engaged in tough bargaining with the Mengistu government for access to the northern provinces where a long-standing civil war was combined with harsh climatic conditions. There was considerable civilian famine, and the ICRC demanded to be able to control humanitarian assistance rather than just turn that program over to the pro-government Ethiopian Red Cross; the ICRC wanted to ensure that food and medical relief was administered without regard to political factionalism. The government refused, and the ICRC felt compelled to withdraw its presence and its foodstuffs. But at this point the League of Red Cross Societies, without consultation with the ICRC a few city blocks away in Geneva, agreed to provide supplies but without procedures to guarantee humanitarian impartiality in distribution. The ICRC, faced with this fait accompli, tried to save face by turning over its supplies to the League and arguing in public that the Red Cross movement had demonstrated flexibility. Privately, ICRC officials were incensed that the League had undercut their position.

Despite this example, one of the relatively firm traditions of the movement is that the ICRC is the lead Red Cross agency when the situation is characterized by armed conflict or political detention. In the language of the Red Cross, where there is need for a "neutral humanitarian intermediary," the ICRC has primary responsibility for action in the name of the Red Cross. Three situations usually fall under this heading: international war, internal war, and relatively large-scale political detention (the ICRC euphemistically refers to the last as "internal troubles and tensions"). Other situations such as hijackings and hostage taking have arisen in which the ICRC has played a role, but the ICRC tries generally to limit its activities to victims of war and detained victims of politics plus their families. Because of this focus, the ICRC has developed expertise in three functional areas: visiting detainees (prisoners of war, civilian detainees, or political/security prisoners), providing material and medical relief in hostile situations, and tracing missing persons. Some might add the fourth category of helping to develop the international law of human rights in armed conflict.[18]

When the subject is prison visits, the ICRC acts as independently as it can. It may receive information from other parts of the Red Cross network or from other private groups like AI. It may seek to utilize contacts through national Red Cross societies, since these are normally close to governments. But only ICRC personnel make the visit unless the agency chooses to enlist outside interpreters.

When the subject is relief in armed conflict, the ICRC may utilize other parts of the movement, but these are at least officially under the ICRC's control. (In Indochina in the 1960s and 1970s, Soviet and East European Red Cross personnel operated without real control by the ICRC.) National societies may provide funds, goods, and personnel, but in an armed conflict, the ICRC is supposed to be in charge for the movement. When an armed conflict is combined with a so-called natural disaster, the latter being normally the domain of the League, the two heads of the Red Cross body are supposed to negotiate an agreement. This transpired reasonably smoothly on the Indian subcontinent in 1971. It was not so smoothly achieved in Ethiopia in 1988.

When the subject is tracing of missing persons, the ICRC is lead agency through its Central Tracing Agency. It does, however, seek to train personnel from national societies in this skill as well.

These three areas of expertise, built up over the years and maintained because of contemporary demands, are affected by international law. This can be seen easily with regard to the first role of visiting prisoners. Law for victims of war entails three types of situations: international armed conflict, noninternational armed conflict, and otherwise.[19] In an international armed conflict, the ICRC has been accorded the right to visit prisoners of war and civilian detainees. The 166 states that are parties to the 1949 Geneva Conventions have recognized that detained foreign combatants and civilians in an international war or occupied territory have a right to communicate directly and privately with the ICRC about their conditions of detention.[20] Persons affected by an international armed conflict have many other human rights recognized in the law—not to be made the object of military attack when they are not combatants—and the ICRC may make appeals on their behalf. But the right to visit detainees is the most important procedural right granted to the ICRC in the law of international armed conflict. The procedural right is ancillary to the numerous substantive rights found in the Third and Fourth Geneva Conventions from 1949 and Protocol I from 1977.

Because of this law and the long traditions associated with it, the ICRC operates with a high expectation of being allowed to act in such situations. As a first-order generalization, the ICRC normally visits civilian and combatant detainees, as seen in the 1982 war in the south Atlantic between the United Kingdom and Argentina. There are exceptions, both more historical and more contemporary. The ICRC never visited detained U.S. combatants in what was then North Vietnam. It was barred from Afghanistan for much of that war, although it acted in-country both early and late during the ten-year involvement of Soviet troops. In wars in the Horn of Africa and the western Sahara and between China and Vietnam, the ICRC was also prevented from visiting some or all of those supposedly protected by the law of human rights in international armed conflict.

More mixed cases also exist. In the Persian Gulf war, both Iran and Iraq admitted the ICRC to prisoners of war in particular, but all sorts of difficulties arose. Iran withheld ICRC access to several thousand Iraqi prisoners of war, whereupon Iraq began to withhold partial access in retaliation, despite the prohibition in the Geneva Conventions against reprisals directed at protected persons. Iran even accused the ICRC of being responsible for a riot among prisoners.[21] With regard to Israel after 1967, that state refused to agree that the Fourth Geneva Convention of 1949 applied to territory taken by it in war, despite the views expressed by the ICRC and also the U.N. General Assembly. But Israel did allow the ICRC in principle to visit detainees. All sorts of difficulties ensued, which can be traced in ICRC publications and other sources.[22]

Despite these examples of problems of ICRC access in helping to implement the human rights of detainees in international armed conflict, the generalization remains valid that the ICRC is usually active in those situations. As seen clearly when dealing with Israel after 1967, the ICRC is more interested in helping individuals even if it is viewed as private agency by the public authority in question than in awaiting final resolution of all legal questions.

By comparison, if the situation if legally viewed as a noninternational armed conflict, fighting parties are not legally obligated—even under the 1977 law—to admit the ICRC to territory they control for prisoner visits (or other humanitarian purposes). The ICRC is authorized to request such access, but the parties are not obligated to grant it. It is probably accurate to say that in these internal wars, the ICRC is more likely to see prisoners than not, as in El Salvador during the 1980s. There are exceptions, of course, as in Sri Lanka in the 1980s where the government delayed for many years ICRC access to detained Tamils and others in obvious armed struggle against the government. Again there are mixed cases in two respects. Some situations seem to be a mixture of internal and international armed conflict, as in Nicaragua and Angola in the 1980s. And in some situations, the ICRC is granted partial but not total access to prisoners, as seen not only in Nicaragua and Angola but also in Peru, Chile, and many other nations.

If the ICRC would like to see prisoners not regarded by public authorities as falling under the aegis of the international law for armed conflict, the ICRC normally presents itself as a private humanitarian agency and makes no reference to any international law. It may do this in any event if it believes that this will improve access to detainees. Thus in Afghanistan after 1979, the ICRC was more interested in visiting prisoners in Pul-I-Charki prison in Kabul than in discussing their legal status under international law. This approach has become traditional where prisoners are regarded by the detaining authority as political or security prisoners unrelated to the Geneva law for victims of war. And the ICRC, to my knowledge, has never tried to base its approach explicitly on the international law for human rights in peacetime, under which it has no procedural rights anyway. The ICRC acts in a de facto way to advance those rights, but it does so implicitly rather then explicitly.

Despite the lack of authorization in international law for ICRC access to those "detained by reason of political events," since 1919 and mainly since 1945 the ICRC has visited approximately half a million such persons in ninty-five countries.[23] It does so by permission of controlling authority, not by legal right. For example, the ICRC saw security detainees in Northern Ireland with British permission, Basque security detainees with Spanish permission, and martial law detainees in Poland with the usual governmental permission. If the ICRC believes that such victims of politics might benefit from a neutral humanitarian intermediary, it presents itself to the authorities despite the absence of clear legal foundation.

Thus, in retrospect with regard to ICRC prison visits, it is clear that international law can facilitate—but not guarantee—those visits, can mention the ICRC without giving it any real procedural rights, or can remain silent. The law does affect ICRC operations, but probably more important than the law is essentially private tradition and practice. After 130 years of prison visits, the ICRC is associated with prisoners of war, civilian detainees, prisoners in civil wars, now increasingly, political prisoners and their families. An ICRC presence is frequently (but not always) accepted as normal by those detaining authorities that value their international reputation, that wish to control better their lower officials, or that want to reduce costs by accepting ICRC nutritional, material, and medical assistance that sometimes accompany the prison visits. It now maintains a constant presence in some forty-five countries around the world, and in addition about sixty special missions are ordered by Geneva each year. Its Geneva staff is 600 and its Swiss field staff about 500. The great bulk of this operation is normally directed to prisoner problems.

In any given year, relief in armed conflict, or in some type of mixed situation (man-made and natural disaster), can greatly affect the agency. Here, too, international law can affect operations, as it did historically in the Nigerian civil war (1967–1970)[24] and more recently in the Angolan situation. International law has much to say about medical and material relief in armed conflicts, but it does not accord clear procedural rights to the ICRC. Its activity must be negotiated with the fighting parties, as has been shown already with regard to Ethiopia. What transpires is bargaining between an essentially private actor and a de jure or de facto public authority. Here again tradition helps the ICRC, as it does with the tracing of missing persons also, since the ICRC is usually accepted for some relief (and tracing) in international armed conflict and frequently in internal armed conflict as well.

The difficulties are demonstrated not only by the situation in Ethiopia in 1988 but also in the neighboring Sudan at approximately the same time. In the latter case, international food relief to civilians in territory held by rebels (the Sudanese Peoples Liberation Army) was regarded by the established government in Khartoum as aid to the rebels. Thus political and logistical difficulties impeded Red Cross assistance, designed to implement de facto the socioeconomic rights of starving civilians.

This review of the position of the ICRC in the Red Cross movement, against the background of international law, sets the stage for a discussion of the leading critiques of ICRC activity. It should be clear by now that international law recognizes the still essentially private ICRC. That recognition itself is a reflection of a long tradition of involvement in armed conflict and political detention. But this historical record, legal and practical, should not suggest that the ICRC's mètier is an easy one or that there are few problems. On the contrary, the ICRC is faced with many difficult choices that have given rise to troubling critiques.

Leading Issues

What the ICRC does and the way it does it have provoked considerable discussion, for many reasons. The ICRC concentrates on the material and psychological conditions of detainees and does not directly raise questions about the legal or political reason for detection. The ICRC places an emphasis on in-country activity. As a result, it does not normally release to the public the details of what its delegates have witnessed. This is the price it has agreed to pay for the permission to get into prisons and other installations—and return to them. The organization gives great weight to the wishes of individuals it is trying to help. As long as some good is being achieved for some individuals or—and this is even more difficult to fathom—as long as some bad is being prevented, it is reluctant to withdraw from a situation on the grounds that it is being prevented from doing further good. The ICRC is associated with the larger Red Cross movement, parts of which are not widely regarded as either politically astute or especially sympathetic to human rights.

We can organize the subject into three related points: ICRC action pursuant to its mandate, its choice of mandate and style, and the organization of the house.

Activity In-Country

There is no more troubling question about the ICRC than whether it maximizes leverage on public authorities on behalf of those it is trying to help. At least for purposes of discussion, we can put forth the criticism boldly: Is the ICRC manipulated by public authorities into routine and relative unimportant tasks while major and egregious violations of human rights go untended? It is public knowledge that in the Sandinistas' Nicaragua, the ICRC was allowed to visit prisoners in the regular penal system but not other detainees held by the police and military. So the argument runs, the ICRC's limited presence in-country allows the authorities to deflect criticism of their policies but to keep the ICRC away from places where torture and mistreatment are more likely to occur. And in South Africa for about two decades, the ICRC was allowed to visit convicted security prisoners and those in preventive detention but no other categories of prisoners—and certainly not those being interrogated shortly after arrest.

This critique cannot be treated scientifically or even in a very scholarly fashion, since neither the ICRC nor the authority in question will release the total facts—or a reasonably approximation thereof—of the situation. It seems fairly obvious that ruling authorities, as well as those who would like to rule, will try to manipulate the ICRC according to their perceived self-interests. And the "one more blanket school of morality" can logically lead to problems. If the ICRC will stay in-country as long as it can provide one more blanket to one in need, it can be funneled off into routine duties.

At a minimum, tough choices are sometimes required. Perhaps the most oft-cited situation was that of World War II in which the ICRC was given access to prisoners considered by Nazi Germany to be prisoners of war but denied access to others, including Jews, consigned to the concentration camps. Debate has long raged over whether the ICRC exerted enough effort in behalf of the Jews and, in particular, whether the ICRC should have withdrawn from POW visits, especially once it received reliable reports about what was occurring in the concentration camps. Complicating the subject was the fact that Nazi Germany was not obligated under international law to give the ICRC access to the camps. The ICRC has recently reviewed this situation and cooperated in new studies involving archival material. Several ICRC officials have concluded that they were legally or morally obligated to continue the POW visits.[25]

In more recent years, the ICRC has faced similar dilemmas. It has never, on its own initiative, completely withdrawn from a situation in which it was given access to persons expressly under the law for international armed conflict. It has, however, withdrawn from more ambiguous situations as a policy statement indicating serious human rights or humanitarian problems. For example, for a time it curtailed its activities for political prisoners in South Vietnam, given deplorable conditions and lack of prospect for beneficial change after repeated quiet efforts. It suspended its activities in Portuguese Mozambique until certain problems were corrected. In 1988, it reevaluated its work for political prisoners in South Africa. In the early 1980s it threatened to withdraw from El Salvador at the height of death squad activity.[26] It interrupted visits in places like Afghanistan and Iran. (The agency maintains it did not withdraw from Ethiopia but was effectively thrown out by the terms set by the government.)

When compared with the sixty to ninety countries in which the ICRC may be active in a year, these examples constitute a very small sample of withdrawals or suspensions over time. Obviously the ICRC is reluctant to withdraw as a symbol of protest. It is at least possible in many situations that conditions are so bad that even a limited ICRC presence helping some is to be preferred over a symbolic action that would help none—at least in the short run. These judgments are difficult to second-guess from a great distance.

There is some further evidence that is relevant to this debate. As long as the ICRC is active in-country, there is virtually no evidence that it softens its views to accord with the powers that be. We know on occasion the reverse is true. Some published reports show that the ICRC is careful about prison inspections, cross-checks various claims thoroughly, and presents candid reports to authorities. In Iran under the shah, we know from reports first published by the Islamic Republic and then more completely by the ICRC that the agency reported clearly to the shah the horrors inflicted upon some 30,000 political prisoners by the secret police (SAVAK).[27] And we know that the comprehensive and systematic reports led to the termination of torture and mistreatment, once they came to the attention of the shah. In other situations in the past involving French Algeria, Uruguay, and Greece, we know from ICRC reports that found their way into the public domain that the ICRC was exceedingly candid in its discrete reports to ruling authorities.

On occasion the ICRC undergoes friction with its interlocutors in ruling circles. It is unlikely that the ICRC would have been barred from certain places of internment in countries like El Salvador, Uruguay, Uganda, and Greece unless it has proved itself an assertive watchdog. Such friction is circumstantial evidence in behalf of a conscientious agency, and similar evidence against the notion that the ICRC would accommodate public authorities for the sake of maintaining a largely symbolic presence. There are long-term dangers to the agency's reputation should it become too deferential to ruling authorities, since some information eventually becomes public.

Furthermore, while some observers might be incredulous about the political sophistication of ICRC personnel, ICRC officials meet regularly in Geneva with governmental representatives to review political factors affecting its tasks. My own travels with ICRC delegates as well as interviews in Geneva convinced me that they were—on balance during the 1970s and 1980s—as politically astute as any functionary of a national government. As one ICRC official is reported to have said, "It takes a lot of politics to keep politics out of humanitarian activity." Within the ICRC, there is widespread awareness of what East Europeans like to call the "constellation of political forces," meaning what elite is under what political pressures and constraints—and therefore how hard the ICRC can push on the various issues. It was not by accident that there was a public push on the government of El Salvador to clean up its act, at a time when that government was under severe criticism for its human rights record by the U.S. public and U.S. Congress and in other places. Also the ICRC was fully aware of the lack of U.S. pressure on Israel to improve its human rights record in the occupied territories, and the insensitivity of Iran to all outside opinion during the early stages of the Persian Gulf war.

These examples lead back to the original point concerning the inevitability of tough choices. The ICRC is certainly aware, from its own considerable experience and from the reports of others like AI, where real problems are likely to exist in a given country. One of these is during time of arrest and interrogation. It is not by accident that the ICRC sought and obtained from the Greek junta in the late 1960s written permission to visit all places where political detainees were held, including police stations.[28] ICRC delegates did, in fact, appear at such installations during interrogations—and, one may safely assume, during applications of torture.

It is also no accident that the ICRC entered into agreement with Israel guaranteeing ICRC access to detainees from the occupied or administered territories no later than fourteen days after detention. Apparently bowing to the reality that Israel will seek information from these prisoners during this period, that effective countervailing pressures from inside Israel or from abroad are absent, that delayed access is better than no access, and that delayed access will deter at least some mistreatment, the ICRC has practiced humanitarian politics as the art of the possible. This deal is not free from moral criticism, and the ICRC itself reported at one point that it was unsatisfactory. But some ICRC officials are prone to repeat in private what Nelson Mandela supposedly told a visiting ICRC delegate in South Africa: "It is not so much the good you do, as the bad you prevent." One can only assume that since the ICRC has continued prison visits in Israel and Israeli-controlled territory, it believes there is enough bad being prevented over time to warrant its continued presence.

In El Salvador the ICRC agreed with the government on access to detainees eight days after detention. The agency publicly reported that after a "shaky start," the agreement was being implemented.[29] Evaluating such an agreement may entail evaluating the larger context. Given the operation of death squads, or in Afghanistan the philosophy of taking no prisoners, almost any agreement may be morally justified if it leads to any improvement at all in fundamental human rights.

There is no implicit suggestion that the ICRC has constituted a collective Metternich as the epitome of diplomatic cunning. It has contributed at times to its own difficulties, perhaps most markedly in the Nigerian civil war when its chief delegate proved abrasive toward the federal government, cut corners on some agreements, winked at some provisions of the Geneva Conventions, and—after a Red Cross plane was shot down with loss of life—was declared persona non grata. Other ICRC policies from that situation are also debatable.[30] It may also turn out to be true that the ICRC did not push very hard, and certainly not publicly, on North Vietnam when it was brutalizing U.S. airmen detained during the Vietnam War.

While any given situation may give rise to difficult choices by the agency as well as to an outside debate about the wisdom of its policies, most observers would probably find an improvement in the ICRC's field record over time. This was certainly the conclusion of an independent evaluation team commissioned by the Red Cross in the 1970s.[31] Later independent authors have reached similar conclusions, on subjects ranging from political prisoners in general to ICRC operations on the Thai-Cambodian border.[32]

My overall evaluation on this point is generally sympathetic but not totally comfortable with routine visits to regular prisons while there is no access to other police and military installations. The ICRC is always hoping for an expansion of its tasks, but a shrewed adviser in a repressive government could probably safely advise severe limitations on the agency's access to persons and get away with it for a considerable time. The more the ICRC "hangs tough," as in Ethiopia, the greater will be its respect as a human rights actor in the international community, although there is a short-term price to be paid in terms of individuals left temporarily unprotected. Without access to the ICRC's archives, it is impossible to make a firm evaluation.

Mandate and Style

A second criterion related to the first is that the mandate and style of the ICRC is tied too much to the past and hence out of step with the increased emphasis on human rights. This criticism has to do with the overall philosophy and orientation guiding the institution. The problem, in this view, is that the ICRC is too amateurish in policymaking. Hence it is said to drift with a tradition that seeks only minimum protection of rights, only indirectly, and only by discrete actions that give great deference to governments.

At first glance there seems something to this argument. Some social history and administrative politics are relevant. The ICRC grew out of an upper-class background. Although Henry Dunant was a pauper for part of his life, those who come to dominate the ICRC were upper- and upper-middle-class Swiss, frequently from Geneva. Even today the ICRC president usually comes from prestigious banking, medical, or governmental circles. He is essentially an amateur when he assumes the presidency. The collective body, the assembly, which sets general policy for the organization, is made up mostly of law professors, former diplomats, bankers, and others from the normally traditional and conservative strata of Swiss society. Assembly members contribute their time to the ICRC in a volunteer capacity. There have been no political radicals, no members of racial minorities, few women, and no radical feminists co-opted into membership of the assembly. Those who are well off, who have power and wealth, have not usually been champions of human rights. At the start of their tenure with the ICRC, they may have no claim to special expertise on humanitarian policy.

It is probably true that in the past a sense of Christian charity combined with noblesse oblige animated the work of the ICRC. These traits did not prevent the emergence of world-class personalities such as Max Huber, who were both impressive scholars and familiar with the practical problems of Red Cross protection and assistance.[33] Yet there was at times a kind of aristrocratic amateurism that affected the agency. The top officials, after all, were volunteers to a charitable organization. At least theoretically, this amateurism could lead to excessive caution, perhaps exemplified by activities during World War II, or to excessive assertiveness, perhaps exemplified by activities during the Nigerian civil war. The key factor was a lack of professionalism and expertise in policymaking. As late as 1970 perhaps, this orientation still had its representatives within the organization.

Two events undermined the strength of the traditionalists in the early 1970s: they did not handle well the situation in Nicaragua, and one of their more distinguished members, Pierre Boissier, who might have been elected president and who might have been expected to carry on in a traditional manner, died in an accident while on civil defense training in Switzerland.[34] Since that time two further developments account for more carefully considered ICRC policy. First, those co-opted into the assembly and the presidency have shown increased sensitivity to the international push for human rights and to the agency's reputation within the international community. Some of those who have power and wealth can be sensitive to those who do not, and sensitive as well to a changing international relations. Observers denying this possibility would be surprised at assembly debates concerning how to get an ICRC presence in Kampuchea, how to counteract South African racism, how to devise a long-term strategy for political prisoners. Probably under the impact of the Nigerian war, increased concern for effective policy, in the context of criticism of the agency, could be seen at the highest levels of the ICRC.

Second, by the early 1970s the ICRC had evolved a structure of policymaking that entailed essentially a president and an assembly given to general rather than specific policy and a strong directorate made up of professional staff. The situation was personified by President Alexander Hay on the one hand, and Jean-Pierre Hocke and Jacques Moreillon on the other, respectively, director of operations and director for general affairs for much of the time being discussed. Hocke and Moreillon represented the experienced, politically astute, internationally aware ICRC professional official who had great influence on what the ICRC said and did—even though the formal decision might be made by others.

Thus in both the assembly and in the directorate, one could find increased concern for effective policy (in reaction to criticism). The relatively young, well-educated staff exercised considerable influence on the more traditional elements holding top official positions. Christian charity and noblesse oblige, while perhaps not dead, were joined by professional experience and awareness of changing normative and political conditions. Symptomatic of changes was the addition of a new motto, "per humanitatem ad pacem" alongside the old one, "inter arma caritas."

Moreover, regardless of how the ICRC historically came to define its mission as seeking a minimum of human dignity in certain situations, a defense can be made of this approach, especially when joined by the historical trend toward improved policy. First, the word *minimum* may be used as an equivalent to *fundamental*. What the ICRC seeks is protection of the basic rights to life and other basic rights necessary for human dignity. It has sought both a civil and socioeconomic meaning to human dignity. It has sought freedom from summary execution, from torture and mistreatment, from inhumane and degrading conditions, and from unfair trials (for those protected by the law of international armed conflict). It has also sought to implement rights to adequate diet and health care, communication with family, and access to religious officials. While the ICRC has been helping to implement these civil and socioeconomic standards for some time, sometimes without mentioning rights to the authorities involved, it has now begun to link expressly its activities to rights, at least in public explanations.[35]

Sometimes it is very difficult for the ICRC to get authorities to give even minimum attention to rights, even if rights are not explicity mentioned. In the Persian Gulf war, Iran and Iraq used poison gas; Iran sent juveniles into battle with little training and without air or artillery support against entrenched positions. It was the horrors of World War I all over again; Verdun became Basra. Both sides also attacked civilian centers. In that situation, it was a remarkable achievement to get some attention to the rights of prisoners of war and to civilians in need. In the former states of South Vietnam and Rhodesia, where many prisoners were viewed as subhuman, it was exceedingly difficult to get authorities to give serious attention to improvement of conditions. In Afghanistan where there was tendency for the antigovernment forces to take no prisoners, it was not easy to get the various parties involved to agree to an arrangement whereby captured Soviet personnel were sent first to Pakistan and then to Switzerland for humane detention.[36]

Particularly where elites or would-be elites feel insecure and threatened, as in war and domestic instability, it frequently proves difficult enough to implement minimum standards for human dignity. And more advanced standards are taken up by other NGOs like AI or the International Commission of Jurists or by states and intergovenmental organizations like the United Nations.

Relevant here is a discussion of the ICRC position on publicity, as an example of a carefully considered policy in behalf of fundamental rights. When there has been a clear pattern of violation of the international law for human rights in war and when discrete demarches have not been successful over time, the ICRC will engage in an effort to mobilize public pressure against the violator if it believes such a policy will help victims. According to one source, between 1945 and 1980 the ICRC made thirty-five formal protests; in the subsequent eight years, the agency issued thirty-seven public protests.[37] Either the ICRC was becoming more assertive, or violations of human rights standards were getting worse, or both.

If one really wanted to know, one could easily enough affirm that Iraqi prisoners of war in Iranian hands were mistreated and even killed; Iraq for its part had attacked civilians.[38] During the war for Zimbabwe, forces of the Patriotic Front killed some civilians and also combatants who were hors de combat, shot down civilian aircraft, kept some detainees away from the ICRC, took civilian hostages, and put military installations intentionally in civilian areas. On the Rhodesian side, the death penalty was applied to political offenses, the ICRC was prohibited from seeing detainees under emergency regulations, the food supply was interrupted to certain civilian areas thought to be supportive of the Patriotic Front, and civilians were attacked.[39] Israel military and security personnel used psychological and physical pressure against Arab detainees, committed perjury about these offenses in court, made prisoners confess in the Hebrew language even though they did not understand it, deported Arabs from occupied territory, destroyed Arab property without judicial proceedings, engaged in collective punishment involving guilt by association, employed inhumane detention conditions, and so on.[40]

Moreover, apart from formal public protests, the ICRC does release a considerable amount of information through its publications. It does not normally release the details of what its delegates have seen. (There are two exceptions. In international armed conflict, it sends its reports on detention conditions to both the detaining authority and the authority of origin; this may have the effect of indirectly releasing details to the public, since the aggrieved state may go public, although it risks reciprocal disclosure of its own violations. And if a state publishes a distorted record, the ICRC will correct the distortion in public.)

But the ICRC tells the public where it is making prison visits and how frequently, where its overtures have been rebuffed, where it is not allowed to supervise humanitarian relief, whether it stopped visits because interviews without witnesses were denied, and so on. An informed journalist, official, or citizen can tell a great deal about the ICRC from such public records. If one reads, for example, that the ICRC is making daily visits to detainees in southern Lebanon, one can fairly conclude that there is a problem. If, on the other hand, the ICRC's visits occur every six months, one can fairly conclude that the situation is normalized. All sorts of controversial matters are on the public record. Israel ordered the ICRC out of Palestinian refugee camps in Lebanon the day before massacres occurred.[41]

Naturally all the details of its various negotiations are not publicized, and many other facts remain unadvertised. The ICRC has a long-term view; it is interested in maintaining access to persons in need over time, and this affects its action in any one situation. It is also true that if the situation is not regulated by the international law of armed conflict or if the treatment of persons is not a clear violation of such law or if its quiet diplomacy has not been fully tested, the ICRC exercises a tendency toward discretion.

The central issue with regard to publicity by the ICRC is whether the rights of protected persons can be better advanced by publicity or discretion. (The secondary issue is how the ICRC can act with discretion and yet build support for itself as a means to protect victims of war and politics.) In the Persian Gulf war, the ICRC helped bring about a certain amount of pressure on the belligerents from the states of the European Community.[42] The superpowers, on the other hand, seemed more interested in geostrategic calculus than in curtailing violations of the laws of war. Thus the answer to the question of whether ICRC efforts to generate public pressure on the fighting parties had much effect is very much open to debate. Certainly with regard to the use of chemical weapons, the general consensus is that Iraq showed that such violations were rewarded militarily and politically. At least the ICRC was not barred from either Iran or Iraq because of its public protests. (It was barred partially and temporarily for other reasons.) While the ICRC may argue that states have a legal obligation not only to observe the Geneva law but to make it observed by others, states give priority to their own raison d'état rather than humanitarian law in situations of armed conflict.[43] This leaves the ICRC in an isolated position. Its public protests in the war for Zimbabwe seemed to have had little effect.

In the mid-1980s the ICRC became so concerned about abuses to persons within its mandate that it undertook a public campaign to direct attention to these violations. The agency's president made speeches about the problems in general, without naming names, and various contacts were made with public and private organizations.[44] It was difficult for an observer to see any clear results from this public campaign, at least in the short run. At least the agency protected its own integrity, and in no situation did a formal, public statement by the ICRC result in its expulsion from a nation where it was active. (The ICRC was barred from Uruguay for a time after an ICRC internal report was leaked by someone into the public domain.)

Historically some public action by the ICRC has secured dramatic results. An ICRC public protest about the use of poison gas in the Yemeni civil war caused the Egyptians to reverse policy. ICRC reports about brutal French behavior in the Algerian war, which appeared in the French press, led to the reduction of torture by the French and the dismantling of the infamous Fifth Office in the French military establishment.[45] These may be the exceptions that prove the general rule to the contrary. It is very difficult to get outside parties, as well as the principal protagonists, to give high priority to fundamental human rights in times of war or domestic problems.

The central point remains that the ICRC will go public in several ways about major violations of human rights if this seems the only recourse left to it to advance the interests of persons within its mandate. It has been a carefully considered policy, especially recently, and it appears to be coordinated with its political context. There is continued misunderstanding of the policy, however, either intentionally or otherwise.[46]

Even if one concludes that top ICRC officials and professional staff have considered its mandate, style, and overall position in international relations carefully, and even if one believes that the ICRC is correct to focus only on minimum standards in war and political difficulties, one comes back repeatedly to the central problem of how difficult it is to get public authorities to emphasize those standards in those situations. This is relevant to the critique that the ICRC should attempt more through more assertive tactics. In some situations, a revisionist party wants the situation to deteriorate in human rights terms in order to discredit the ruling authorities and thus hasten the revolution. On the other hand, in El Salvador some U.S. military advisers told journalists the human policy would be to wage a totally brutal war in the short run and then institute a more humane government afterward; moderating policy and thus prolonging the war was inhumane in their view.[47] The ICRC was caught in the middle of these views.

Organization and Membership

One of the criticisms of the ICRC is that its being mononational reduces its wisdom and influence. Another is that it is not well organized for its tasks.

The criticism of the all-Swiss membership is a hoary one. Its validity depends on the organization's record. If the all-Swiss ICRC recruits and retains cosmopolitan personnel with political acumen and more technical ability and if as a result it is widely perceived as doing the best that can be expected in difficult situations, there will not be a significant move to change the nature of membership. This appears to be the situation now. If, on the other hand, the ICRC reflects some of the more parochial elements of Swiss political culture and nationalism, there could arise increased pressures for change. This has happened in the past—after World War I, for example, and in a more muted way around 1970. The ICRC sees itself as working for victims of war and politics, but it must also work with and satisfy its major supporters, which come from governmental, intellectual, and human rights circles in the West.

One of the brakes on any movement for change in ICRC membership is state fear about new composition. At least with a mononational membership, a state does not have to worry that an adversary or its ally might be a member of the agency. This is a strong pillar of the status quo, yet from time to time there is discussion of the merits of some form of international membership.

Since the Nigerian civil war, the ICRC has undergone important changes in personnel and organization. In general between 1970 and 1990, the more traditional, parochial, and amateurish elements receded in influence and the more professional and cosmopolitan elements dominated. This was achieved partly through retirements, partly through restructuring, and partly through fate. The training of delegates was improved. Relations with the component parts of the Red Cross movement were improved, especially with national Red Cross societies, even if a certain competition with the league remained. Relations with journalists and academics were improved in an effort to inform the public better about what the agency did and why and in relation to which laws.

Most important, the ICRC avoided major criticisms about its work in the field. There were frictions and controversies, of course, stemming from the very nature of its activities. But there appeared to be no brouhahas similar to the Nigerian civil war. There were few substantiated or persuasive arguments that the ICRC was unprepared for the political difficulties of the non-Western world, that it was biased toward one party or another, that it had not carefully considered its courses of action, that it was too legalistic, or that it lagged behind the evolution of international relations. It was active in some way in most of the violent or potentially violent situations in the Third World. While historically experiencing difficulties in developing close relations with many Marxist states, the ICRC did make prison visits in Poland under martial law, in the Sandinistas' Nicaragua, in Afghanistan after the rise of Gorbachev, in China to Vietnamese prisoners of war, and in Cuba in the late 1980s. After the European political revolutions of 1989, the ICRC improved its relations with the Soviet Union and East European states; it played a sizable relief role in the Rumanian upheavals of late 1989. Relations remained good with most Western circles.

The ICRC managed to scrape together enough financial support to get its tasks accomplished in at least a minimal way. Operating on regular and emergency budgets funded through voluntary contributions, the ICRC got about 65 percent of its resources from governments—mainly Western ones such as the United States, Switzerland, Canada, Japan, Norway, Sweden, and West Germany. About 40 percent of the governments representing states parties to the Geneva Conventions made no financial contribution. Most of the rest of ICRC material resources came about equally from national Red Cross societies, again primarily Western, and from the European Community. By the late 1980s the ICRC had a regular budget about the equivalent of one F-16 fighter aircraft, an emergency budget roughly approximating three AH-64 helicopters, and a total budget roughly in the range of one B-1 bomber. The total operating budget in 1985 amounted to about $360 million, figured at 1988 exchange rates, or somewhat less than half of the regular U.N. annual budget. Costs were escalating, however, with expenditures tripling between the early- and mid-1980s, due mainly to increased conflicts and instability. It was always a question of whether material support would keep up with humanitarian demand. The ICRC's record of action has led to sufficient, if less than luxurious, financial support.

One of the factors contributing to this support was that it was difficult to think of an existing agency that could replace ICRC tasks across the board. Protecting powers (neutral states to assist in implementing humanitarian law in international armed conflict) frequently were not appointed and/or did not function.[48] AI had made a few prison visits, but its policy on publicity made it unacceptable to many parties, and it lacked the ICRC's expertise in this domain. The Inter-American Commission on Human Rights had made a number of prison visits but on an unsystematic basis and with no jurisdiction beyond the OAS. U.N. agencies were viewed by many states as too governed by partisan or strategic politics, although representatives of the U.N. Human Rights Commission had made a few prison visits. These were not, however, systematic. Some church or charitable groups were widely seen as insensitive to political or legal factors. Many of these types of agencies, such as UNICEF, UNHCR, Oxfam, and Church World Service, were active concerning humanitarian relief in implementing socioeconomic human rights. None of them exactly duplicated the status and reputation of the ICRC. Even the new European Commission on Torture did not exactly duplicate the ICRC, even within Western Europe.[49]

When the ICRC was barred from Nazi concentration camps, it suggested that a multinational team drawn from other neutral states such as Sweden might be utilized. This was unacceptable to Berlin. It was not the all-Swiss ICRC that was unacceptable but rather the idea of transnational inspection of those camps. By rough analogy, if the ICRC is not given access to certain detainees in places like South Africa or Angola, it is not because of the all-Swiss ICRC but because no human rights monitoring of those persons will be allowed by the authorities.

While there is now no significant push to change the mononationality of the ICRC, the all-Swiss ICRC is not guaranteed immunity from criticism. Three important personnel shifts occurred in the late 1980s. Jean-Pierre Hocke resigned to become the U.N. High Commissioner for Refugees; Jacques Moreillon resigned to become the secretary-general of the World Scout Movement; and Cornelio Sommaruga left government service in Bern and subsequently became an activist ICRC president. It remains to be seen how the new administrative structure will acquit itself.

Moreillon, in a complicated and uncoordinated series of events, had earlier thought about leaving the ICRC but had wound up being nominated to become president. Although he and Sommaruga were not bitter rivals for the top post, the comparison between the two represented a choice between the experienced staff and the traditional amateur. During twenty-five years, Moreillon had carried out more than two hundred ICRC missions in seventy countries and had been head of delegation in Israel and Syria, regional delegate in South America, delegate general in Africa, and director of the department of principles and law before becoming director for general affairs.[50] He had developed such rapport with the leading national Red Cross societies that he had been asked previously to stand for secretary-general of the Leauge of Red Cross Societies.

Sommaruga quickly established from 1987 that he intended to be much more than a figurehead president. For almost thirty years, he had held various positions with the Swiss Confederation, mainly in the economic field. He was experienced in dealing in international relations, especially with other governments, but he was an amateur as far as the ICRC and human rights were concerned. While Sommaruga did not drive out Moreillon, shortly after the former took control of much policy, the latter left. The ICRC thus found itself without the two staff members who had effectively made much policy in the preceding fifteen years (Moreillon and Hocke).

It could be hoped that the new structure of a hands-on president and a necessarily weaker staff would maintain the more recent track record of the ICRC. Some of the members of the assembly (including Moreillon, who was co-opted there after resigning from the staff) were experienced themselves, and the assembly had started using more or less permanent committees to develop specialized expertise in order to supervise activities better. Several staff changes were made in 1989 and 1990 to try to compensate for the departure of Hocke and Moreillon. The new structure of policymaking is too recent for full evaluation.

Conclusion

In the mid-1970s I wrote:

> The climate of opinion concerning international interest in human rights has been changing. There is increasing interest in human rights on a global scale, even if that interest is not sufficiently strong to guarantee that violations of fundamental human rights are successfully countered. . . . [I]f the ICRC does not respond to some of the aspirations of some circles of opinion—like IGOs, other NGOs, and attentive publics—it is going to lose the support of these groups. Increasingly it is not just governmental opinion that the ICRC must respond to, but other informed opinion as well.

In the last analysis, the ICRC must make a difficult judgment about when the climate of opinion permits it a more assertive defense of human rights—assertive behavior that, because it is carefully considered and executed, improves a particular situation and also moves the international consensus in support of human rights one more step forward.[51]

Some fifteen years later, I see no reason to revise this perspective. Moreover, it seems to me that the ICRC has become more assertive, as shown, for example, by its policies on public protests and public information. Yet this has occurred in conjunction with a continuing caution based on the reality of what governments and other authorities demand.

Many ICRC policy judgments transpire at the juncture between a tradition emphasizing caution in the face of governmental power and an assertiveness based on the changing nature of international relations. For example, in the mid-1970s the ICRC did not want to assume the position, under the First Protocol of 1977, as automatic substitute for a protecting power. It did not want to be forced upon an unwilling belligerent. Yet a number of Western states pushed this proposal, ultimately unsuccessfully, on the ground that such a measure would improve the protection of the human rights of victims of war. I thought then, and still think now, that the ICRC took the wrong position. The ICRC as automatic substitute would increase pressure on a belligerent to do something about human rights in war, even if some friction ensued between the ICRC and the belligerent. After all, the ICRC's first duty is to victims, not to conflict avoidance. In any event, these are the types of policy choices that must be evaluated, by both the ICRC and those who would critique it.

I continue to believe that on a number of subsequent occasions, the ICRC has been too cautious. In 1983 there was a debate about health policy in Israeli-occupied territory.[52] The ICRC was willing to send a team of doctors to evaluate why so many persons, supposedly protected by the Fourth Geneva Convention, were being hospitalized, but it was not willing to conduct a formal inquiry and made no public report on the situation. Yet it did make formal inquiries on all sorts of other matters pertaining to the occupied territories and published all sorts of clear conclusions about Israeli compliance with that convention. It was not at all evident why this one incident led to so much ICRC caution and meaningless statements.

Similarly, if in Lebanon the ICRC issues a public protest about a specific attack on protected persons, it seems rather pointless not to name the offending party.[53]

Yet on balance I believe the ICRC has been moving in tandem with the evolution of international relations with regard to human rights. It has now formally linked itself to the same fundamental rights recognized in the major international instruments. It has improved its contacts with national Red

Cross societies and also with NGOs and IGOs active on human rights. At the same time it has secured much cooperation from public authorities. It has given evidence of careful consideration of policy and of many planned efforts to develop an ongoing dialogue on fundamental rights with public and private persons in key positions. There is considerable public information available about the agency itself and the law it tries to promote. It is not perfectly clear that bringing in another president from Swiss governmental circles, while downgrading the influence of the professional staff, is necessarily a step in the right direction, but time will give us a basis for wrestling with that question too.

Notes

1. See further Harold K. Jacobson, *Networks of Interdependence: International Organizations and the Global Political System,* 2d ed. (New York: Knopf, 1984) chap. 1, appendix B.

2. From a voluminous literature, see especially Robert Gilpin, *The Political Economy of International Relations* (Princeton: Princeton University Press, 1987), chap. 6.

3. See Lowell W. Livezey, *Nongovernmental Organizations and the Idea of Human Rights* (Princeton: Princeton University Press, 1988). See also David P. Forsythe, *Human Rights and World Politics,* 2d ed. (Lincoln: University of Nebraska Press, 1989), chap. 6, for a discussion of types of interest groups.

4. David D. Newsom, ed., *The Diplomacy of Human Rights* (Lanham, Md.: University Press of America, 1986), 237.

5. One can track the interplay of governmental and nongovernmental action in *New York Times,* March 31, 1989, 2; July 13, 1989, 3; September 21, 1989, 6; October 3, 1989, 4.

6. Forsythe, *Human Rights and World Politics.*

7. Egon Larsen, *A Flame in Barbed Wire: The Story of Amnesty International* (London: Frederick Mueller, 1978).

8. Forsythe, *Human Rights and World Politics.*

9. Lars Schoultz, *Human Rights and United States Policy toward Latin America* (Princeton: Princeton University Press, 1981), esp. chap. 2.

10. Jacques Moreillon, "The Fundamental Principles of the Red Cross, Peace, and Human Rights," *International Review of the Red Cross,* no. 217 (1980): 179.

11. David P. Forsythe, *Humanitarian Politics: The International Committee of the Red Cross* (Baltimore: Johns Hopkins University Press, 1977), 6. See further James Avery Joyce, *Red Cross International and the Struggle for Peace* (New York: Oceana, 1959); and Forsythe, "The Red Cross as Transnational Movement," *International Organization* 30, 4 (Autumn 1976): 607–30.

12. See ICRC and Henry Dunant Institute, *Bibliography of International Humanitarian Law Applicable in Armed Conflicts* (Geneva: Red Cross, 1987).

13. Quoted by Paul Fussell in *New Republic,* August 22, 29, 1981, 30.

14. An official history of earlier periods is by Pierre Boissier, *De Solferino à Tshoushima: Histoire du Comité de la Croix-Rouge* (Paris: Plon, 1963; English translation in 1985; and André Durand, *From Sarajevo to Hiroshima* (Geneva: Henry Dunant Institute, 1984). See further André Durand, *The International Committee of the Red Cross* (Geneva: ICRC 1981); and Jacques Freymond, *Guerres, Revolutions, Croix-Rouge: Reflexions sur le Rôle du Comité International de la Croix-Rouge* (Geneva: ICRC, n.d.).

15. Donald D. Tansley et al., *Final Report: An Agenda for Red Cross* (Geneva: Red Cross, 1975), 46–51.

16. Jacques Moreillon, "Different Perceptions of the Same Event," *International Review of the Red Cross,* no. 257 (1987): 133–51; ICRC, *Annual Report* (Geneva: ICRC, 1988), 16.

17. ICRC, *Statutes and Rules of Procedure of the International Red Cross and Red Crescent Movement,* (Geneva: ICRC, n.d.).

18. The independent team that evaluated the Red Cross movement was not much impressed with the role of the ICRC during the last diplomatic conference on humanitarian law; Tansley, *Final Report,* 69; Forsythe, *Present Role of the Red Cross in Protection* (Geneva: Red Cross, n.d.), 13. Since that time (1974–1977), the ICRC has shown more dynamism in staying in touch with governmental experts and in discussing the prospects for new and related legal instruments. It has also been diligent in trying to secure adherences to the laws already drafted. The central issue is whether the ICRC should be essentially a drafting secretariat, recording mostly what others want, or a more active lobbyist.

19. The two concepts of international and internal war are clearly recognized in international law. The ICRC has been trying to employ the concept of internal troubles and tensions as an intermediate notion between international and domestic jurisdiction. This last notion is a matter of Red Cross practice rather than public international law.

20. Third Geneva Convention, 1949, Article 126; Fourth Geneva Convention, 1949, Articles 76, 143. The procedural details of ICRC detention visits, such as confidential interviews, stem from practice rather than convention.

21. For an independent view, see "Prisoners of War in Iran and Iraq: The Report of a Mission Dispatched by the Secretary-General," U.N. Security Council, S/16962, February 19, 1985. The ICRC was absolved of any wrongdoing.

22. See, e.g., ICRC, *Five Years of Activity 1981–1985* (Geneva: ICRC, 1986), 37–38.

23. ICRC, *International Review of the Red Cross,* no. 262 (1988): 14. See further J.D. Armstrong, "Political Prisoners and the Red Cross," *International Organization* 39, 4 (Autumn 1985): 615–42, and Jacques Moreillon, *Le Comité International de la Croix-Rouge et la Protection de Detenus Politiques* (Lausanne: L'age d'homme, 1973).

24. On the activity of the ICRC in the Nigerian civil war against the background of the Geneva conventions, see especially Thierry Hentsch, *Face au Blocus: La Croix-Rouge Internationale dans le Nigeria en Guerre* (1967–1970) (Geneva: Institut Universitaire, 1973).

25. ICRC, "The ICRC and the Victims of Nazi Persecution," press release, August 1988. The book in question is by Jean-Claude Favez, *Une Mission Impossible?*

Le CICR, Les Deportations, and les Camps de Concentration Nazis (Lausanne: Payot, 1988). See further Arieh Ben-Tov, *Facing the Holocaust in Budapest* (Leyden: Marinus Nijhoff, 1988).

26. ICRC, *Annual Report, 1982* (Geneva: ICRC, 1983), 26. "As there was no improvement in conditions in the places of temporary detention, the ICRC sent one of its members . . . to make an appraisal. . . . He let it be understood by the authorities that if there was no improvement, the ICRC might reconsider continuing its humanitarian and protective work in El Salvador in 1982."

27. ICRC, "Iran: Publication of an ICRC Report," press release, January 1980: "The ICRC wishes to draw attention to the fact that its delegates' findings in places of detention are set forth in confidential reports. . . . Should . . . an incomplete version of such reports be published, the ICRC reserves the right to publish the reports concerned in full." Prisoners were subjected to electrical shocks, burnings with flammable liquids, sexual abuse, and psychological pressures.

28. See Forsythe, *Humanitarian Politics,* 76–84, appendix D.

29. "Prisoners of War in Iran and Iraq."

30. See Hentsch, *Face au Blocus.*

31. Tansley, *Final Report.*

32. See Armstrong, "Political Prisoners and the Red Cross," and William Shawcross, *The Quality of Mercy: Cambodia, Holocaust and Modern Conscience* (New York: Simon and Schuster, 1984). Shawcross presented much more criticism of the UNHCR and its activity on the Thai-Cambodian border than of the ICRC.

33. See further Max Huber, *The Red Cross: Principles and Problems* (Geneva: ICRC, n.d.).

34. I had enormous respect for Boissier, for whom I worked for a time. Boissier had considerable field experience, and it is always difficult to predict how one would perform in a given office. In certain respects, however, Boissier was a European aristocratic traditionalist.

35. In addition to Moreillon, "The Fundamenteal Principles of the Red Cross, Peace, and Human Rights," see D. Schindler, "The International Committee of the Red Cross and Human Rights," *International Review of the Red Cross,* no. 208 (1979): 3–14; André Durand, "Human Rights as Perceived by the Founders of the Red Cross," *International Review of the Red Cross,* no. 266 (1988): 435–51; and ICRC, "The Red Cross and Human Rights," *Working Document,* prepared for the Red Cross Council of Delegates, Geneva, August 1983.

36. See especially ICRC, *Annual Report 1982,* 39–40.

37. *Economist,* May 21, 1988, 80.

38. ICRC, "Second Memorandum from the International Committee of the Red Cross to the States parties to the Geneva Conventions of 12 August 1949 concerning the conflict between the Islamic Republic of Iran and the Republic of Iraq," Geneva, February 10, 1984."

39. ICRC, "Rhodesia/Zimbabwe: Appeal by the International Committee of the Red Cross," Geneva, March 19, 1979.

40. ICRC, *Five Years;* in addition see numerous more recent statements such as ICRC, *Bulletin,* no. 146 (March 1988): 1; and *Bulletin,* no. 148 (May 1988): 4.

41. ICRC, *Five Years,* 38.

42. *International Herald Tribune,* December 8–9, 1984, 2.

43. Alexandre Hay, "The ICRC and International Humanitarian Issues," *International Review of the Red Cross,* no. 238 (1984): 3–10.

44. For an example, see "The ICRC and International Humanitarian Issues."

45. *Le Monde,* January 5, 1960, 1; January 6, 1960, 2; February 10, 1960, 2; February 12, 1960, 2.

46. *Insight,* published by the *Washington Times,* on October 3, 1988, ran an erroneous account (pp. 34–35) of the ICRC policy on public statements in the Middle East, after the reporter who wrote the article had been given a correct explanation of that policy.

47. *Washington Post,* June 7, 1981, A-21, 27. According to a U.S. adviser, in guerrilla wars "where the existing government has won, it has won by terribly brutal methods. . . . The point is that we won't do it. We've all become humanists."

48. See among others David P. Forsythe, "Who Guards the Guardians: Third Parties and the Law of Armed Conflict," *American Journal of International Law* 76, 1 (January 1976): 41–61.

49. When the European Convention on Torture enters into force, the European Commission on Torture would be able to visit prisons on demand in state parties.

50. ICRC, *Bulletin,* no. 149 (1988): 1.

51. Humanitarian Politics, 246–47.

52. *International Review of the Red Cross,* no. 234 (1983): 161.

53. ICRC, press release, July 27, 1982.

7
Conclusion: Understanding
Human Rights

International relations, by whatever name, is not what it was. The overall process can be called world politics, global politics, international politics, postinternational politics, or something else. Those engaging in rhetorical differentiation no doubt have been trying to capture some of the major changes occurring in political interactions. And it is true that in many ways the interaction of those exercising influence in the making of public policy across national boundaries has been characterized by enormous changes. Among the many changes occurring since the end of World War II, the increased internationalization of human rights has been the focus in this study.

I noted in chapter 1 and elsewhere the major international movements prior to 1945 concerned with such human rights as freedom from slavery and to medical assistance in armed conflict and equitable labor conditions.[1] Since 1945, governments, along with other political actors, have taken more international action in support of more human rights than ever before in world history. The modern period has seen an explosion in international attention to human rights by comparison even with the immediately previous interwar period (1919–1939). One has only to compare the hesitant international action on human rights at the start of the U.N. era with subsequent broad action to grasp the outline of change, not to mention that in 1945 there were no regional treaties or declarations on human rights.

To recapitulate, the internationalization of human rights can be detailed in several ways. One can note the changed content of international law and the still-growing number of treaties with monitoring mechanisms concerning human rights. State legal obligations have increased in the name of the fundamental rights of persons, with a view to increasing human dignity. Moreover, the individual, as single entity or as found in private groups, has been given increased authority to act in international relations.

One can track the increased attention given to human rights by intergovernmental organizations, such as the United Nations. This action, which is linked to international law, has helped to change the climate of opinion within which governments and other political actors operate. An official attempt to socialize into increased learning in behalf of human rights is clearly in process. This U.N. effort to promote and protect human rights has not so much reduced state formal authority as it has politically circumscribed state exercise of authority. One can also analyze the construction, evolution, and impact of international regimes dealing with human rights—in this book, the one associated with the OAS. Intergovernmental organizations can be viewed as distinct entities or as part of broader regimes. While the dynamics of different regimes vary, the number of human rights regimes has increased, and the cumulative effect of their operation should be noted, even if that requires a long-term perspective. Because of the actions of the Inter-American Commission and Court on Human Rights, as well as because of state foreign policy acting under regional human rights norms, the internationalization relations of the Western Hemisphere is not what it was.

One can struggle to comprehend the overall meaning of the vast number of national policy decisions oriented toward human rights in foreign policy—legislative statutes, executive decisions, and court judgments. There is no denying that human rights is more integrated into U.S. foreign policy than ever before, although its significance varies with time and place. The evolution of the Reagan administrations, in particular, shows that even when a superpower starts with the desire to ignore international standards and actors on a broad range of human rights, it finishes by achieving some sort of accommodation with them.

One can wrestle with the preplexing question of the role and influence of private groups acting to further the promotion and protection of human rights on an international basis. The ICRC is only one of the many private human rights groups that are active in many parts of the world in different ways. While the ICRC has its own distinctions, so does AI, which is not at all like the International Commission of Jurists or Physicians for Human Rights. The increasing professionalization, political sophistication, and breadth of action of the ICRC is symptomatic of important changes in the world of private transnational human rights groups of all types.

The sum total of these changes—and others not covered here—can be captured in a brief comparison. In the interwar period of 1919–1939, there were sporadic diplomatic efforts to increase the dignity of individuals through such measures as new treaties about the laws of war or new resolutions by the ILO. Since 1945, internationally recognized human rights have become a routinized part of the warp and woof of international relations on a broad scale. Most states and most other actors in an expanded international relations have to be aware of, and sensitive to, the subject of human rights.

To take one typical example, in the interwar years, there was international action for refugees, but that action was diplomatic, without explicit and specific legal foundation, and on a small scale with minor impact. In the postwar period, the international law in behalf of refugees has been extensively developed, the U.N. High Commissioner for Refugees, has been an active and respected office, and many states in many parts of the world are under considerable pressure from public and private groups, foreign and domestic, to treat refugees in accordance with human rights norms. There is, post-1951, a well-developed and complicated international regime to promote and protect the human rights of refugees.

By the 1980s, the human rights situation played a large role in how various actors evaluated the situation in such places as Iran, the Philippines, Nicaragua, Panama, China, and throughout the Soviet Union and Eastern Europe. To recognize this increased importance of human rights is not to suggest that human rights became the only game in town. Strategic and economic considerations, especially, continued to play a very large role in international relations. It was not so unusual for some elites to calculate how much they could pursue their more traditional strategic and economic interests without genuine attention to human rights as demanded by some other party.

Increasingly, however, it became difficult for any actor to pursue either business as usual or politics as usual, including traditional alliance building, without regard for the human rights aspect of the situation. For example, provision of foreign economic assistance was affected by human rights conditions, not only through decisions in Washington but also in Bonn and Tokyo. Membership in the European Economic Community was conditioned upon meeting the human rights standards as found in the Council of Europe; Spain and Portugal were admitted to the EEC only after jettisoning dictatorship, and Turkey failed to gain admittance in large part because of its continuing violations of civil and political rights. In 1990, states coming to the collective defense of Kuwait in the face of Iraqi aggression had to address the question, Why defend Kuwait when that country has ignored civil and political rights?

Moreover, human rights was frequently at the center of the struggle to make foreign policy in national capitals. In Washington from the early 1970s, there was persistent friction between Congress and the president for control of U.S. foreign policy. Whether the subject was how to encourage change in South Africa, or how to deal with China, or what groups merited support in Central America, human rights was central to policy debate.

Perception and Reality

It is not at all clear, however, that this important dimension of change in international relations has been correctly perceived, by many "experts," despite its significance. This affects what students and other citizens perceive about international relations. Table 7–1 surveys coverage of human rights in some

Table 7–1

Coverage of Human Rights in Leading Textbooks of International Relations in American Political Science.*

Author(s) (edition, date)	Chapter on Human Rights?	Total Pages on Human Rights
Cantor, 1986	No	2
Chan, 1984	Yes	34
Couloumbis/Wolf, 4th, 1990	No	2
Deutsch, 3d, 1988	No	2
Farnsworth, 1988	No	7
Holsti, 5th, 1988	No	1
Jones, 6th, 1988	No	5
Kegley/Wittkopf, 3d, 1988	No	2
Lieber, 1988	No	4
Pearson/Rochester, 2d, 1988	No	4
Ray, 4th, 1990	No (section)	10
Rourke, 2d, 1989	No	8[a]
Rusett/Starr, 3d, 1989	No	0[b]
Stoessinger, 9th, 1990	No	0

[a]Separate section on morality.
[b]Considerable attention to democracy.

leading American textbooks of political science dealing with international relations.

It is reasonably clear from the information contained in the table that most American political scientists who write on international relations do not think human rights is an important part of international relations. In this survey of textbooks, chosen arbitrarily but with an effort at broad coverage, only one book devotes a complete chapter to the subject (only one other contains a separate section within a chapter on the subject). Most authors of these standard texts devote two or slightly more pages to internationally recognized human rights. Some treat democracy, and some treat morality or ethics, but most do not adequately and explicitly treat international human rights.

---

*Sources: Robert D. Cantor, *Contemporary International Politics* (Minneapolis: West Publ. Co.); Steve Chan, *International Relations in Perspective* (New York: Macmillan); Theodore A. Couloumbis and James H. Wolfe, *Introduction to International Relations* (Englewood Cliffs, N.J.: Prentice-Hall); Karl W. Deutsch, *The Analysis of International Relations* (Englewood Cliffs, N.J.: Prentice-Hall); David N. Farnsworth, *International Relations*, Nelson-Hall); K.J. Holsti, *International Relations* (Englewood Cliffs, N.J.: Prentice-Hall); Walter S. Jones, *The Logic of International Relations* (Glenview, Ill.: Scott, Foresman, & Co.); Charles W. Kegley, Jr., and Eugene R Wittkopf, *World Politics* (New York: St. Martin's Press); Robert J. Lieber, *No Common Power* (Glenview, Ill.: Scott, Foresman); Frederic S. Pearson and J. Martin Rochester, *International Relations* (New York: Random House); James Lee Ray, *Global Politics* (Boston: Houghton Mifflin); John T. Rourke, *International Politics on the World Stage* (Guilford, Conn.: Dushkin Publishing Group); Bruce Russett and Harvey Starr, *World Politics* (San Francisco: Freeman); John G. Stoessinger, *The Might of Nations* (New York: McGraw-Hill).

Also, review of the descriptions of faculty positions open for recruitment as listed in the *Personnel Newsletter* of the American Political Science Association between 1985 and 1989 reveals that not a single position pertaining to international relations was defined in terms of international human rights. This was probably true for a longer period of time as well. There were numerous faculty positions open in the general field of international relations in American colleges and universities, but they were defined in terms of other subfields, usually international political economy or strategic studies. By and large, the political scientists who specialized in international human rights were not recruited because of that interest but rather because they tracked other aspects of international relations. Once employed to teach and do research on such subjects as U.S. foreign policy or international relations, they managed to develop the subfield of international human rights on their own—usually as a derivative of international law or international organization.

Academic traditions die hard. No matter that numerous governments have fallen, quit, or were significantly altered because of, to a considerable extent, human rights issues. In a number of cases, international action contributed to these important changes. Never mind that Congress and the United Nations, among other political actors, spent innumerable hours debating and acting on human rights matters. There was also a proliferation of national and transnational human rights lobbies. Most of this has been screened out by the collective mind-set of American political scientists focusing on international relations. They continue to emphasize security and economics and a few other traditional subjects such as ideology and diplomacy.

There are at least three principal traditions explaining the lack of adequate attention to human rights in the American study of international relations: political realism, crude behavioralism, and grand theory building.

Political realism has been the dominant approach to the study of international relations in the United States since more or less the 1930s.[2] It arose as an attack on idealism, defined as a moral and legal emphasis in the study of international relations. In the view of the fathers of realism such as E.H. Carr, the British historian, and Hans Morgenthau, the German émigré who became a political scientist at the University of Chicago, American writers on international relations had stressed law and traditional Western morality too much and power not enough. The cure was to downgrade traditional norms of individual liberalism, and traditional legal ones as well, and to emphasize the actual exercise of influence pursuant to the national interest, with a heavy orientation to military power. This approach entailed an emphasis on states, since they held most of the military and other forms of power extant in the world from 1930. Realism was and is a statecentric view of the world stressing security and economic policies, implicitly manifesting a bias against nonstate actors and sentimental subjects such as legality and individual rights.

While American political science grew out of constitutional and jurisprudential subjects taught in history departments, the rise of realism via Morgenthau and his disciples such as George Kennan and Henry Kissinger did much to separate the study of international relations from law and human rights. Realism purported to be pure science, devoid of distorting biases by its adherents, while in fact it was more philosophy than science, more a value judgment about an inherent and evil power drive on the part of policymakers.[3] Given this assumed power drive to maximize national power without normative restraint, which became an appealing framework in the era of Hitler, there was a marked tendency to ignore evidence of other motivations, other processes, other changes over time that were more subtle than national violence, more elusive than the economy that sustained war, and less obvious than overall national foreign policies of expansion or containment.

Morgenthau, and many who followed in his steps, as Kissinger did, did not ignore morality so much as they redefined it. What became moral in international context was that which was done to advance the national interest. If war was seen as necessary to advance the interests of the "good" nation (and what national leader would not see his or her nation as good?), that war became a moral act. If killing individuals or lying to them or torturing them was perceived as necessary to defeat a Hitler (or later a Stalin or a Saddam Hussein), then the greater value of the nation, and its existence as a moral entity, prevailed over the lesser value, and moral standing, of an individual. Thus for Kissinger, promoting arms control or détente between the United States and the Stalinist Soviet Union was a moral as well as political act.

It is, therefore, not true that realists like Morgenthau and Kissinger were amoral in their analytical concerns. It is true to say that they regarded individual human rights, as defined by international law, as a sentimental subject unworthy of emphasis in the face of need to balance national power against national power. To the realities, this quest for dominance or equilibrium was a moral as well as strategic pursuit. To emphasize the difference between international and individual morality, and to stress the symbiosis between political and moral action, was part of their principal motivation in developing realism.

It is obvious in retrospect that realism proved appealing as philosophy, morality, and a framework for political analysis. As a philosophy of human nature, it seemed to accord with events in international relations from the 1930s through the Soviet-U.S. cold war. Hitler, Mussolini, the Japanese imperialists, and Stalin, among others, including Saddam Hussein, seemed to confirm the foundational premise that the political being is driven by an impulse to maximize power. As political morality, realism fit with the times of World War II and then the cold war, as the democratic nations most certainly, and probably the Soviet Union as well, had no difficulty in justifying not just the deaths of soldiers but even the firebombing and nuclear bombing of civilian centers in the name of the greater good of preserving one's nation.

And there was no doubt that nation-states possessed most of the military and economic power in the world and employed it in pursuit of perceived national interest.

Because of the resulting predominance of realism in the American study of international relations, international law and individual human rights became marginal to that study. Given the dominant prism of realism, human rights was associated with a naive idealism. To focus on human rights as defined by international law was to retreat to the time of Woodrow Wilson, if not before, when analysis of legal structure substituted for analysis of power relations. This meant, among other things, that how human rights interacted with the exercise of influence, how human rights affected the rise and fall of governments, if not states, was consigned to the margins of American political science. Human rights, mostly implicitly, was considered outside the scope of national interest, with no significant role in international politics.

This is not the place for a complete discourse on human rights and realism. If, as empirical analysis shows, democratic states do not make war on other democracies, then attention to civil and political rights is not a reflection of mere sentiment but rather attention to one of the crucial factors affecting peace and war.[4] If, as impirical analysis shows, perception of relative deprivation can at times contribute to intra- and international violence,[5] then attention to broad range of human rights, socioeconomic as well as civil-political, can deepen our understanding of domestic political stability as well as of interstate behavior. There is no valid reason for viewing human rights as beyond the bounds of national interest or political calculation, and therefore no reason for viewing human rights as a moralistic and legalistic subject divorced from the proper study of power and public policy.[6]

As an empirical matter, in certain times and places, states have included a concern for human rights within their conceptions of national interest. They have in effect said that not all aspects of international relations can be treated as an unbridled attempt to maximize state power. As an empirical matter, in some eras, states have made room for individual human rights, saying in effet that political morality involves not just the preservation of the state but the pursuit of individual human dignity as well. As an empirical matter, most states in contemporary times have given consent for the creation, operation, and authority of nonstate actors in order to promote and protect human rights on an international scale. Thus influence and even authority have come to be shared by state and nonstate actors.

While realism may have been and may still be an appropriate approach—philosophical, moral, and analytical—for a given circumstance, it is by no means sufficient for all types of international relations across different eras. If realism was appropriate for the 1930s and 1940s, that does not mean that its postulates necessarily fit with the international relations of the great powers in the 1990s. Recognition of this point has given rise to efforts trying to distinguish different types of international politics, one of which has been termed a situation of complex interdependence.[7] In this latter situation, the agenda of international politics goes far beyond the high politics of war and national security to include extensively the low politics of socioeconomic subjects; military power does not predominate over other forms of exercising influence; states may not seek to maximize unilateral power but may both cooperate extensively and be content with maintaining rather than extending power; and nonstate actors, including international organizations, may be influential in coordinating international action to reduce transaction costs.

Despite the development of new schools of thought such as complex interdependence, one effect of realism's hegemony in the American study of international relations remains the marginality of human rights studies. Even those who developed the idea of complex interdependence as a type of international relations different from "realistic" international politics have been more interested in economics than human rights. There has been little analysis of how complex interdependence should inform the analysis of the promotion and protection of human rights.

The rise of crude behavioralism compounded the screening out of human rights factors. If the realist attack on idealism constituted the first grand debate in the American study of international relations, the behavioralist attack on traditionalism constituted the second. In the 1950s and 1960s, the growing use of computers in social science analysis, and the accompanying development of refined methodologies to guide their use, led to a widespread attack on nonquantitative studies of politics. Even in the 1990s, some political science departments were known to enforce a doctrinaire view that all faculty members were expected to utilize data-based or statistical analyses. Those studies seeking precise information and understanding but not relying on a science of numbers were criticized in these departments for not being sufficiently scientific. The behavioralist tradition, defined as the statistical study of political behavior, did not seem to lend itself easily to most studies of human rights. Crude behavioralism, defined as an emphasis on a rigorous science of numbers to the exclusion of other approaches, compounded the problem of screening out adequate attention to human rights in international relations.

Almost by definition, human rights seemed to entail more value judgment than numerical measurement. If human rights were most fundamentally moral rights, inherent in the person by virtue of moral integrity,[8] this was seen by some as falling more in the realm of ethics and philosophy than data-based political science. If human rights were trump legal rights, this was seen by some as falling in the domain of traditional law. If the proper implementation of rights depended on such things as historical tradition, cultural diversity, or stage of economic development, then how could this be analyzed by multiple regression analysis, path analysis, or any other sophisticated social science methodology? "Mainstream" American political science, oriented to counting votes or counting opinions uncovered in questionnaires, had great difficulty in accommodating the subject matter of human rights, especially human rights in foreign policy and international relations.

I am distinguishing between behavioralism and crude behavioralism, between use of statistics as the science of numbers and a sole emphasis on that science. There is no doubt that statistical studies can be useful, but there is also no doubt that there are many and formidable problems to an extensive, much less sole, use of statistics in human rights studies.[9]

For several decades, the private organization Freedom House has ranked nations around the world on a scale of 1 to 7 for civil and political rights.[10] Political scientists developed other, more complex scales to try to measure civil and political rights in a different way. While not utilizing the language of rights, the Overseas Development Council, based in Washington, D.C., created the Physical Quality of Life Index.[11] Measuring such things as longevity, literacy, and infant mortality, it compared nations in such a way as to permit a judgment about implementation of such internationally recognized rights as a right to adequate nutrition, to adequate health, and to education. Progressively into the 1980s, some political scientists developed statistical techniques for correlating human rights performance with such things as national foreign assistance.[12] A lively debate developed over the use of statistical analysis for insights into human rights situations, with books and special issues of journals devoted to the question.[13] There was no doubt that some insights into internationally recognized human rights could be gained from statistical approaches.[14]

The central point is not that the use of statistics is inappropriate to all studies of international human rights but rather that the statistical approach is a limited means to understanding a subject matter whose central features call for normative choice—how to blend human rights with security and economic values, or how to evaluate how much human rights progress is enough to justify resumed foreign assistance. It is highly unlikely there will ever be "scientific" and data-based answers to such central questions. Thus human rights studies were dismissed as marginal to the development of a scientific political science by the crude behavioralists.

I wish to emphasize the difference between behavioralism and crude behavioralism—the difference, respectively, between use of statistics where appropriate as a means to understanding and the doctrinaire use of statistics to define what should be studied. One could rigorously quantify, as part of formal theories, some studies dealing with strategic policy if they were based on patterns of military spending. One could rigorously quantify trade patterns and all sorts of financial data encompassed in the international political economy.

But it has proved extremely difficult to use a true science of numbers to get at key issues in the domain of human rights. Should the United States push for human rights in Lithuania in the context of a decreasing Soviet security threat to the Western nations? Should it push for greater human rights in China at a time when it wants Beijing's help in curtailing arms races in the Middle East and creating a new government in Cambodia? What was the impact on human rights of the United Nations and the OAS? These and other important questions about political behavior and influence do not lend themselves easily to the new methodologies and machines of quantitative analysis, and thus most human rights studies dealing with such important questions are dismissed as being too traditional by the crude behavioralists.

If political realism screened out human rights as sentiment, crude behavioralism saw concern with human rights as unscientific. If realism failed to account for concern with human rights in the real conceptions of national interest extant in the world, so crude behavioralism overlooked how human rights affected behavior. Nothing was more unreal than to argue that human rights concerns had no impact on power. Nothing was more unscientific than to argue that concern for human rights did not affect behavior, even though that concern and its results could not always be numerically measured in rigorous fashion.

A third tradition of American political science doomed studies of human rights to the margins of the discipline: the tradition of grand theory building. Far more so than for other fields of political science, international relations has long been influenced by those in search of macrotheory. Among political scientists focusing on international relations, for at least three decades that field has been characterized by pursuit of grand theory and essays decrying the poverty of that theoretical pursuit.[15]

I am not in favor of only descriptive case studies limited to one situation and time frame, although such studies have their uses. Moreover, insights have been gained into such general subjects as the reasons for the rise and decline of nation-states in world history. For example, I take it as proved that, at least in the past, the states that have been able to construct dominant economies have been able also to construct dominant military establishments that through victories in war have allowed them to play a decisive role in international relations for a time.[16] These great powers then decline either because the cost of remaining a great power saps the economic system that allowed them to attain that status (this is Paul Kennedy's "imperial overstretch") or consumer spending leads to the same effect (this is Samuel Huntington's rebuttal to Kennedy).[17]

Whether this type of analysis can be called rigorous theory may be a matter of semantical dispute. To me, this type of study seems less like formal theory and more like interpreting diplomatic history over time. The point of interest for present purposes lies not in an endorsement of systematic interpretation of historical pattern but rather in a critique of the largely barren quest for a grand theory purporting to explain with scientific rigor the workings of the world.

In the past, graduate students have been made to wade through decision-making theory, general systems theory, and other examples of formal-rigorous theory building on a grand scale.[18] While required reading for their day, they failed to provide useful insights into actual policies and situations. They have been abandoned by subsequent generations of students and scholars. It was as if creativity per se merited publication rather than helpful analysis, although one can always argue that new ideas should be tried until proved deficient.

Other concepts proved more useful, such as transnational relations or regimes. But these were not theories; rather, they were static, nondynamic constructs useful for organizing information. But by no means were they able to explain, in and of themselves, the international exercise of influence in behalf of public policy.[19] Particularly regime theory is unable to explain why states consent to principles, rules, and policymaking institutions for the regulation of an issue or issue area. Rather, it is a set of concepts helpful in organizing an analysis of the outcomes of national foreign policy, without being able to say anything about why states create and maintain, or not, the regimes they do.

I do not contest the desire for more general understanding as opposed to limited description. I find useful such questions as: Do we know anything in principle (or in theory) about manipulation of national foreign assistance and implementation of human rights norms? If these sorts of commonsense questions add up to middle-range theories, I have no quibble with pursuit of knowledge on that scale. I do continue to wonder about what is a useful approach to understanding and what is intellectual faddism. For example, at one time, if American political scientists were to publish in certain journals on the subject of the integration of nations in Europe, it had to be within the confines of functionalism or neofunctional theory; then suddenly that framework disappeared from the intellectual map. One was left wondering what was improved understanding of political behavior and what was academic faddism.

The study of human rights does not lend itself to macrotheory since it covers a broad process of interdisciplinary nature. Especially as internationally defined, human rights encompasses civil, political, economic, social, cultural, legal, historical, philosophical, and other phenomena in an untidy mix. While parts of the study of human rights have long concerned those seeking general understanding—the requisites for stable democracy—other parts seemed unlikely candidates for general theory. For example, the rise of ethnic violence in Sri Lanka, closing a period of not only stable democracy but also economic growth with equity, was more likely to be explained by knowledge of Sri Lanka than by a grand theory of ethnic politics. The fate of human rights in Sri Lanka, whether civil-political or socioeconomic, did not seem a likely candidate for explanation by general theory, although I would not rule out some increased understanding about the relationship between intranational violence and human rights violations.

This book has demonstrated that one can apply certain concepts to the study of human rights—concepts like regimes, political socialization, and hegemonic leadership. But in all the literature published on human rights in the last two decades, there is virtually no indication that a grand theory of human rights is on the horizon.[20] This makes the subject matter suspect to those influential political scientists preoccupied with macrotheory building in international relations.

The lack of emphasis on human rights by political scientists interested in international relations, because of an intellectual hegemony comprised of political realism, crude behavioralism, and grand theorizing, has been accompanied by the same result in law faculties but for different reasons. For law faculties, the central problem is that most American law schools are essentially vocational schools and hence not designed for the general study of law in society. This is in marked contrast to the teaching of law in Western Europe, where it is part of the general educational requirement in universities. In Western Europe, law is not treated solely as an advanced subject for career specialists as it is in U.S. law schools, where the emphasis is on torts, contracts, civil procedure, and the other technical subjects, which, in the words of one law professor, constitute the equivalent of auto mechanics.[21]

In most American law schools, public international law is a marginal elective, available in the second or third year of study but certainly not emphasized. (In Western European universities, it is not uncommon to find public international law as a required course in the first or third year of general education requirements.) In the United States there are very few practicing lawyers in public international law. International human rights law, as a subsidiary of public international law, is a still more esoteric elective. Only a handful of lawyers in the United States actually practice human rights law from an international orientation. This means that law schools that offer more than passing attention to internationally recognized human rights are rare indeed. Law schools at Columbia University, the University of Cincinnati, the University of Virginia, New York University, and perhaps a few more do so. To the extent that law schools teach much international law, they emphasize the private international law of economic transactions. This is the kind of international law that is practiced by firms, and thus this is the orientation of American law schools as trade schools.[22]

Therefore because of different reasons, American political scientists and law professors have not kept pace with changes in international relations. Acedemic traditions, sometimes fed by commercial pressures, giving rise to intellectual hegemonies have retarded the perception that human rights matter in world affairs.

New Perceptions

There is some indication that political science, at least, may be catching up with the human rights changes that have so clearly occurred in international relations. James Rosenau, one of the leading theorists of the discipline over the past three decades, has authored a book in which he writes of the importance of micropolitics and in which he tries to separate, at least for analytical purposes, private from public politics.[23] He admits that he does not know what the many changes in international relations add up to in systemic terms. He emphasizes change by referring to postinternational politics and also what he calls turbulence, by which he means that the changes in international relations have caused some sort of transformation of the old international or global political system but without being consolidated yet into a discernible new system. Thus the structure—the fundamental characteristics or properties—of global politics is not what it was but not definitively something new. This is a stimulating, if not always satisfying, new view of international relations that emphasizes, in part, individual and private foci, if not consistently individual rights.

Other theorists such as George Modelski and Theodore N. Von Laue likewise stress change in international relations but with more explicit attention to some internationally recognized human rights. Modelski focuses on the replacement of war as the determinant of long cycles of influence by great powers.[24] He does not stipulate what exactly replaces war as the new determinant in the rise and fall of great powers but rathr argues for multiple causation with new political agendas for individual nations and for the international system as a whole. In stressing the concept of national learning (industrialized and especially democratic nations have learned to avoid war among themselves), he is led into a discussion of human rights, especially the civil and political rights related to democracy.

Von Laue, in a broad historical analysis, argues that the Westernization of the world has entailed, among other things, an emphasis on human rights.[25] His discussion of global politics at the end of the twentieth century emphasizes three clusters of issues: state power; the new agenda items of international community building such as trade, finance, scientific research, disaster relief, the environment; and human rights. The latter subject he considers the softest, or most difficult, to analyze precisely.

These studies seem to be prototypes of new perspectives, at least in American political science, that hold the promise of more adequate attention to internationally recognized human rights. Some authors who were concerned with international order or with international justice had, of course, written about human rights. What seems to be occurring now is that general theorists interested not in order or justice per se but rather in the patterns and structures of international relations are recognizing the importance of internationally recognized human rights.

I doubt, however, that there will be widespread agreement on some of the central propositions offered. Early reactions to Rosenau's typically creative and provocative approach make it likely that it will be seen by several as overstating the extent of change in international relations. While offering some new terminology, it may fail to convince that many of the old structures have really changed.[26]

For example, one question refers to patterns of authority, a subject central to any discussion of any political system. In the 1990s patterns of authority in the world—and the political views that sustain them—are changing somewhat but in global perspective remain statecentric. There has been change but not fundamental change, on balance. There has been change within the overall system but not structural change in the system itself.[27]

While individuals and their private groups have been granted more authority to act in world affairs and while private individuals and their groups do act, states still retain controlling authority to facilitate or retard that private action (whether individual or group) for human rights. It is states acting in ECOSOC that decide which private groups shall have consultative status with the United Nations; it is states that dispose of private human rights petitions in the U.N. Human Rights Commission. Some of the most assertive human rights private groups are still denied consultative status by states, and U.N. agencies still lack the usable authority to enforce or compel states to follow international human rights norms. Thus within intergovernmental organizations, it is still states that control, and they establish and use authority with a fundamental interest in national prerogatives.[28] While there is increased attention to human rights in world politics and while this attention has weakened the play of national sovereignty, this evolution has transpired without replacement of state authority as the central legal feature of international relations.[29] Increased attention to human rights has been accompanied for the most part by consolidation of the legitimacy of state authority, although the exercise of that authority has been affected by human rights values.

It is true that intergovernmental organizations have the potential to exercise decisive authority in behalf of human rights. But not only does the entire process hinge on state policy. Also such authoritative action remains very much the exception rather than the rule. The World Court can give binding judgments on human rights, but it has not because states have not allowed human rights disputes to be supranationally adjudicated. The U.N. Security Council can declare human rights violations a threat to the peace, can mandate change, and can require sanctions in support of its position. This existing authority by the Security Council hinges on state cooperation for its activization, and because of that reason, when combined with other factors, has not been used very often. Even with talk of the end of the cold war and of increased superpower and great power cooperation, state policies have not yet changed much concerning the transfer of independent authority to international organizations. Patterns of authority reflect state predominance and the value of state prerogatives, even if coexisting uneasily with newer values such as human rights.

Admittedly the situation in Western Europe is different. There, state policy does reflect a new perspective and a new (if limited) shift in political values and loyalties. The European Convention on Human Rights can be, and frequently is, interpreted in a supranational process in which the ultimate interpretation is made by an international court comprised of individual experts rather than state representatives. It is true that states remain the building blocks of the sponsoring Council of Europe and that state cooperation is necessary for the creation, implementation, and enforcement of human rights norms.

The point to be stressed, however, is that the situation in Western Europe is thus far exceptional with regard to international relations. Most of the rest of the world has not seen the same willingness of national decision makers to limit their freedom of decision by international authority. This is especially clear with regard to the Western Hemisphere. Authority patterns in most of the world remain traditional: preferential to national rather than supranational authority and to states as a supreme value apart from competing values such as human rights (or environmental protection). Some aspects of micro- and macropolitics may have changed globally, but authority patterns have not. There has been increased internationalization of human rights, but states remain the most important factor in that process.

When Rosenau writes of the greater political skills of individuals, it is not completely clear what he means. Most individuals, even the educated ones in the open societies of the industrialized democracies, are not part of the attentive public interested in foreign policy and international relations, and they do not act consistently in international politics. As Stephen Krasner has argued persuasively, while international transactions have increased relative to the past, national transactions have increased at a much faster pace, leaving international transactions as perhaps weaker as influential factors relative to national factors.[30] A small number of individuals may be acting more in international relations, on the basis of more cosmopolitan values and loyalties, but this does not seem to be true of large numbers of citizens. What counts is not learning per se, as measured in UNESCO figures on education, but political learning as manifested in political attitudes. It is political learning and political skills that affect the structure of international relations, especially authority patterns.

Apart from the exceptional enclave again of Western Europe, there is little evidence that nationalism, national loyalties, and national politics have been altered in fundamental ways in most of the world. When, for example, the U.S. president declares the unilateral use of force to be necessary, the Pavlovian response of popular nationalism is still as strong as ever in the short run, as proved by recent U.S. invasions of Grenada and Panama. Condemnation of such invasions by the U.N. General Assembly and/or OAS, based on correct interpretations of international law, were consigned to oblivion by traditional political factors within the U.S.[31] At least for the moment, Rosenau's data on, for example, higher levels of education on the part of the globe's citizenry should not suggest any transformation of world politics. While the trend for education may point upward and while this may be significant in the long run, for the moment dominant political loyalties remain unaltered, especially between national and supranational choices. Other data show increased participation in international affairs by cities and states as well as by private individuals and groups, but this participation and the more cosmopolitan views that frequently accompany it have not yet signaled a change in authority patterns.[32] Dominant political views and actions remain traditional, although change is, of course, possible.

Some of the more powerful changes in the world are parochial rather than cosmopolitan and reflect a resurgence of ignorance and hate rather than an increase of international tolerance and understanding as based on higher levels of education. The resurgence of subnational group orientation in the Soviet Union and the Balkans, as well as in other parts of the world, has already led to genocidal attacks. This weakening of national authority in favor of here to fore subnational authority may indicate nothing more than the continuing strength of exclusive nationalism but with a smaller and more cohesive definition of the nation. The demand that prevails over time may be for more, more exclusive, and more virulent nation-states. It is difficult to say what the future holds, for while Western Europe manifests a trend in favor of international integration of existing states in a larger authority, trends in other parts of the world manifest contrary patterns.

There are changes in international relations, but they do not add up to a different structure of global international relations, at least in terms of authority patterns and the political views that sustain them. Such structural changes may emerge in the future, and we may be witnessing their very early manifestations, but for the most part, international relations remains a nation-state system, somewhat modified by both intergovernmental and private transnational organizations. Within the nation-state system, there is more attention to human rights. There is more international action on human rights, with action understood to include diplomatic promotion as well as various forms of protection (implementation and enforcement). But it is still states that retain most formal authority and also most power (influence).

There are also problems with Modelski's interesting new theoretical writings. When Modelski builds his neo-Kantian theory of international relations around the concept of learning and presents this as the new key feature of world politics, learning constitutes an expansive concept encompassing anything and everything. Modelski argues that it is learning, not anarchy (derived from national sovereignty) or war, that is the central and defining characteristic of world politics. Change (or the lack thereof) results from learning (or not learning) something.

But this still leaves open the prior question of what accounts for learning (or its lack). Learning consists of perceptions and resulting behavior, but this is too large a process to yield many specific insights. To answer the question of why most Americans have not learned to give up nationalism, I find myself dealing with the traditional subject matter of political socialization. To answer the question of why the Iraqi government has not learned the folly of arms races and brutally militaristic policies, one has to go back to the traditional subjects of threat perception, quest for national prestige, and personal megalomania. And if learning the benefits of democracy is the key for international peace and stability, how do we account for the difficulties democracies encounter outside the culture of the North Atlantic area (and related areas such as Australia and New Zealand)? How do we account for the "unlearning" of democracy repeatedly in so many Western Hemispheric nations in the Southern Hemisphere, not to mention in other parts of the world as well? These questions can be answered only by delving into traditional subject matter such as requisites for stable democracy.

Modelski's new theory is useful as an organizing device to systematize discussion. But his "learning," like Morgenthau's "national interest," is too amorphous a concept to provide much precise guidance. The concept of learning turns out to be another layer of language, below which one must return to traditional and perplexing subjects. At a certain level of analysis, the improved implementation of human rights depends on more widespread learning of the notion that individuals have rights and it is the duty of public authorities to protect them. But the concept of learning itself does not tell us why this notion was practically learned—implemented—first in the North Atlantic area and why that process of learning human rights values has proved so difficult in, say, the nations of Islamic culture. For precise analysis, one has to return to the historical and cultural factors feeding into particular political cultures.[33]

In my view, macrotheories of international relations, whether they revolve around turbulence, a bifurcation of micro- and macropolitics, or learning, do not add great clarity to understanding international relations, especially as it encompasses international human rights. Although each theorist usually provides some helpful insights for understanding part of international relations, the sum of these theories is usually less than isolated parts of the whole. The situation is not advanced by developing a poststructural or postmodern philosophy calling into question observation of events and attitudes.[34] As K.J. Holsti has argued, "There is no foundation of theory superior to a keen understanding of the facts of international relations, past and present."[35] It is therefore not surprising that recent and major contributions to understanding international relations have been based on observation of empirical patterns over time and that authors like Paul Kennedy and Robert Gilpin are very well read in history.

For some 300 years, international relations has been a nation-state system in which most authority and power, and the political attitudes and loyalties that affect them, have been put at the service of national prerogatives and national prestige. There have been partial alterations of this nation-state system of international relations in different eras because of colonialism, empire, intergovernmental organization, or transnational ideology (which proves frequently a mask for nationalism, whether one speaks of Marxism and Soviet-Russian nationalism or Shiism and Iranian nationalism). But the overall structure of international relations has been best captured in the concept of nation-state system linked to national competition for power and prestige. This has not been fundamentally altered, although other values have been joined to those associated with the nation-state. Thus one can see a significant modification of the nation-state system in the addition of competing values such as human rights, but the authority patterns of the system remain mostly statecentric, reflecting the still-powerful pull of nationalism.

Two aspects of international relations have changed in significant ways, even as the legal and political structure of the overall system remains mostly or fundamentally the same. (Not only do patterns of authority favor the nation-state but also patterns of power.) First, the range of legitimate values pursued through foreign policy has increased. There are growing expectations that state authority in world affairs, while still valued in and of itself by most politically aware persons, should be exercised with regard for attention to human rights (and environmental protection). Second, the scope of the international political system has increased. Individuals, private groups, and intergovernmental organizations all participate in world politics to a relatively greater extent.

These two changes can be demonstrated by reference to the United States and El Salvador in the 1980s and early 1990s. The United States considered a noncommunist government in El Salvador to be in its national interest: no more Cuban-model states. But pursuit of this state-to-state policy was affected by growing expectations, in the Congress and in significant parts of American public opinion, that U.S. foreign policy toward El Salvador had to include a human rights component. Simple pursuit of U.S. security through material and diplomatic assistance to the government and military of El Salvador was deemed insufficient by important parts of the U.S. policymaking process. Over time a concern for human rights, distinct from but linked to security policy, came to be a feature of U.S. policy toward El Salvador. A relatively larger amount of U.S. time and money was directed to such matters as reducing the operation of death squads linked to the state's army and trying to increase the operation of independent courts. There was some attention to land reform, health care, medical neutrality, and other subjects falling under the concept of human rights in peacetime or armed conflict. The official goal of U.S. policy became the creation and support of not just any noncommunist government in San Salvador but one committed to internationally recognized human rights.

In this pursuit, any number of nongovernmental organizations and private individuals were active in a transnational process. The ICRC, Americas Watch, and AI were three of the better-known human rights groups that took an active interest in the situation in El Salvador. Lesser-known groups such as the Commission for Medical Neutrality and the Humanitarian Law Project were also active on selected human rights issues. All of them, and all nonpartisan, were political actors in the sense of trying to mobilize parts of Salvadoran and U.S. societies to support their human rights concerns. All of them tried to make contact with influential persons in the two nations in order to circulate their information and enlist support for human rights. National frontiers and visa requirements had to be observed, but the political process was a transnational one. Lobbying, de facto and otherwise, occurred across national boundaries. The Commission for Medical Neutrality, based in Washington, linked up with a member of Congress in order to try to generate influence on both the U.S. executive and the Salvadoran military.

Intergovernmental international organizations were also involved with El Salvador. The U.N. Human Rights Commission appointed a special rapporteur to report on the human rights situation in that country, and both Washington and San Salvador had to deal with his creation, terms of reference, report, reappointment, and related factors that affected the legitimacy of the government of El Salvador and the reputation of U.S. policy. The Inter-American Commission on Human Rights also paid attention to the human rights situation in El Salvador, both through its country reports and its handling of private petitions.

The scope of the political process was large concerning the international relations between the U.S. and El Salvador. Whereas as late as the interwar years of 1919–1939 such relations were dominated by government-to-government relations of a traditional sort, by the 1980s there were two new features: human rights values were a central part of the process, and nonstate actors, both private and public, were deeply involved and generated some influence, although that influence is difficult to measure precisely.

It remained true, however, that the most important decisions were taken in Washington and in San Salvador by state officials. There was no decision maker, no would-be policymaker who could substitute for national decision makers in the two countries. No U.N. or OAS official, and certainly no private person, could replace U.S. and Salvadoran officials. The process was one of trying to influence national decision makers, not substitute for them.

The process remained statecentric at the same time that nonstate values—human rights—and nonstate actors (both public and private) played larger roles. This situation was typical of international relations in general.

Final Thoughts

There is no theory, and especially no macrotheory, for understanding the internationalization of human rights in all its dimensions, and there never will be. There is no computer program or no mathematical formula that can encompass the complex political process central to the recognition and implementation of human rights norms on a global scale, and there never will be. While limited range theory and quantitative analysis can surely shed light on some aspects of human rights, in general there is no substitute for non-quantitative analysis on a less-than-macro basis of human rights situations and relationships.

Analysis of internationally recognized human rights, and their implementation, is aided by recalling at least five rules of thumb, which can fruitfully guide analysis.

1. Most important decisions are still made by national public authority. National authority may be, and usually is, fragmented or divided. Some important decisions may be made by legislatures or courts rather than executives. One may need to take note of factions within executives. But national authorities retain most authority and power regarding universal human rights. Much analysis should be focused at this level.

2. Private persons and groups can be influential at the margins, and more rarely at the center, of human rights policies. Nongovernmental organizations can exercise influence as sources of information and as mobilizers of sympathetic opinion, whether mass or elite. If protection of human rights most fundamentally depends on the learning of values, analysts should not overlook the role of those who consistently emphasize some variation of the idea of human rights.

3. General intergovernmental organizations have increased their activity in the human rights domain, and they may have some long-term influence on international relations. Most remain weak, however, in terms of short-term protection, usually referred to as enforcement. Nevertheless, they have devised a number of initiatives in order to contribute to implementing universal human rights.

4. Most overall situations, and most human rights matters, are intermestic. There is an international dimension, perhaps consisting of appeals to international standards or action by an international or transnational organization. Key elements remain domestic, such as the decisions of national

authorities, the role of opposition groups, and the status of national public opinion. The human rights situation evolves from this intermestic play of factors.

5. Human rights has become broadly important in contemporary international relations. In historical perspective, the changes of the last fifty years constitute an incremental revolution in the nature of international relations. Within the extent and resilient modified nation-state system, the broadly defined rights of persons matter as never before. Concern for human rights is intertwined with concern for state security, economic health, and a sound environment. Human rights has arrived as one of the major subjects of world affairs.

Notes

1. David P. Forsythe, *Human Rights and World Politics,* rev. 2d ed. (Lincoln: University of Nebraska Press, 1989), 7–10.

2. See Robert O. Keohane, "Realism, Neorealism and the Study of World Politics," in Keohane, ed., *Neorealism and Its Critics* (New York: Columbia University Press, 1986), 1–27.

3. The key work is Hans Morgenthau, *Scientific Man vs. Power Politics* (Chicago: University of Chicago Press, Midway Reprint, 1974).

4. Michael Doyle, "Liberalism and World Politics," *American Political Science Review* 80, 4 (December 1986): 1151–70.

5. Ted Robert Gurr, *Why Men Rebel* (Princeton: Princeton University Press, 1970).

6. Rogers M. Smith, "Morality, Humanitarianism, and Foreign Policy: A Purposive View," in Bruce Nichols and Gil Loescher, eds., *The Moral Nation: Humanitarianism and U.S. Foreign Policy Today* (Notre Dame, Ind.: University of Notre Dame Press, 1989), 41–62.

7. See Robert O. Keohane and Joseph Nye, *Power and Interdependence,* 2d ed. (Glenview, Ill.: Scott, Foresman, 1989).

8. See, Jack Donnelly, *Universal Human Rights* (Ithaca, N.Y.: Cornell University Press, 1989).

9. See the convincing essay by Robert Justin Goldstein, "The Limitations of Using Quantitative Data in Studying Human Rights Abuses," *Human Rights Quarterly* 8, 4 (November 1986): 607–28.

10. See Raymond D. Gastil, ed., *Freedom in the World* (Westport, Conn.: Greenwood Press, annual).

11. The PQLI is applied to the analysis of human rights in David P. Forsythe, "Human Rights and Development: A Concluding View," in Forsythe, ed., *Human Rights and Development: International Views* (London: Macmillan; New York: St. Martin's, 1989), 349–69.

12. See David Carleton and Michael Stohl, "The Foreign Policy of Human Rights: Rhetoric and Reality from Jimmy Carter to Ronald Reagan," *Human Rights*

Quarterly 7, 2 (May 1985): 205–29; and David Cingranelli and Thomas Pasquarello, "Human Rights Practices and the Distribution of U.S. Foreign Aid to Latin American Countries," *American Journal of Political Science* 29, 3 (August 1985): 540–63.

13. See David Louis Cingranelli, *Human Rights: Theory and Measurement* (New York: St. Martin's 1988); and Richard P. Claude and Thomas B. Jabine, "Statistical Issues in the Field of Human Rights," *Human Rights Quarterly* 8, 4 (November 1986): 551–699.

14. David P. Forsythe, "US Economic Assistance and Human Rights," in Forsythe, ed., *Human Rights and Development: International Views* (London: Macmillan 1989), 171–95.

15. See the symposium by six authors in "Exchange on the 'Third Debate,'" *International Studies Quarterly* 33, 3 (September 1989): 235–328.

16. See especially Paul Kennedy, *The Rise and Fall of the Great Powers: Economic Change and Military Conflict From 1500 to 2000* (New York: Random House, 1987), and Robert Gilpin, *War and Change in World Politics* (Cambridge: Cambridge University Press, 1983).

17. In addition to Kennedy, *Rise and Fall of Great Powers,* see Samuel P. Huntington, "The U.S.—Decline or Renewal?" *Foreign Affairs* 67, 2 (Winter 1988–1989): 76–96.

18. For an overview, see James E. Dougherty and Robert L. Pfaltzgraff, Jr., eds., *Contending Theories of International Relations,* 2d ed. (New York: Harper & Row, 1981).

19. See Robert O. Keohane and Joseph S. Nye, "Power and Interdependence Revisited," *International Organization* 41, 4 (Autumn 1987): 725–53.

20. A reviewer in *Foreign Affairs* 69, 2, (Spring 1990): 168, referred to Jack Donnelly's *Universal Human Rights* as a theory. This is debatable. What Donnelly does is to define human rights analytically as moral rights, to relate moral rights to legal rights, to show how there can be universal human rights in a multicultural world, to argue that most human rights can be implemented despite different economic situations, and to argue for priority to national rather than international action. This useful study, based largely on personal insights into empirical patterns does not constitute a macro- or even middle-range theory explaining why certain actors do or do not acknowledge and/or implement international human rights.

21. Francis A. Boyle, book review, *American Journal of International Law* 83, 2 (April 1989): 403.

22. The American Society of International Law carried out a study of the teaching of international law during 1989–1991. Some of the results will be published in the *American Journal of International Law* when available.

23. James N. Rosenau, *Turbulence in World Politics* (Princeton: Princeton University Press, 1990).

24. George Modelski, "Is World Politics Evolutionary Learning?" *International Organization* 44, 1 (Winter 1990): 1–24.

25. Theodore H. von Laue, *The World Revolution of Westernization: The Twentieth Century in Global Perspective* (Oxford: Oxford University Press, 1987).

26. Some of Rosenau's views have already been published and have already provoked disagreement. See Ernst-Otto Czempiel and James N. Rosenau, eds., *Global Changes and Theoretical Challenges: Approaches to World Politics for the 1990s* (Lexington, Mass.: Lexington Books, 1989).

27. On the important difference between systemic and intrasystemic change, see Gilpin, *War and Change*.

28. I do not accept the view that the practice of majority voting within the U.N. signifies great inroads on state sovereignty and great advances for international authority. On important questions of national security, the veto in the Security Council controls, and on other important questions like financing, an informal veto has replaced majority voting in the General Assembly. See, however, Lawrence S. Finkelstein, ed., *Politics in the United Nations System* (Durham, N.C.: Duke University Press, 1988).

29. The point is well made in R.J. Vincent, *Human Rights and International Relations* (Cambridge: Cambridge University Press, 1986).

30. See Janice E. Thomson and Stephen D. Krasner, "Global Transactions and the Consolidation of Sovereignty," in Czempiel and Rosenau, *Global Changes and Theoretical Challenges,* 195–220.

31. For detailed analysis, see David P. Forsythe, *The Politics of International Law: U.S. Foreign Policy Reconsidered* (Boulder, Colo.: Lynne Rienner Pub. Co., 1990).

32. Chadwick Alger, "U.S. Public Opinion on the U.N.: A Mandate for More Creative U.S. Participation in the U.N. System?" (paper presented at the International Studies Association annual convention, April 1990, Washington, D.C.).

33. See further Forsythe, *Human Rights and Development*.

34. See especially James Der Derian and Michael J. Shapiro, *International/ Intertextual Relations: Postmodern Readings of World Politics* (Lexington, Mass.: Lexington Books, 1989).

35. Holsti, "Exchange on the 'Third Debate,' " 261.

Appendix:
Researching Basic Sources
on Human Rights

Basic Compendia and Commentary

Brownlie, Ian, ed. *Basic Documents on Human Rights*. 3d ed. Oxford: Oxford University Press, 1989.

Council of Europe. *Human Rights in International Law: Basic Texts*. Strasbourg, France: Council of Europe, 1985.

Franck, Thomas M. *Human Rights in Third World Perspective*. 3 vols. Dobbs Ferry, N.Y.: Oceana, 1982.

Joyce, James Avery, ed. *Human Rights International Documents*. 2 vols. Dobbs Ferry, N.Y.: Oceana Publications, 1978.

Laqueur, Walter, and Rubin, Barry, eds., *The Human Rights Reader*. New York: New American Library, Meridian, 1990.

Lawson, Edward H. *Encyclopaedia of Human Rights*. New York: Taylor and Francis, 1990.

Lillich, Richard B., ed. *International Human Rights Instruments: A Compilation*. New York: William S. Hein & Co., 1983, with periodic supplements.

Sieghart, Paul. *The International Law of Human Rights*. Oxford: Oxford University Press, 1985.

Sohn, Louis B., and Buergenthal, Thomas. *Basic Documents on International Protection of Human Rights*. New York: Bobbs-Merrill, 1973, with periodic supplements.

United Nations. *Compilation of Human Rights Instruments*. Publication Sales No. E-88, ST/HR/1. Geneva: United Nations, 1988.

U.S. Congress. Committee on Foreign Affairs. *Human Rights Documents*. Washington, D.C.: Government Printing Office, 1983.

General Commentary

Buergenthal, Thomas. *International Human Rights*. St. Paul, Minn.: West, 1988.

Claude, Richard, and Weston, Burns, eds. *Human Rights in the World Community: Issues and Action*. Philadelphia: University of Pennsylvania Press, 1989.

Dominguez, Jorge, et al. *Enhancing Global Human Rights.* New York: McGraw-Hill, for the Council on Foreign Affairs, 1979.

Donnelly, Jack. *Universal Human Rights.* Ithaca, N.Y.: Cornell University Press, 1989.

Donnelly, Jack, and Howard, Rhoda, eds. *International Handbook on Human Rights.* Westport, Conn.: Greenwood Press, 1987.

Forsythe, David P. *Human Rights and World Politics.* 2d ed. Lincoln: University of Nebraska Press, 1989.

Glaser, Kurt, and Possony, Stefan. *Victims of Politics: The State of Human Rights.* New York: Columbia University Press, 1979.

Henkin, Louis. *The Rights of Man Today.* Boulder, Colo.: Westview, 1978.

———, ed. *The International Bill of Rights.* New York: Columbia University Press, 1981.

Joyce, James Avery. *The New Politics of Human Rights.* New York: St. Martin's, 1979.

Meron, Theodor, ed. *Human Rights in International Law: Legal and Policy Issues.* Oxford: Clarendon Press, 1984.

Nanda, Ved, ed. *Global Human Rights.* Boulder, Colo.: Westview, 1981.

Newberg, Paula, ed. *The Politics of Human Rights.* New York: NYU Press, 1981.

Ramcharan, B.G. *The Concept and Present Status of the International Protection of Human rights.* Dordrecht: Kluwer, 1989.

———. *Human Rights.* Boston: Nijhoff, 1979.

Robertson, A.H. *Human Rights in the World.* 2d ed. New York: St. Martin's, 1982.

Sieghart, Paul. *The International Law of Human Rights.* Oxford: Oxford University Press, 1985.

Tutle, James C., ed. *International Human Rights Law and Practice.* Philadelphia: ABA, 1978.

Vasak, Karel, and Alston, Philip, eds. *The International Dimensions of Human Rights.* 2 vols. Paris: UNESCO; and Westport, Conn.: Greenwood, 1982.

Vincent, R.J. *Human Rights and International Relations.* Cambridge: Cambridge University Press, 1986.

Bibliographies

Basic Bibliography of International Humanitarian Law. Geneva: Henry Dunant Institute, 1985.

Choice. "Bibliography on Human Rights." Edited by Claude E. Welch. 1990.

Facts on File, "International Protection of Human Rights," 1987.

Human Rights: A Topical Bibliography. Center for the Study of Human Rights, Columbia University. Boulder, Colo.: Westview Press, 1983.

Human Rights: An International and Comparative Law Bibliography. Westport, Conn.: Greenwood Press, 1985.

Public Source Materials

Interamerican Yearbook on Human Rights. Washington, D.C.: OAS, annual.
International Labour Standards. Geneva: ILO, 1984.
Report on Human Rights Practices. Washington, D.C.: Government Printing Office,
    annual. This is a report compiled by the State Department and published by Con-
    gress in about February of each year, covering countries for the previous calendar
    year.
The United Nations and Human Rights. Geneva: United Nations, several editions.
    This is an official description of various U.N. agencies and programs.
United Nations Yearbook on Human Rights. Geneva: United Nations, biennial.
Yearbook of the European Convention on Human Rights, Strasbourg, France: Coun-
    cil of Europe; The Hague: Nijhoff, annual.

Private Source Materials

Periodic publications on particular countries, situations, problems, or rights
can be obtained from the following:

American Association for the International Commission of Jurists, Inc.,
777 United Nations Plaza, New York, New York 10017.

Amnesty International, 322 Eighth Avenue, New York, New York
10001.

International Human Rights Law Group, 1700 K St. N.W., #801, Washington, D.C. 20006.

International League of Human Rights, 432 Park Avenue South, New
York, New York 10016.

Lawyers Committee for Human Rights, 330 Seventh Ave., Tenth floor,
New York, New York 10001.

Watch Committees (Americas Watch, Asia Watch, Helsinki Watch), 36
West Forty- St., New York, New York 10036.

Serial Publications

Amnesty International Report
Canadian Human Rights Yearbook
Freedom in the World
Harvard Human Rights Yearbook

Human Rights in Developing Countries
Human Rights Internet Reporter
Human Rights Law Journal
Human Rights Quarterly
International Committee of the Red Cross Annual Report
International Review of the Red Cross
Israeli Yearbook on Human Rights
Review of the International Commission of Jurists
World Bank World Development Report

Selected Recent Books

Alston, Philip, and Tomasevski, Katarina, eds. *The Right to Food*. Dordrecht: Kluwer, 1984.

Cingranelli, David L., ed. *Human Rights: Theory and Measurement*. New York: St. Martin's, 1988.

Donnelly, Jack. *The Concept of Rights*. London: Croom, Helm, 1985.

Forsythe, David P. *Human Rights and U.S. Foreign Policy: Congress Reconnsidered*. Gainesville: University Press of Florida, 1988.

————, ed. *Human Rights and Development: International Views*. London: Macmillan; New York: St. Martin's, 1989.

Harris, D. *The European Social Charter*. Charlottesville: University Press of Virginia, 1984.

Heinz, Wolfgang. *Indigenous Populations, Ethnic Minorities and Human Rights*. Berlin: Quorum Verlag, 1988.

Hevener, Natalie Kaufman. *International Law and the Status of Women*. Boulder, Colo.: Westview, 1983.

Howard, Rhoda. *Human Rights in Commonwealth Africa*. Totowa, N.J.: Rowman and Littlefield, 1986.

Hsiung, James C., ed. *Human Rights in East Asia: A Cultural Perspective*. New York: Paragon, 1986.

Humphrey, John. *The United Nations and Human Rights: The Great Adventure*. New Brunswick, N.J.: Transnational, 1984.

Kuper, Leo. *The Prevention of Genocide*. New Haven: Yale University Press, 1985.

Lauren, Paul Gordon. *Power and Prejudice: The Politics and Diplomacy of Racial Discrimination*. Boulder, Colo.: Westview, 1988.

LeBlanc, Lawrence J. *The United States and the Genocide Convention*. Durham, N.C.: Duke University Press, forthcoming.

Livezey, Lowell W. *Nongovernmental Organizations and the Idea of Human Rights*. Princeton: Princeton University Press, 1988.

Loescher, Gil, and Monahan, Laila, eds. *Refugees and International Relations*. Oxford: Oxford University Press, 1989.

Luard, Evan. *Human Rights and Foreign Policy*. Oxford: Pergamon Press, 1981.

Mastny, Votech. *Helsinki, Human Rights, and European Security*. Durham, N.C.: Duke University Press, 1986.

Mathews, Robert O., and Pratt, Cranford, eds. *Human Rights in Canadian Foreign Policy*. Toronto: McGill-Queens, 1988.

Mower, A. Glenn, Jr. *Human Rights and American Foreign Policy: The Carter and Reagan Experiences*. Westport, Conn.: Greenwood, 1987.

——. *International Cooperation for Social Justice: Global and Regional Protection of Economic/Social Rights*. Westport, Conn.: Greenwood, 1985.

Muravchik, Joshua. *The Uncertain Crusade: Jimmy Carter and the Dilemmas of Human Rights Policy*. Lanham, Md.: Hamilton Press, 1986.

Newsome, David D., ed. *The Diplomacy of Human Rights*. Lanham, Md: University Press of America, 1986.

Nichols, Bruce and Loescher, Gil, eds. *The Moral Nation: Humanitarianism and U.S. Foreign Policy Today*. Notre Dame, Ind.: University of Notre Dame Press, 1989.

Nickel, James. *Making Sense of Human Rights*. Berkeley: University of California Press, 1987.

Quiroga, Cecilia M. *The Battle for Human Rights: Gross Systematic Violations and the Inter-American System*. Dordrecht: Kluwer, 1988.

Ramcharan, B.G. *The Right to Life in International Law*. Dordrecht: Kluwer, 1985.

Schoultz, Lars. *Human Rights and United States Policy toward Latin America*. Princeton: Princeton University Press, 1981.

Shawcross, William. *The Quality of Mercy: Cambodia, Holocaust, and Modern Conscience*. New York: Simon and Schuster, 1984.

Shepard, George W., Jr., and Nanda, Ved, eds. *Human Rights and Third World Development*. Westport, Conn.: Greenwood, 1985.

Shue, Henry. *Basic Rights*. Princeton: Princeton University Press, 1980.

Stover, Eric, and Nightingale, Elena, eds. *The Breaking of Bodies and Minds*. New York: Freeman, 1985.

Sundberg, Jacob, ed. *Laws, Rights and the European Convention on Human Rights*. Littleton, Colo.: F.B. Rothman, 1986.

Tolley, Howard, Jr. *The U.N. Commission on Human Rights*. Boulder, Colo.: Westview, 1987.

Van Dyke, Vernon. *Human Rights, Ethnicity, and Discrimination*. Westport, Conn.: Greenwood, 1985.

Vincent, R.J. *Foreign Policy and Human Rights: Issues and Responses*. Cambridge: Cambridge University Press, 1986.

Welch, Claude E., and Meltzer, Ronald I., eds. *Human Rights and Development in Africa*. Albany, N.Y.: SUNY Press, 1984.

Index

About the Author

David P. Forsythe is professor of political science at the University of Nebraska. He is the author or editor of twelve books and over forty articles and chapters on international relations. Among his recent books are *Human Rights and World Politics* (1989), which was reviewed as "the best recent undergraduate textbook in the field"; *Human Rights and U.S. Foreign Policy* (1988), which won the Manning J. Dauer prize; and *The Politics of International Law: U.S. Foreign Policy Reconsidered* (1990). Dr. Forsythe previously held fellowships from the Ford Foundation and the National Endowment for the Humanities, and in 1989 he was awarded a grant fro the U.S. Institute for Peace to study human rights and peace. He has won both distinguished teaching and research awards from the University of Nebraska. A former consultant to the International Red Cross on human-rights matters, Dr. Forsythe is currently advisor to several private human-rights agencies.